SEPTEMBER MOURNING™

The Complete Collection

Created by
MARC SILVESTRI
& EMILY LAZAR

COVER BY
MARC SILVESTRI

Published By
TOP COW PRODUCTIONS, INC.
Los Angeles

SEPTEMBER MOURNING

For Top Cow Productions, Inc.

For Top Cow Productions, Inc.
Marc Silvestri - CEO
Matt Hawkins - President & COO
Elena Salcedo - Vice President of Operations
Vincent Valentine - Lead Production Artist
Henry Barajas - Director of Operations
Dylan Gray - Marketing Director

www.topcow.com

To find the comic
shop nearest you, call:
1-888-COMICBOOK

Want more info? Check out:
www.topcow.com
for news & exclusive Top Cow merchandise!

CHAPTER 1
A MURDER OF REAPERS

MARIAH McCOURT
Writer

SUMEYYE KESGIN
Artist

BETSY GOLDEN
Colorist

TROY PETERI
Letterer

BETSY GOLDEN · SHAHRIAR FOULADI
Editors

TRICIA RAMOS · ERIKA SCHNATZ
Production Art & Design

ROM
Cover Art

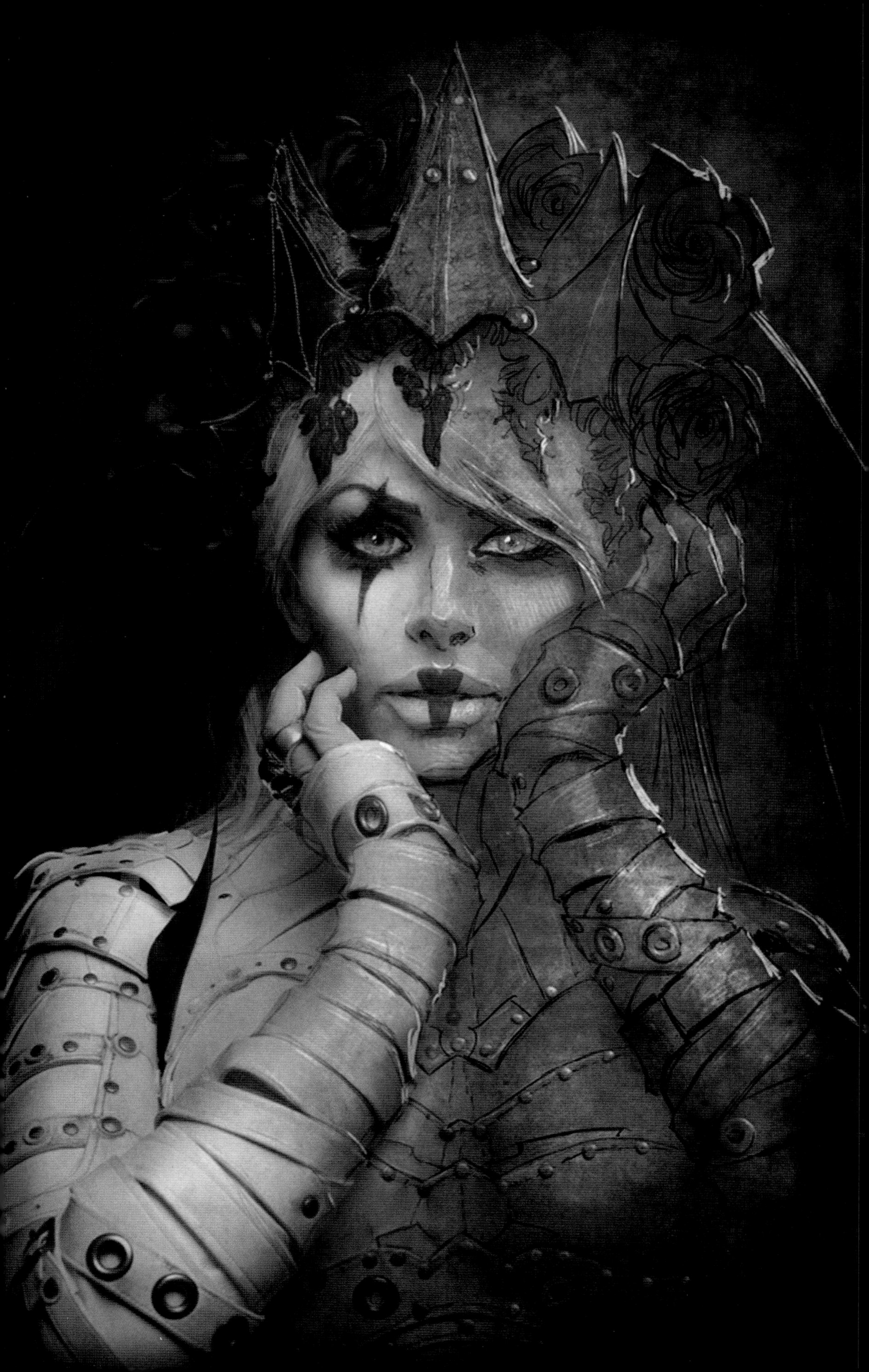

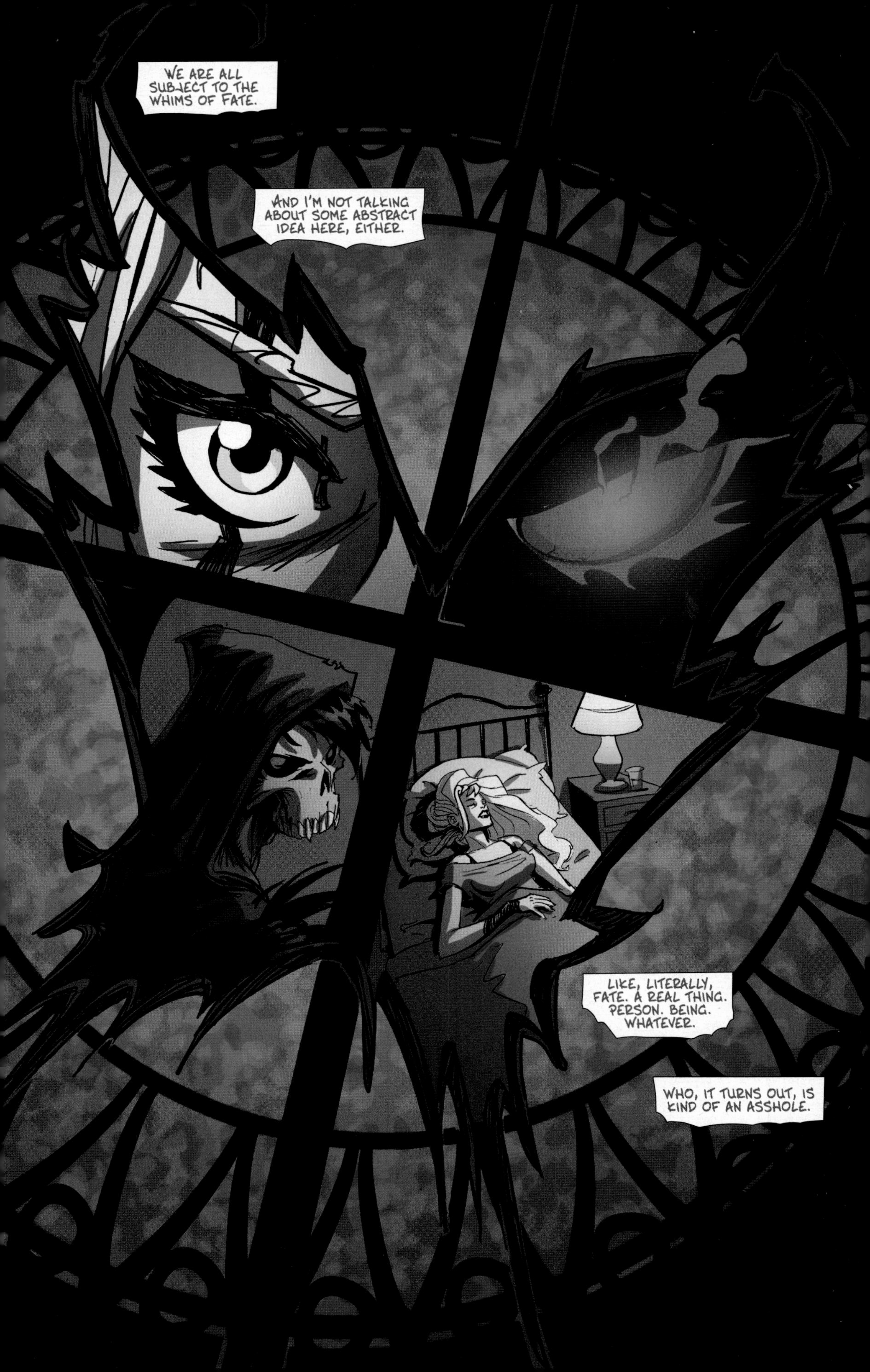
WE ARE ALL SUBJECT TO THE WHIMS OF FATE.
AND I'M NOT TALKING ABOUT SOME ABSTRACT IDEA HERE, EITHER.
LIKE, LITERALLY, FATE. A REAL THING. PERSON. BEING. WHATEVER.
WHO, IT TURNS OUT, IS KIND OF AN ASSHOLE.

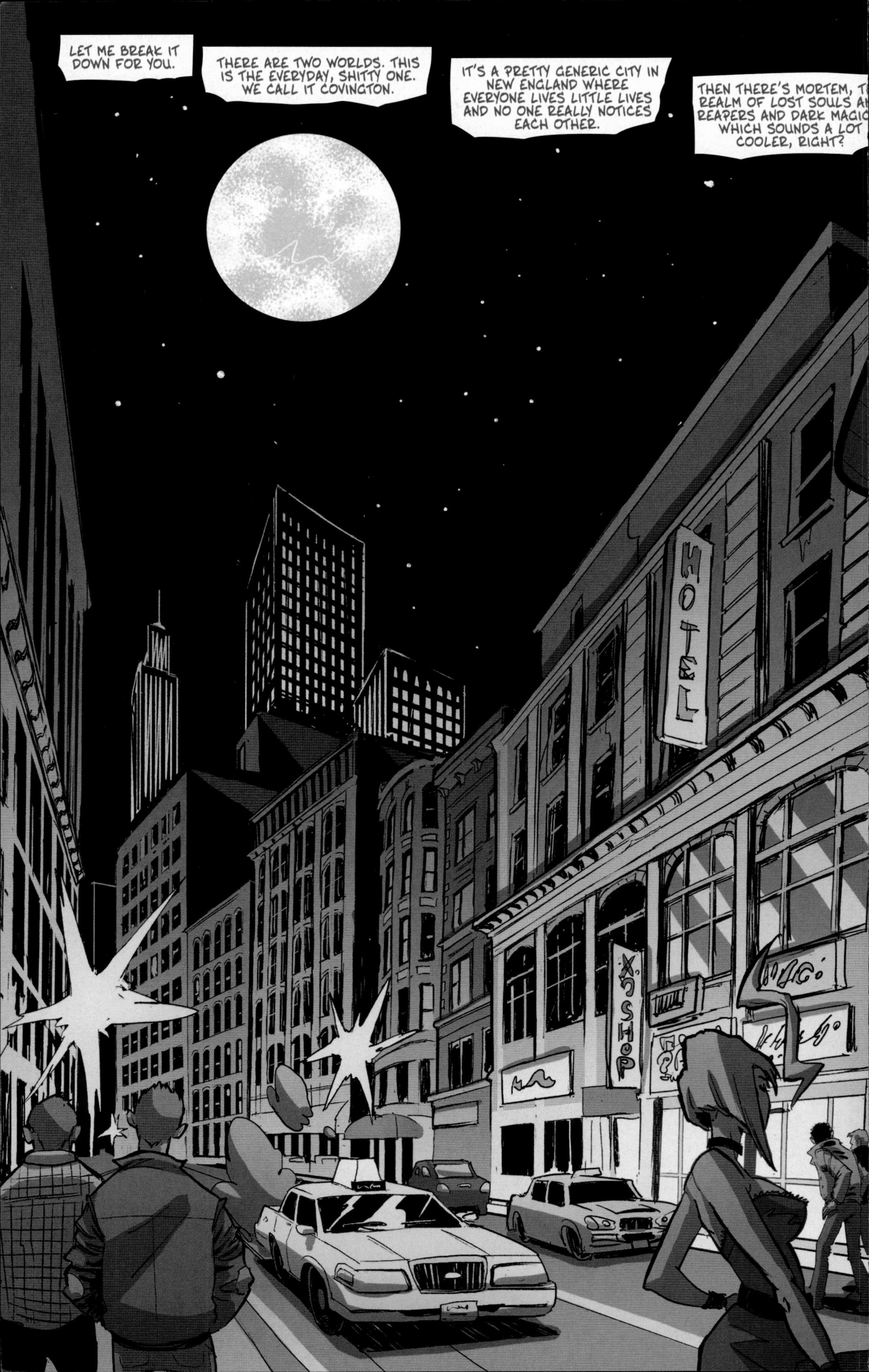
LET ME BREAK IT DOWN FOR YOU.
THERE ARE TWO WORLDS. THIS IS THE EVERYDAY, SHITTY ONE. WE CALL IT COVINGTON.
IT'S A PRETTY GENERIC CITY IN NEW ENGLAND WHERE EVERYONE LIVES LITTLE LIVES AND NO ONE REALLY NOTICES EACH OTHER.
THEN THERE'S MORTEM, T REALM OF LOST SOULS A REAPERS AND DARK MAGIC WHICH SOUNDS A LOT COOLER, RIGHT?
HOTEL
SHOP

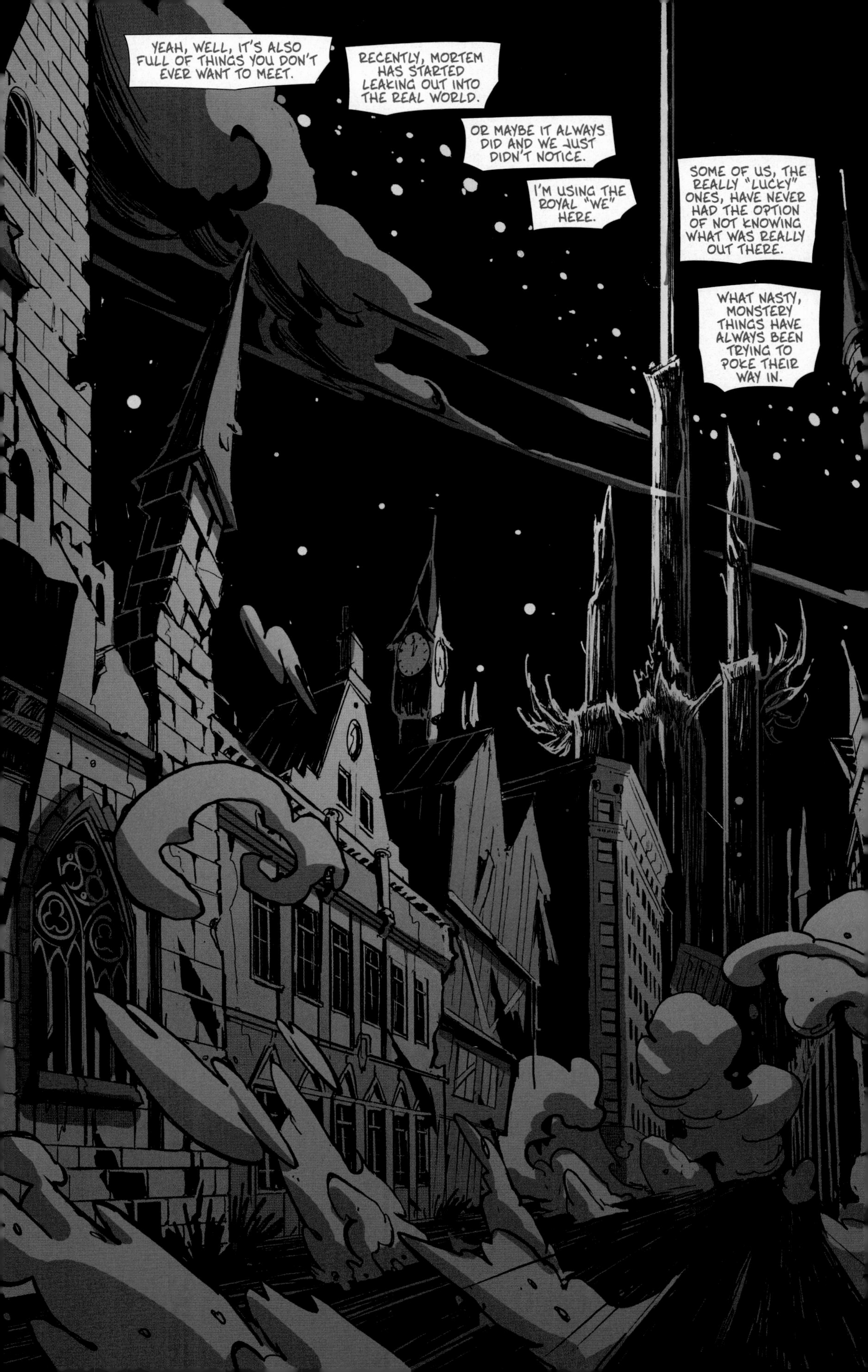
YEAH, WELL, IT'S ALSO FULL OF THINGS YOU DON'T EVER WANT TO MEET.
RECENTLY, MORTEM HAS STARTED LEAKING OUT INTO THE REAL WORLD.
OR MAYBE IT ALWAYS DID AND WE JUST DIDN'T NOTICE.
I'M USING THE ROYAL "WE" HERE.
SOME OF US, THE REALLY "LUCKY" ONES, HAVE NEVER HAD THE OPTION OF NOT KNOWING WHAT WAS REALLY OUT THERE.
WHAT NASTY, MONSTERY THINGS HAVE ALWAYS BEEN TRYING TO POKE THEIR WAY IN.

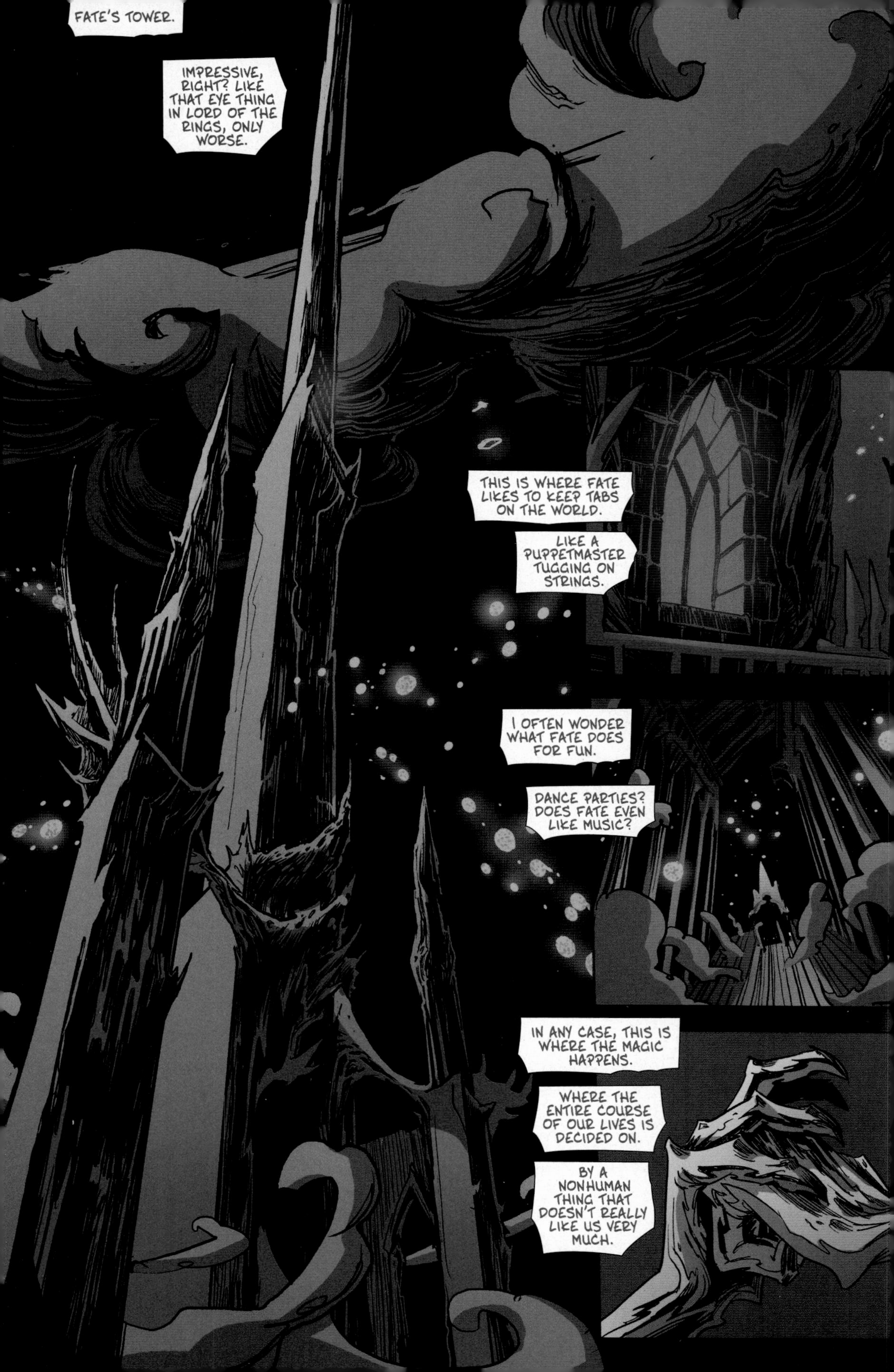
FATE'S TOWER.
IMPRESSIVE, RIGHT? LIKE THAT EYE THING IN LORD OF THE RINGS, ONLY WORSE.
THIS IS WHERE FATE LIKES TO KEEP TABS ON THE WORLD.
LIKE A PUPPETMASTER TUGGING ON STRINGS.
I OFTEN WONDER WHAT FATE DOES FOR FUN.
DANCE PARTIES? DOES FATE EVEN LIKE MUSIC?
IN ANY CASE, THIS IS WHERE THE MAGIC HAPPENS.
WHERE THE ENTIRE COURSE OF OUR LIVES IS DECIDED ON.
BY A NONHUMAN THING THAT DOESN'T REALLY LIKE US VERY MUCH.

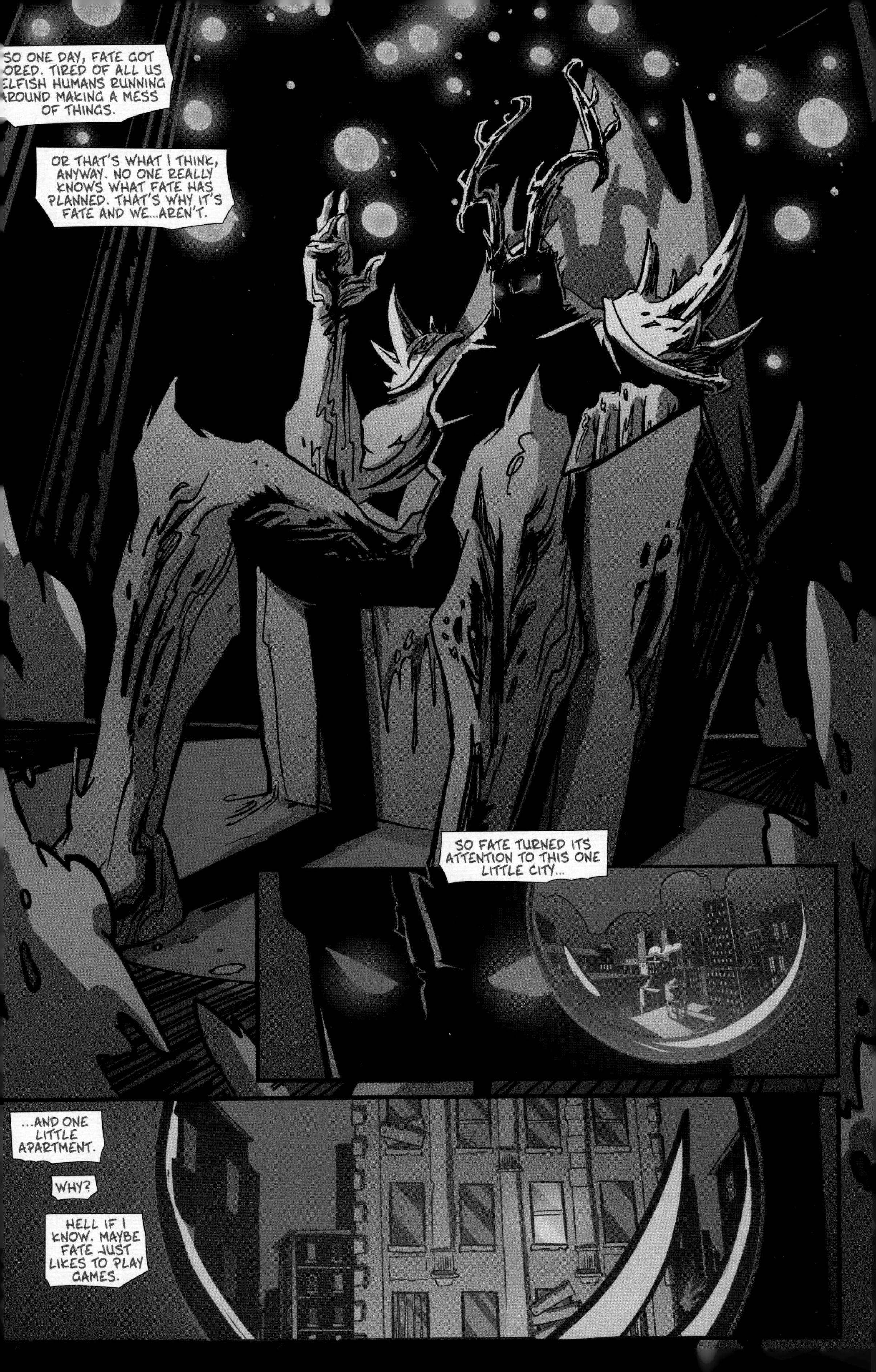
SO ONE DAY, FATE GOT BORED. TIRED OF ALL US SELFISH HUMANS RUNNING AROUND MAKING A MESS OF THINGS.
OR THAT'S WHAT I THINK, ANYWAY. NO ONE REALLY KNOWS WHAT FATE HAS PLANNED. THAT'S WHY IT'S FATE AND WE...AREN'T.
SO FATE TURNED ITS ATTENTION TO THIS ONE LITTLE CITY...
...AND ONE LITTLE APARTMENT.
WHY?
HELL IF I KNOW. MAYBE FATE JUST LIKES TO PLAY GAMES.

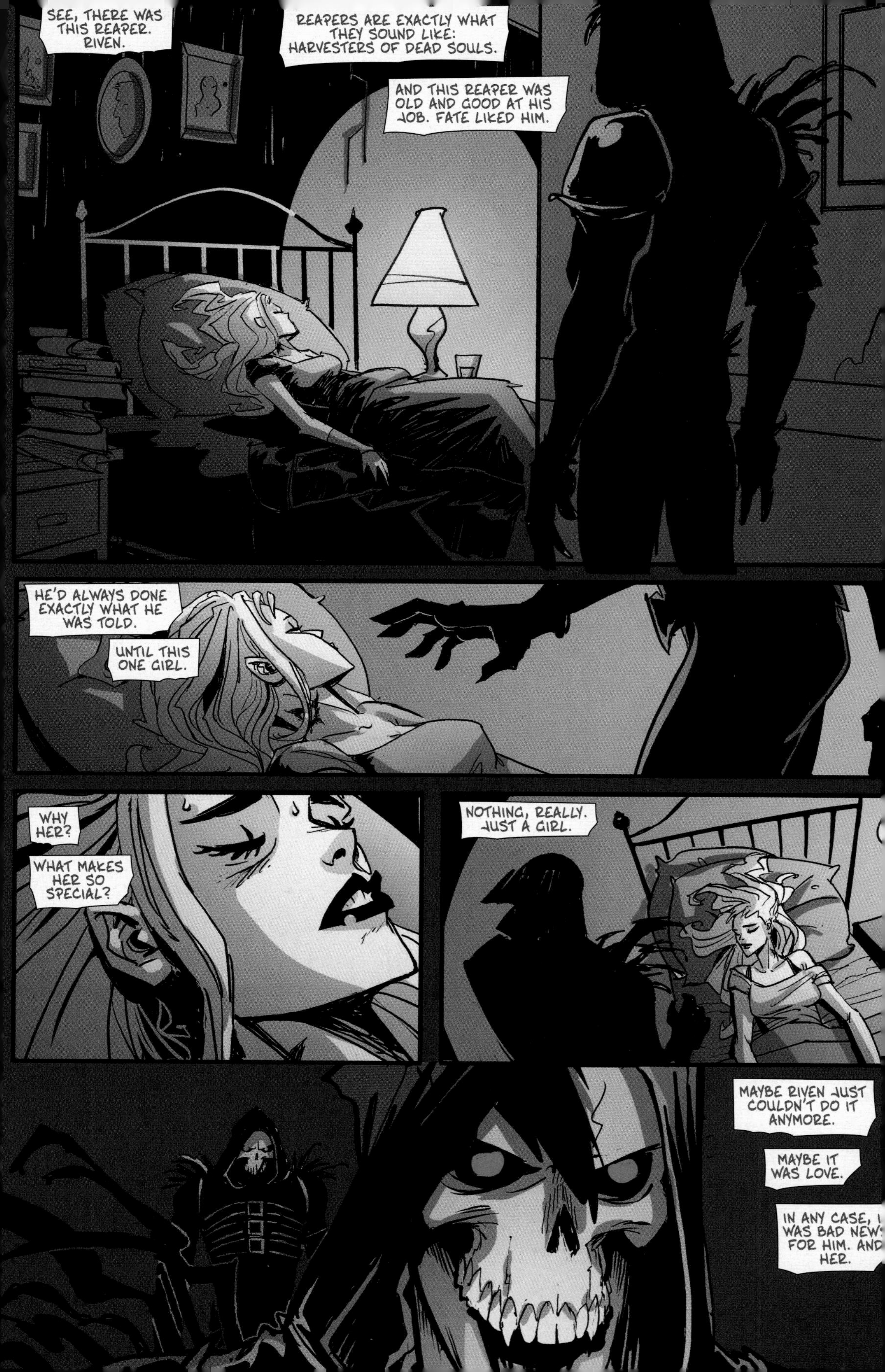
SEE, THERE WAS THIS REAPER. RIVEN.
REAPERS ARE EXACTLY WHAT THEY SOUND LIKE: HARVESTERS OF DEAD SOULS.
AND THIS REAPER WAS OLD AND GOOD AT HIS JOB. FATE LIKED HIM.
HE'D ALWAYS DONE EXACTLY WHAT HE WAS TOLD.
UNTIL THIS ONE GIRL.
WHY HER?
WHAT MAKES HER SO SPECIAL?
NOTHING, REALLY. JUST A GIRL.
MAYBE RIVEN JUST COULDN'T DO IT ANYMORE.
MAYBE IT WAS LOVE.
IN ANY CASE, I WAS BAD NEWS FOR HIM. AND HER.

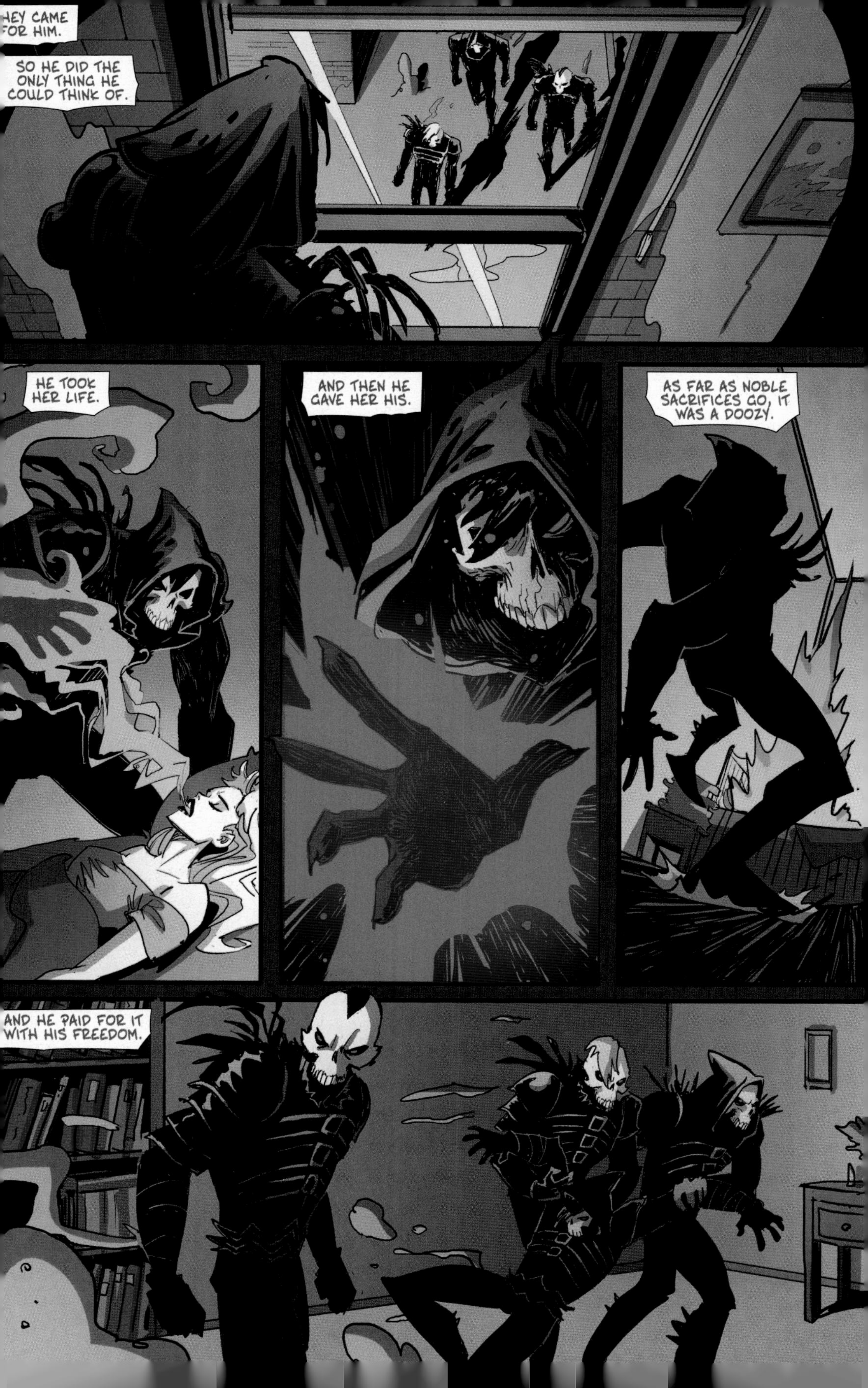
HEY CAME FOR HIM.
SO HE DID THE ONLY THING HE COULD THINK OF.
HE TOOK HER LIFE.
AND THEN HE GAVE HER HIS.
AS FAR AS NOBLE SACRIFICES GO, IT WAS A DOOZY.
AND HE PAID FOR IT WITH HIS FREEDOM.

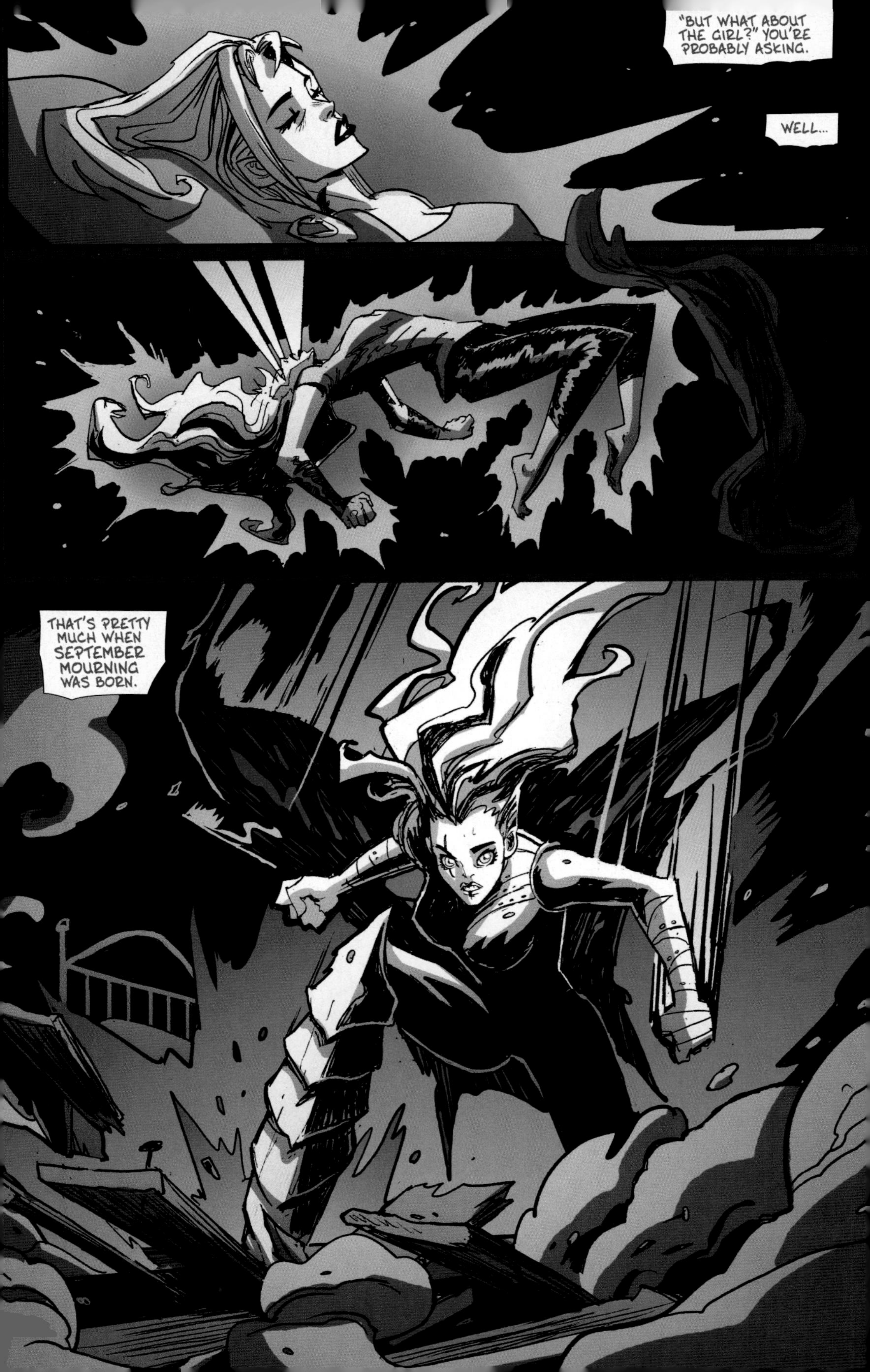
"BUT WHAT ABOUT THE GIRL?" YOU'RE PROBABLY ASKING.
WELL...
THAT'S PRETTY MUCH WHEN SEPTEMBER MOURNING WAS BORN.

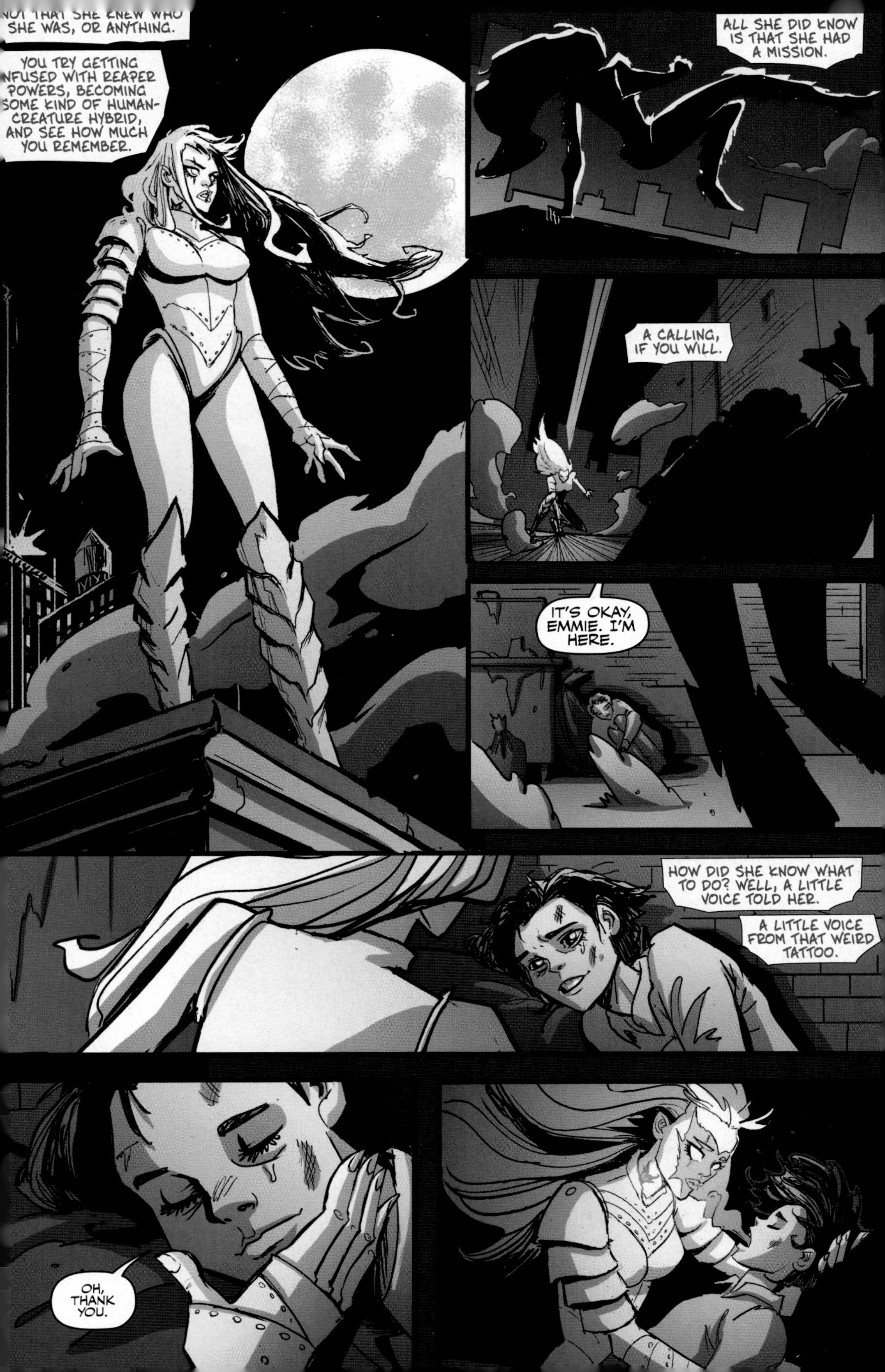
NOT THAT SHE KNEW WHO SHE WAS, OR ANYTHING.
YOU TRY GETTING INFUSED WITH REAPER POWERS, BECOMING SOME KIND OF HUMAN-CREATURE HYBRID, AND SEE HOW MUCH YOU REMEMBER.
ALL SHE DID KNOW IS THAT SHE HAD A MISSION.
A CALLING, IF YOU WILL.
IT'S OKAY, EMMIE. I'M HERE.
HOW DID SHE KNOW WHAT TO DO? WELL, A LITTLE VOICE TOLD HER.
A LITTLE VOICE FROM THAT WEIRD TATTOO.
OH, THANK YOU.

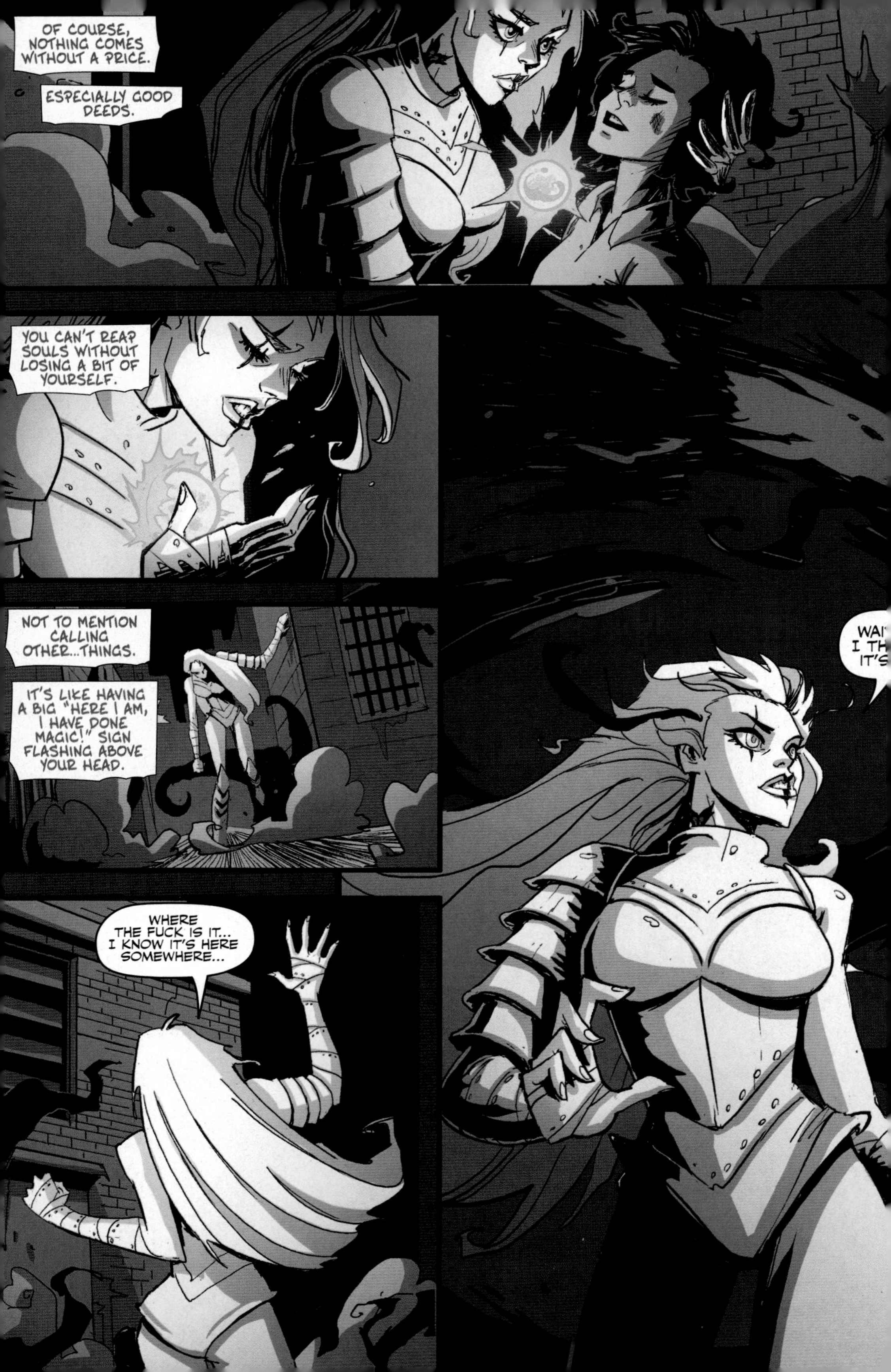
OF COURSE, NOTHING COMES WITHOUT A PRICE.
ESPECIALLY GOOD DEEDS.
YOU CAN'T REAP SOULS WITHOUT LOSING A BIT OF YOURSELF.
NOT TO MENTION CALLING OTHER...THINGS.
IT'S LIKE HAVING A BIG "HERE I AM, I HAVE DONE MAGIC!" SIGN FLASHING ABOVE YOUR HEAD.
WHERE THE FUCK IS IT... I KNOW IT'S HERE SOMEWHERE...

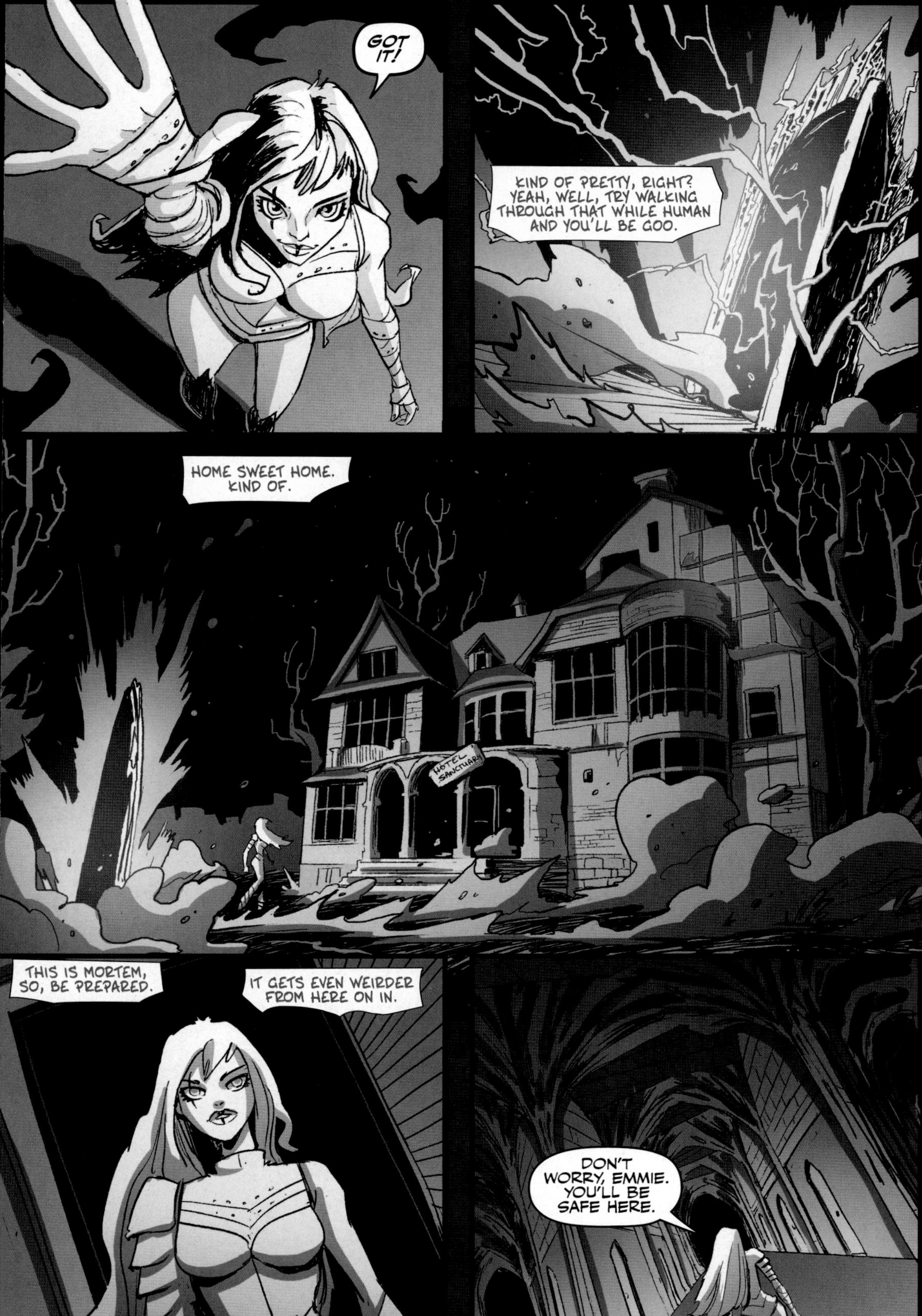
GOT IT!
KIND OF PRETTY, RIGHT? YEAH, WELL, TRY WALKING THROUGH THAT WHILE HUMAN AND YOU'LL BE GOO.
HOME SWEET HOME. KIND OF.
HOTEL SANCTUARY
THIS IS MORTEM, SO, BE PREPARED.
IT GETS EVEN WEIRDER FROM HERE ON IN.
DON'T WORRY, EMMIE. YOU'LL BE SAFE HERE.

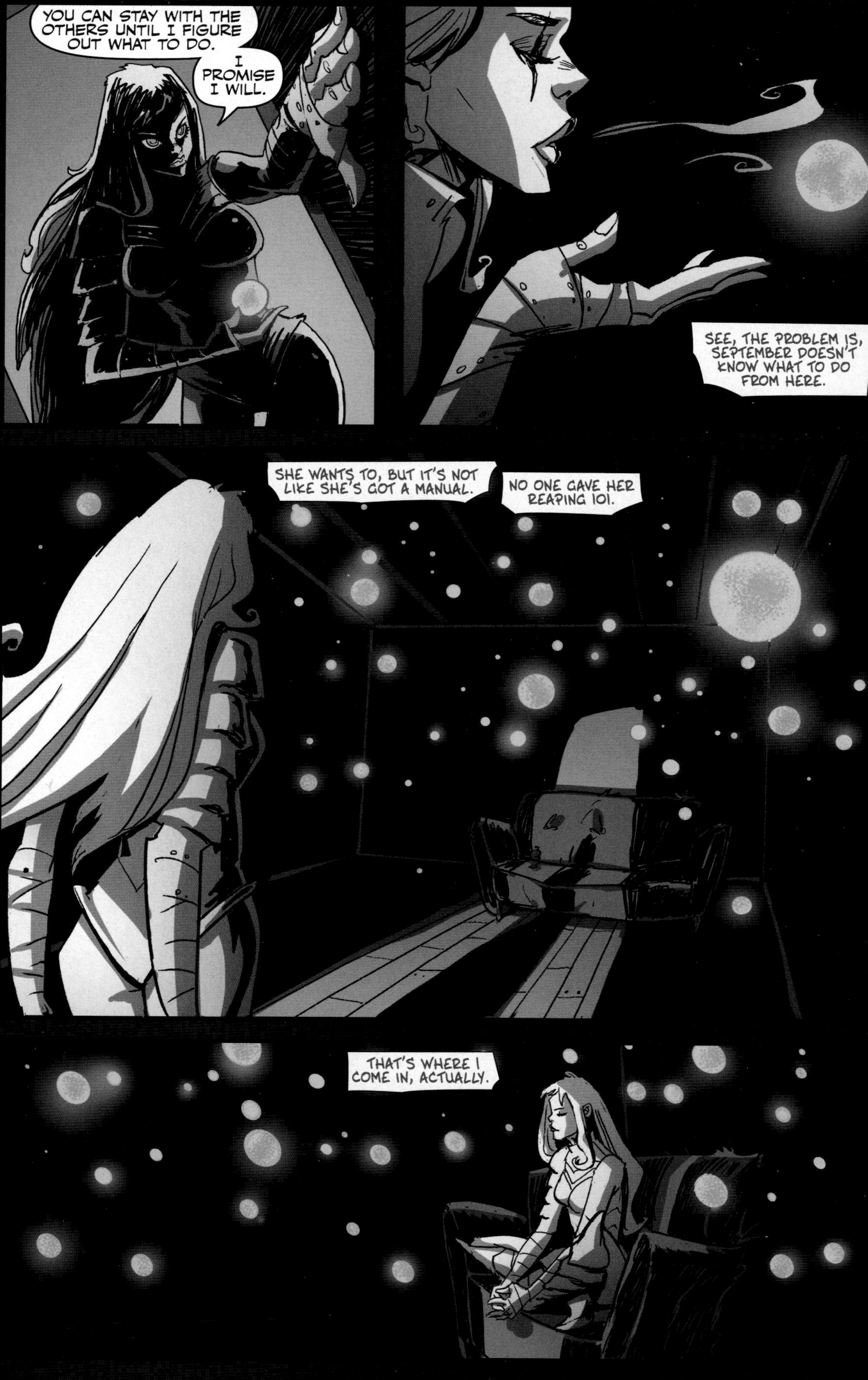
YOU CAN STAY WITH THE OTHERS UNTIL I FIGURE OUT WHAT TO DO.
I PROMISE I WILL.
SEE, THE PROBLEM IS, SEPTEMBER DOESN'T KNOW WHAT TO DO FROM HERE.
SHE WANTS TO, BUT IT'S NOT LIKE SHE'S GOT A MANUAL.
NO ONE GAVE HER REAPING 101.
THAT'S WHERE I COME IN, ACTUALLY.

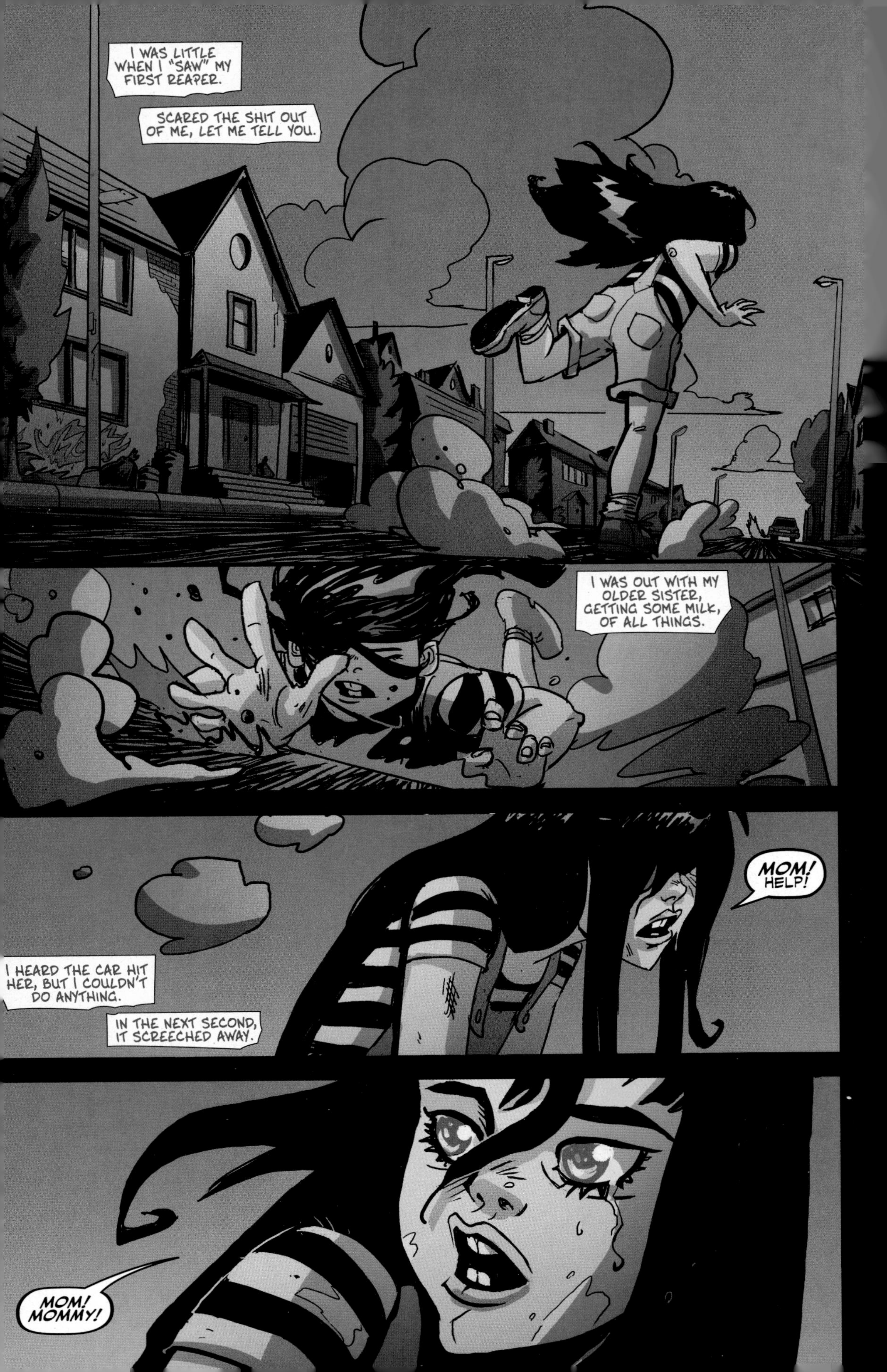
I WAS LITTLE WHEN I "SAW" MY FIRST REAPER.
SCARED THE SHIT OUT OF ME, LET ME TELL YOU.
I WAS OUT WITH MY OLDER SISTER, GETTING SOME MILK, OF ALL THINGS.
MOM! HELP!
I HEARD THE CAR HIT HER, BUT I COULDN'T DO ANYTHING.
IN THE NEXT SECOND, IT SCREECHED AWAY.
MOM! MOMMY!

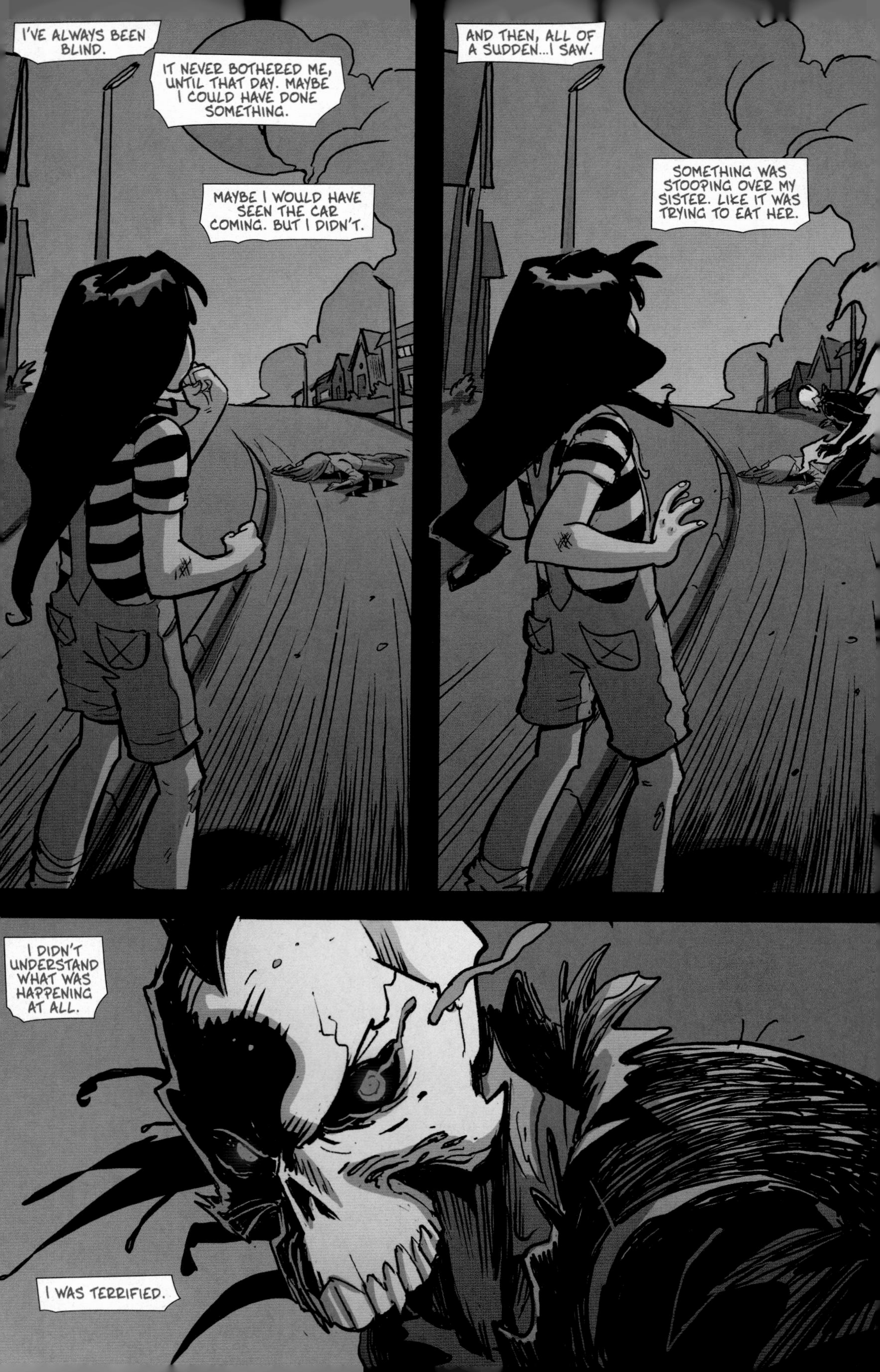

I'VE ALWAYS BEEN BLIND.
IT NEVER BOTHERED ME, UNTIL THAT DAY. MAYBE I COULD HAVE DONE SOMETHING.
MAYBE I WOULD HAVE SEEN THE CAR COMING. BUT I DIDN'T.
AND THEN, ALL OF A SUDDEN...I SAW.
SOMETHING WAS STOOPING OVER MY SISTER. LIKE IT WAS TRYING TO EAT HER.
I DIDN'T UNDERSTAND WHAT WAS HAPPENING AT ALL.
I WAS TERRIFIED.

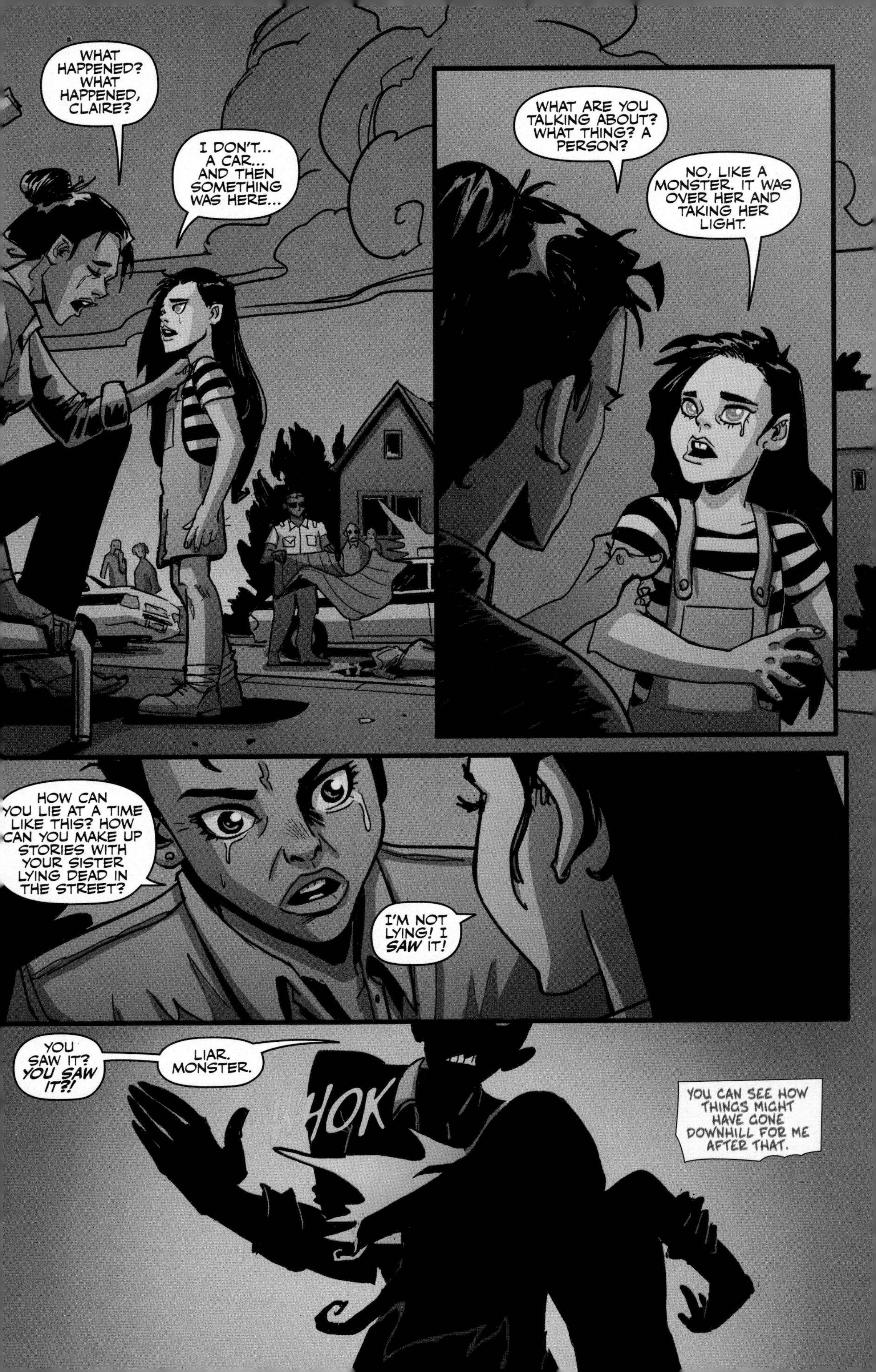
WHAT HAPPENED? WHAT HAPPENED, CLAIRE?
I DON'T... A CAR... AND THEN SOMETHING WAS HERE...
WHAT ARE YOU TALKING ABOUT? WHAT THING? A PERSON?
NO, LIKE A MONSTER. IT WAS OVER HER AND TAKING HER LIGHT.
HOW CAN YOU LIE AT A TIME LIKE THIS? HOW CAN YOU MAKE UP STORIES WITH YOUR SISTER LYING DEAD IN THE STREET?
I'M NOT LYING! I *SAW* IT!
YOU SAW IT? *YOU SAW IT?!*
LIAR. MONSTER.
WHOK
YOU CAN SEE HOW THINGS MIGHT HAVE GONE DOWNHILL FOR ME AFTER THAT.

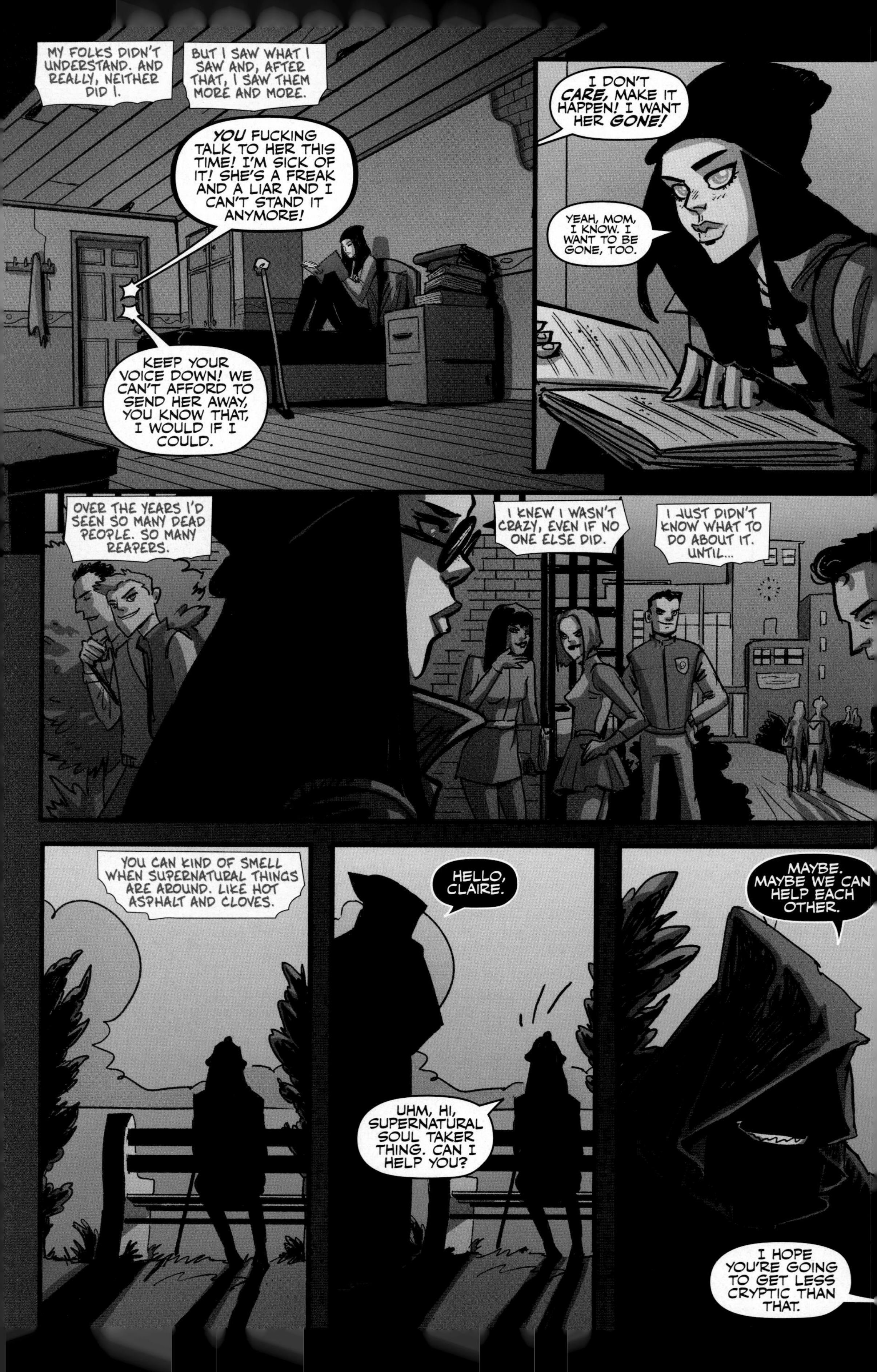
MY FOLKS DIDN'T UNDERSTAND. AND REALLY, NEITHER DID I.
BUT I SAW WHAT I SAW AND, AFTER THAT, I SAW THEM MORE AND MORE.
YOU FUCKING TALK TO HER THIS TIME! I'M SICK OF IT! SHE'S A FREAK AND A LIAR AND I CAN'T STAND IT ANYMORE!
KEEP YOUR VOICE DOWN! WE CAN'T AFFORD TO SEND HER AWAY, YOU KNOW THAT, I WOULD IF I COULD.
I DON'T CARE, MAKE IT HAPPEN! I WANT HER GONE!
YEAH, MOM, I KNOW. I WANT TO BE GONE, TOO.
OVER THE YEARS I'D SEEN SO MANY DEAD PEOPLE. SO MANY REAPERS.
I KNEW I WASN'T CRAZY, EVEN IF NO ONE ELSE DID.
I JUST DIDN'T KNOW WHAT TO DO ABOUT IT. UNTIL...
YOU CAN KIND OF SMELL WHEN SUPERNATURAL THINGS ARE AROUND. LIKE HOT ASPHALT AND CLOVES.
HELLO, CLAIRE.
UHM, HI, SUPERNATURAL SOUL TAKER THING. CAN I HELP YOU?
MAYBE. MAYBE WE CAN HELP EACH OTHER.
I HOPE YOU'RE GOING TO GET LESS CRYPTIC THAN THAT.

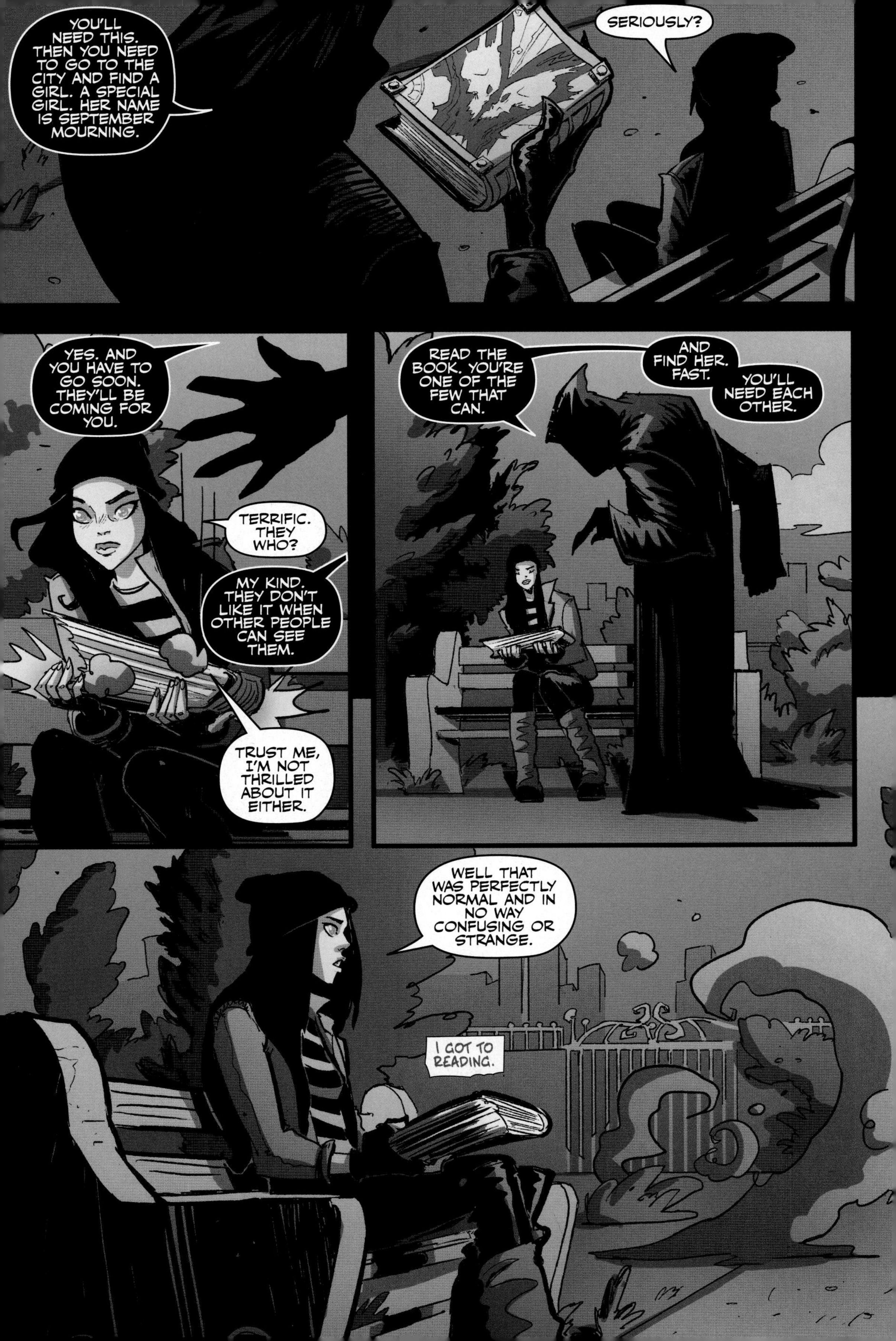
YOU'LL NEED THIS. THEN YOU NEED TO GO TO THE CITY AND FIND A GIRL. A SPECIAL GIRL. HER NAME IS SEPTEMBER MOURNING.
SERIOUSLY?
YES. AND YOU HAVE TO GO SOON. THEY'LL BE COMING FOR YOU.
TERRIFIC. THEY WHO?
MY KIND. THEY DON'T LIKE IT WHEN OTHER PEOPLE CAN SEE THEM.
TRUST ME, I'M NOT THRILLED ABOUT IT EITHER.
READ THE BOOK. YOU'RE ONE OF THE FEW THAT CAN.
AND FIND HER. FAST.
YOU'LL NEED EACH OTHER.
WELL THAT WAS PERFECTLY NORMAL AND IN NO WAY CONFUSING OR STRANGE.
I GOT TO READING.

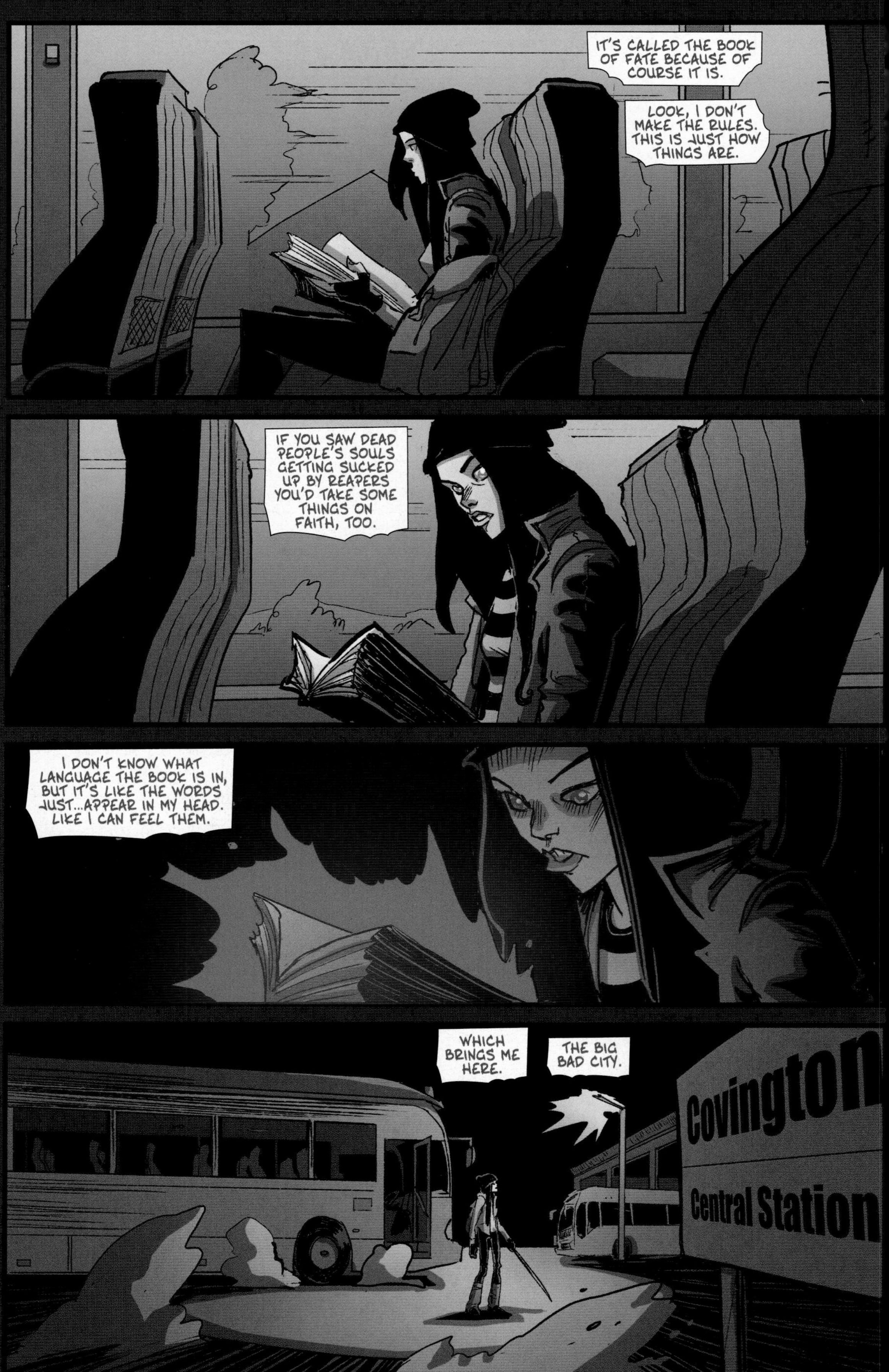
IT'S CALLED THE BOOK OF FATE BECAUSE OF COURSE IT IS.
LOOK, I DON'T MAKE THE RULES. THIS IS JUST HOW THINGS ARE.
IF YOU SAW DEAD PEOPLE'S SOULS GETTING SUCKED UP BY REAPERS YOU'D TAKE SOME THINGS ON FAITH, TOO.
I DON'T KNOW WHAT LANGUAGE THE BOOK IS IN, BUT IT'S LIKE THE WORDS JUST...APPEAR IN MY HEAD. LIKE I CAN FEEL THEM.
WHICH BRINGS ME HERE.
THE BIG BAD CITY.
Covington
Central Station

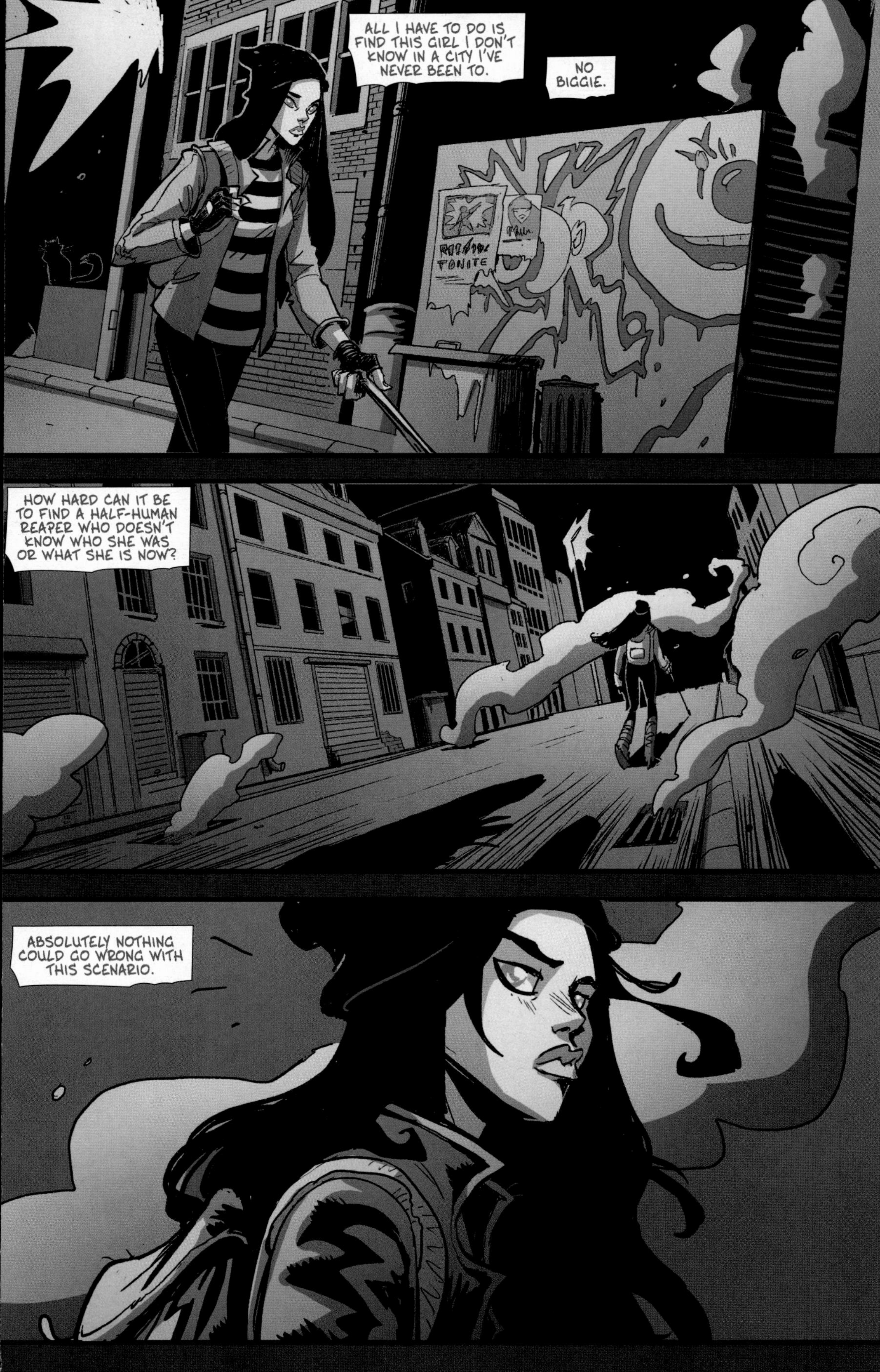
ALL I HAVE TO DO IS FIND THIS GIRL I DON'T KNOW IN A CITY I'VE NEVER BEEN TO.
NO BIGGIE.
TONITE
HOW HARD CAN IT BE TO FIND A HALF-HUMAN REAPER WHO DOESN'T KNOW WHO SHE WAS OR WHAT SHE IS NOW?
ABSOLUTELY NOTHING COULD GO WRONG WITH THIS SCENARIO.

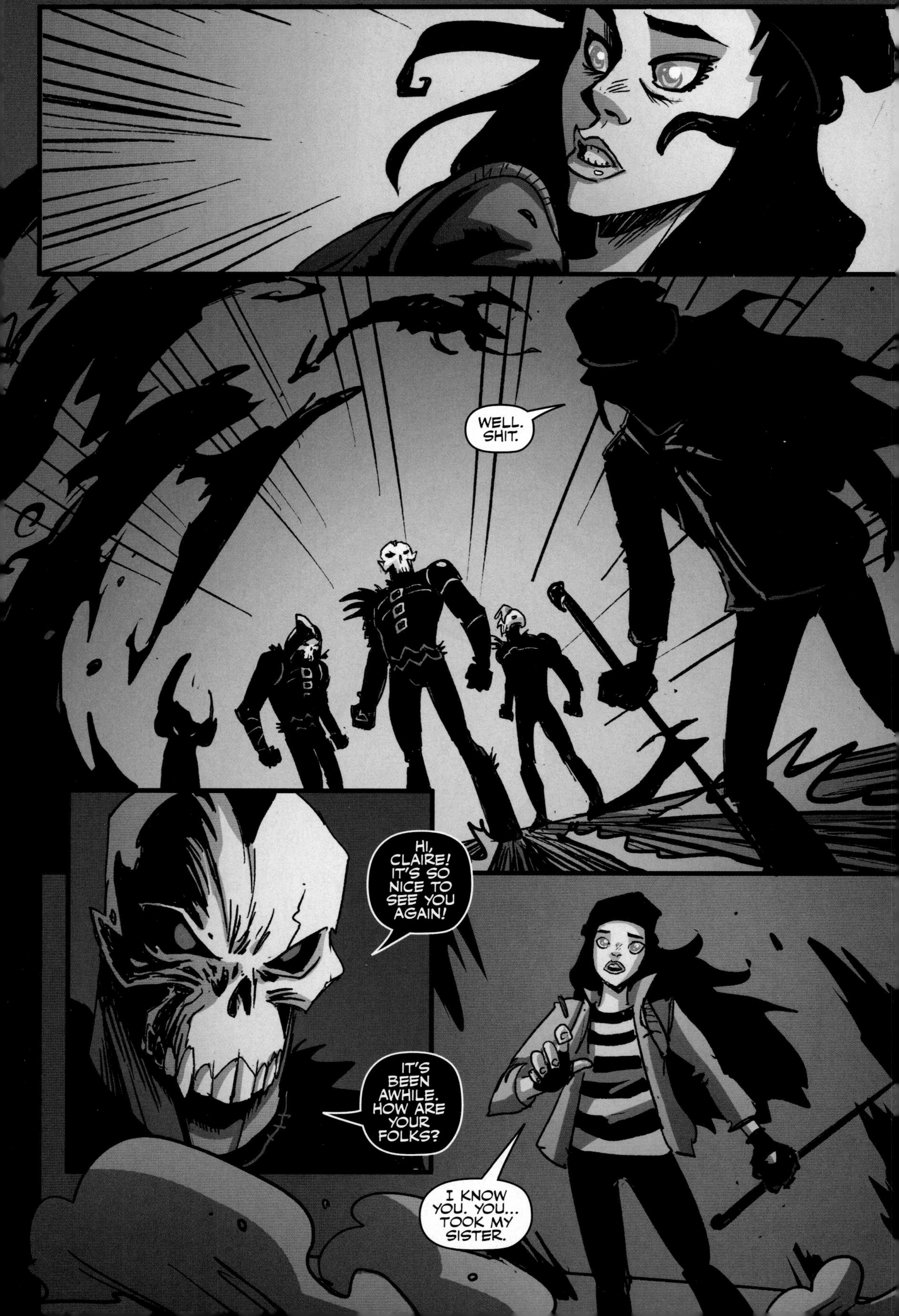
WELL. SHIT.
HI, CLAIRE! IT'S SO NICE TO SEE YOU AGAIN!
IT'S BEEN AWHILE. HOW ARE YOUR FOLKS?
I KNOW YOU. YOU... TOOK MY SISTER.

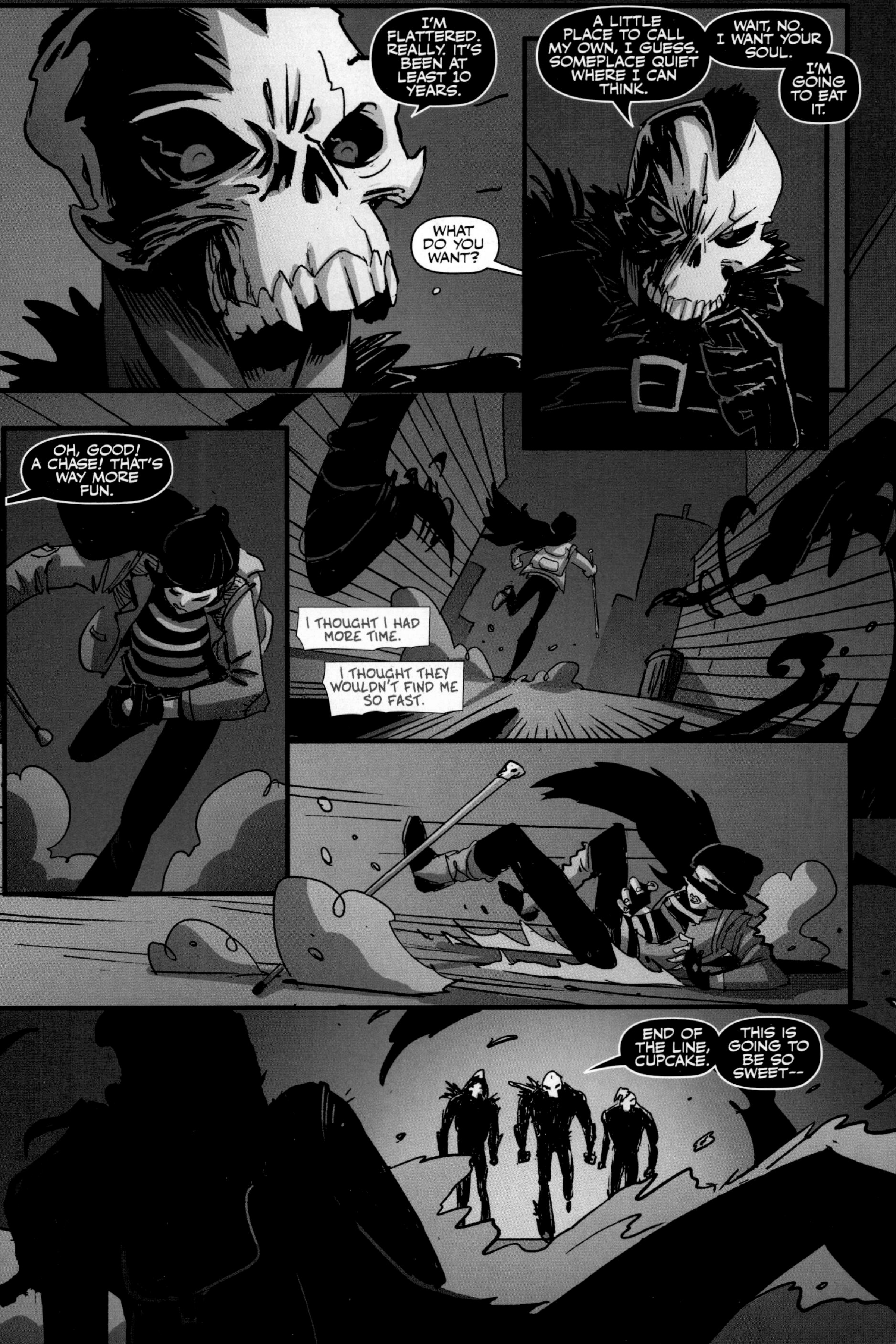
I'M FLATTERED. REALLY. IT'S BEEN AT LEAST 10 YEARS.
A LITTLE PLACE TO CALL MY OWN, I GUESS. SOMEPLACE QUIET WHERE I CAN THINK.
WAIT, NO. I WANT YOUR SOUL.
I'M GOING TO EAT IT.
WHAT DO YOU WANT?
OH, GOOD! A CHASE! THAT'S WAY MORE FUN.
I THOUGHT I HAD MORE TIME.
I THOUGHT THEY WOULDN'T FIND ME SO FAST.
END OF THE LINE, CUPCAKE.
THIS IS GOING TO BE SO SWEET--

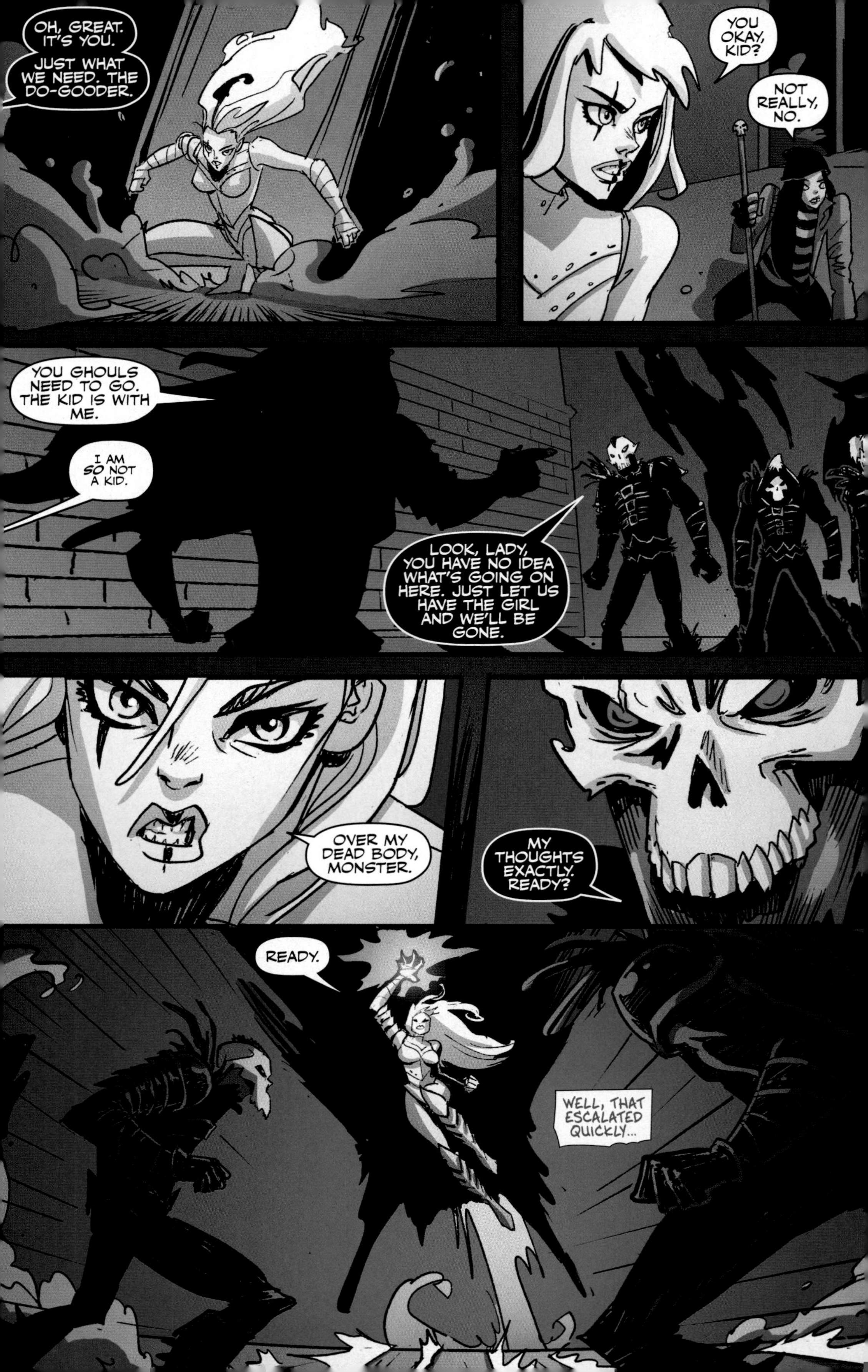
OH, GREAT. IT'S YOU.
JUST WHAT WE NEED. THE DO-GOODER.
YOU OKAY, KID?
NOT REALLY, NO.
YOU GHOULS NEED TO GO. THE KID IS WITH ME.
I AM SO NOT A KID.
LOOK, LADY, YOU HAVE NO IDEA WHAT'S GOING ON HERE. JUST LET US HAVE THE GIRL AND WE'LL BE GONE.
OVER MY DEAD BODY, MONSTER.
MY THOUGHTS EXACTLY. READY?
READY.
WELL, THAT ESCALATED QUICKLY...

CHAPTER 2
THE HAND OF FATE

EMILY LAZAR & MARIAH McCOURT
Writers

SUMEYYE KESGIN
Artist

KATARINA DEVIC
Colorist

TROY PETERI
Letterer

RYAN CADY
Editor

VINCENT VALENTINE · TRICIA RAMOS
Production Art & Design

SUMEYYE KESGIN & KATARINA DEVIC
Cover Art

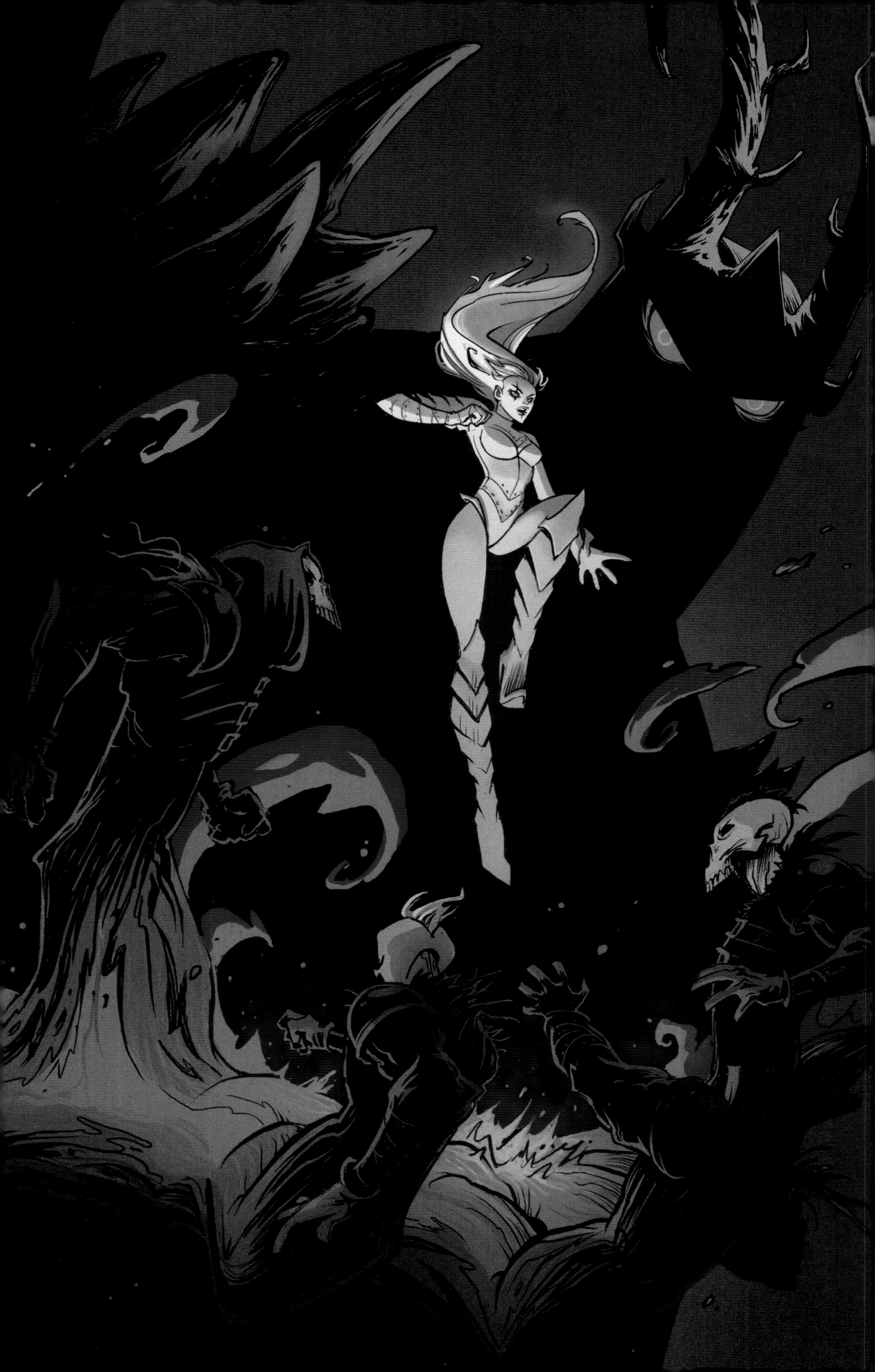

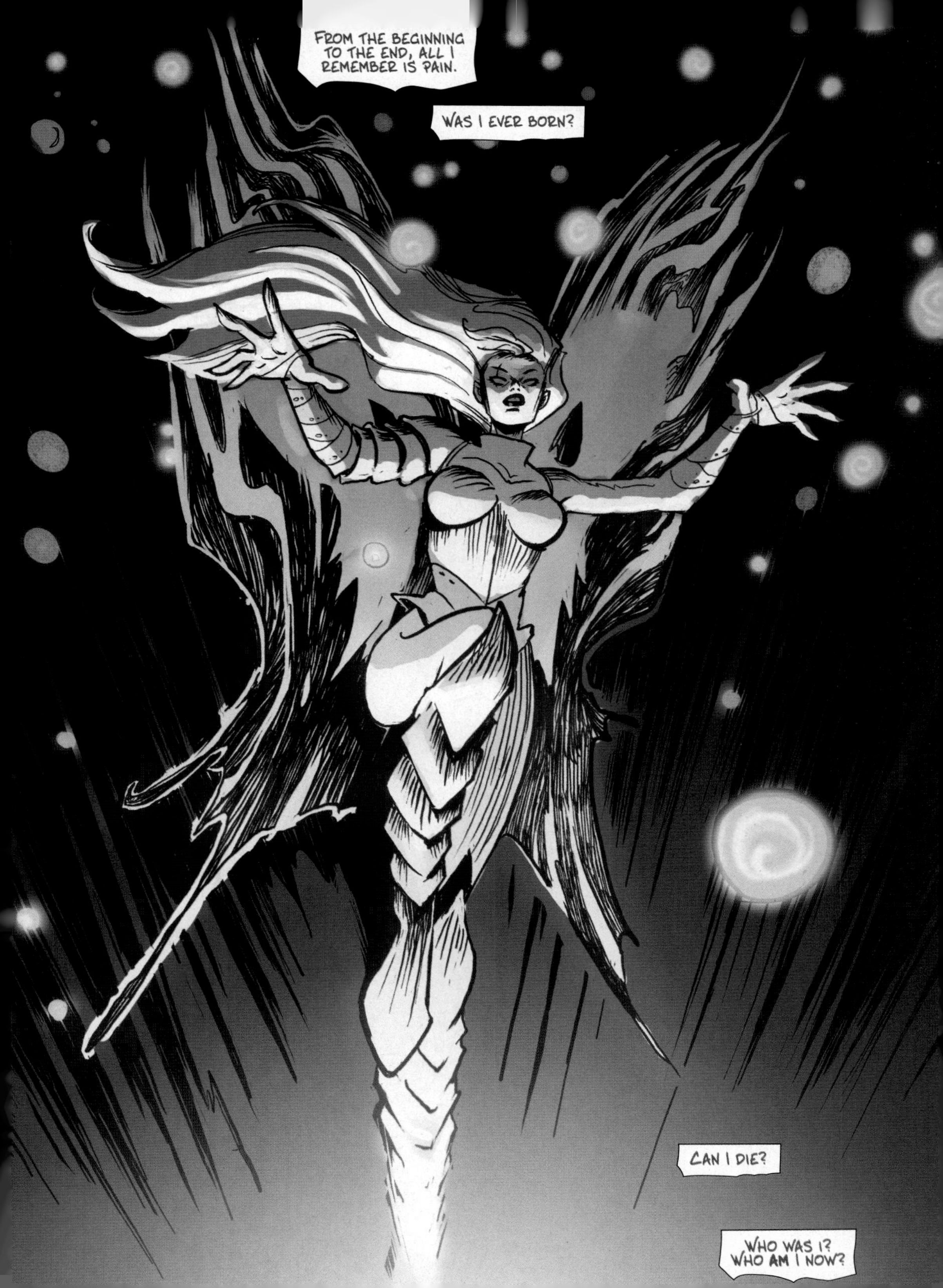
FROM THE BEGINNING TO THE END, ALL I REMEMBER IS PAIN.
WAS I EVER BORN?
CAN I DIE?
WHO WAS I? WHO AM I NOW?

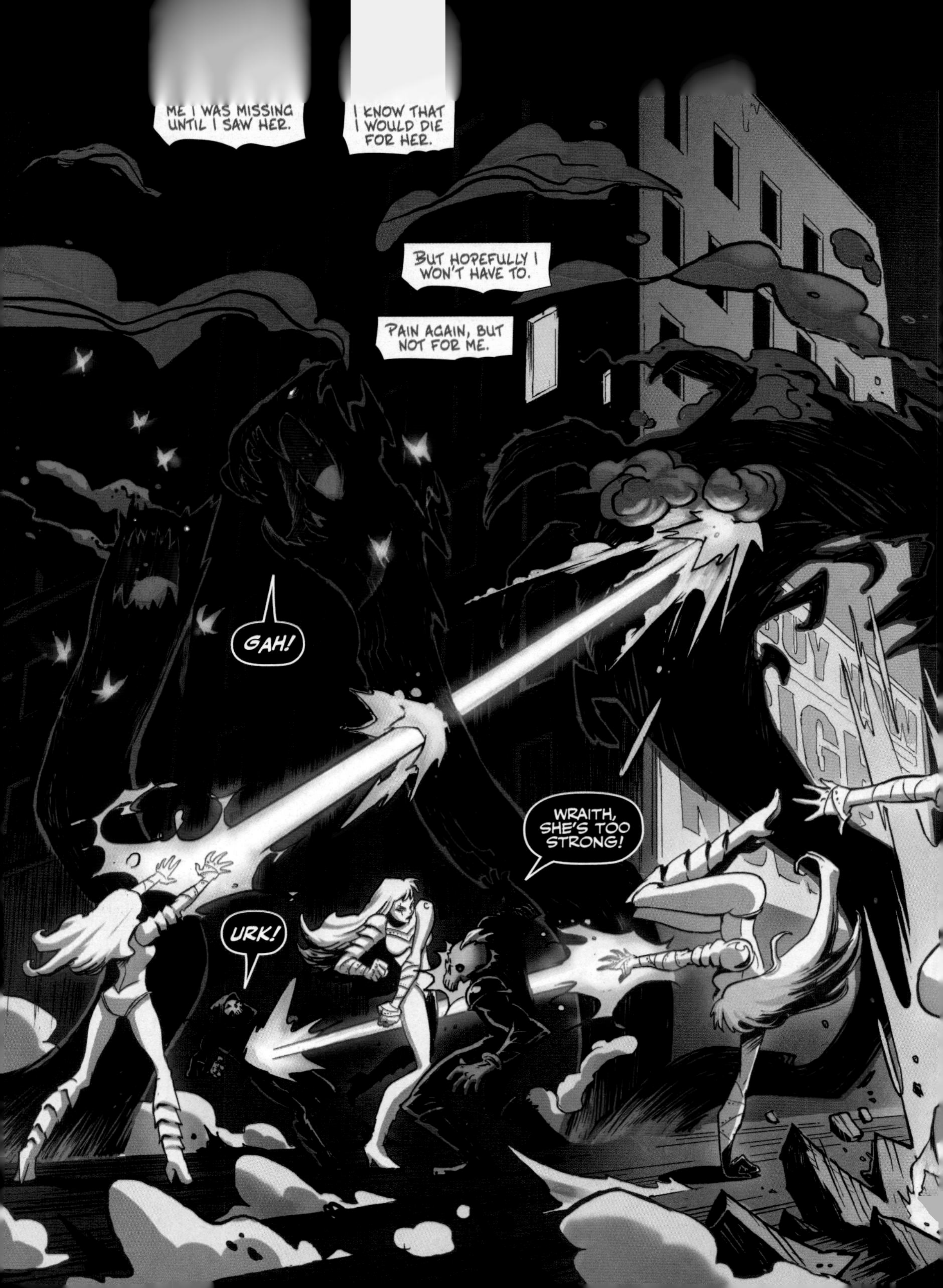
ME I WAS MISSING UNTIL I SAW HER.
I KNOW THAT I WOULD DIE FOR HER.
BUT HOPEFULLY I WON'T HAVE TO.
PAIN AGAIN, BUT NOT FOR ME.
GAH!
WRAITH, SHE'S TOO STRONG!
URK!

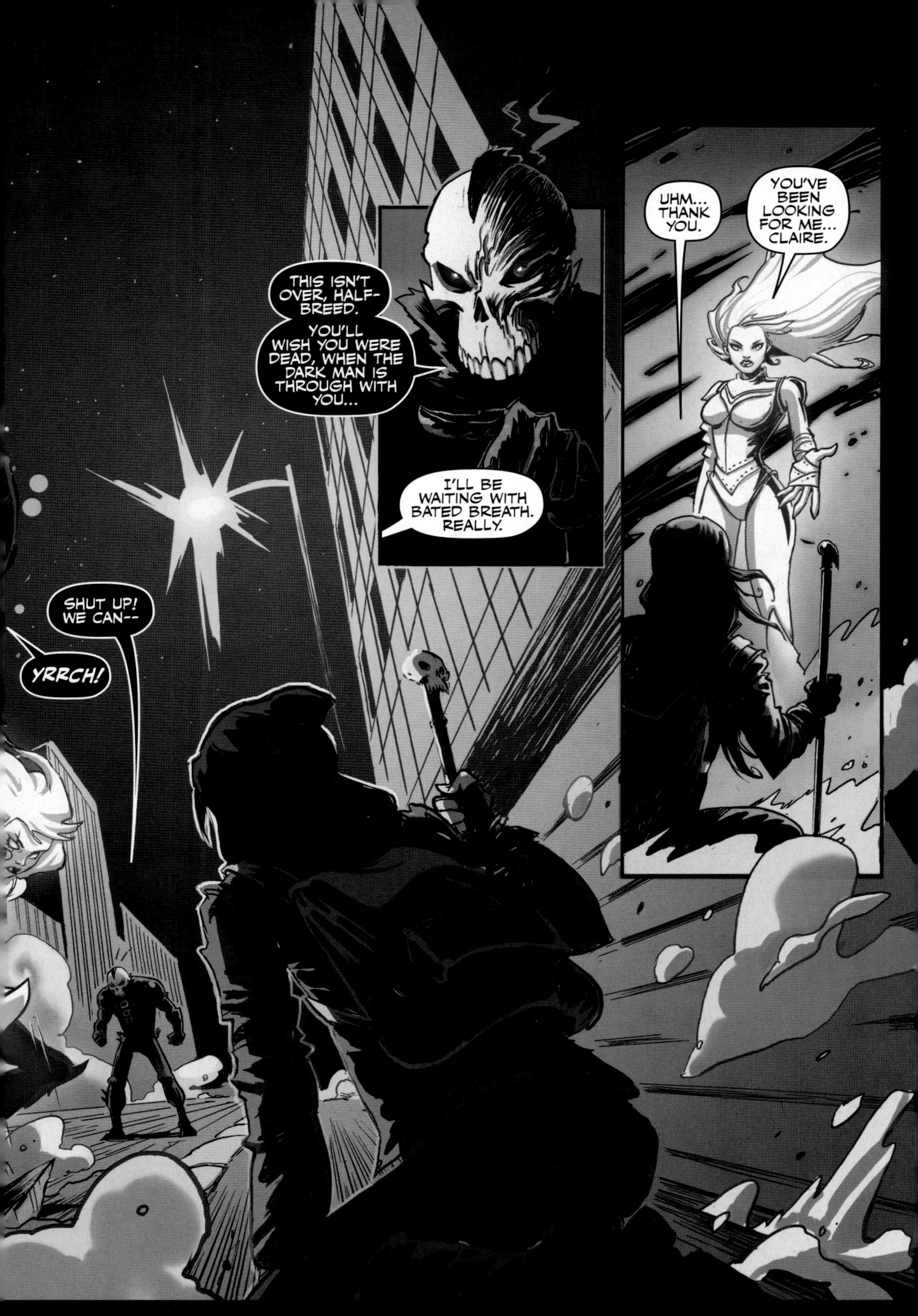

THIS ISN'T OVER, HALF-BREED.
YOU'LL WISH YOU WERE DEAD, WHEN THE DARK MAN IS THROUGH WITH YOU...
I'LL BE WAITING WITH BATED BREATH. REALLY.
UHM... THANK YOU.
YOU'VE BEEN LOOKING FOR ME... CLAIRE.
SHUT UP! WE CAN--
YRRCH!

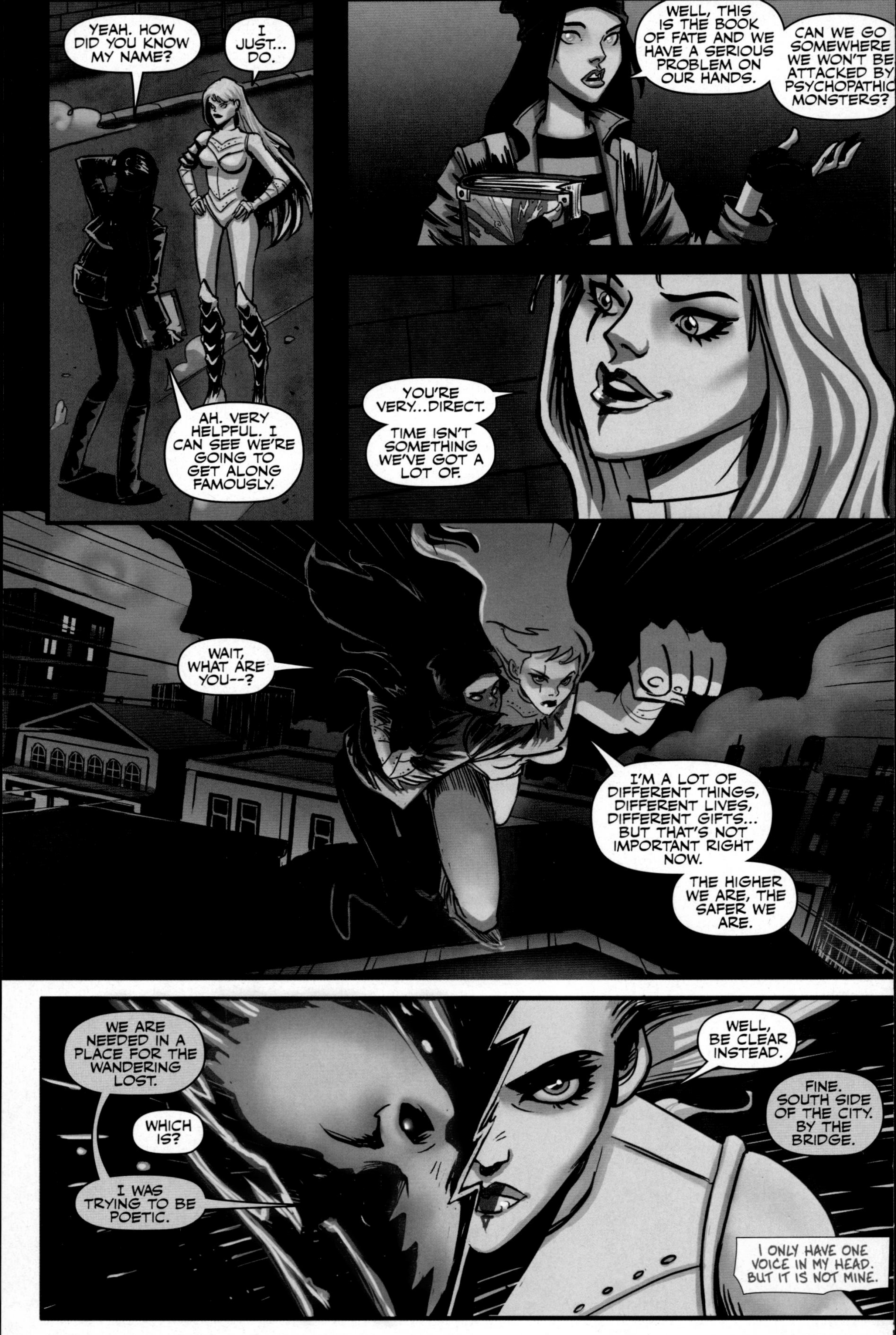
YEAH. HOW DID YOU KNOW MY NAME?
I JUST... DO.
AH. VERY HELPFUL. I CAN SEE WE'RE GOING TO GET ALONG FAMOUSLY.
WELL, THIS IS THE BOOK OF FATE AND WE HAVE A SERIOUS PROBLEM ON OUR HANDS.
CAN WE GO SOMEWHERE WE WON'T BE ATTACKED BY PSYCHOPATHIC MONSTERS?
YOU'RE VERY...DIRECT.
TIME ISN'T SOMETHING WE'VE GOT A LOT OF.
WAIT, WHAT ARE YOU--?
I'M A LOT OF DIFFERENT THINGS, DIFFERENT LIVES, DIFFERENT GIFTS... BUT THAT'S NOT IMPORTANT RIGHT NOW.
THE HIGHER WE ARE, THE SAFER WE ARE.
WE ARE NEEDED IN A PLACE FOR THE WANDERING LOST.
WHICH IS?
I WAS TRYING TO BE POETIC.
WELL, BE CLEAR INSTEAD.
FINE. SOUTH SIDE OF THE CITY. BY THE BRIDGE.
I ONLY HAVE ONE VOICE IN MY HEAD. BUT IT IS NOT MINE.

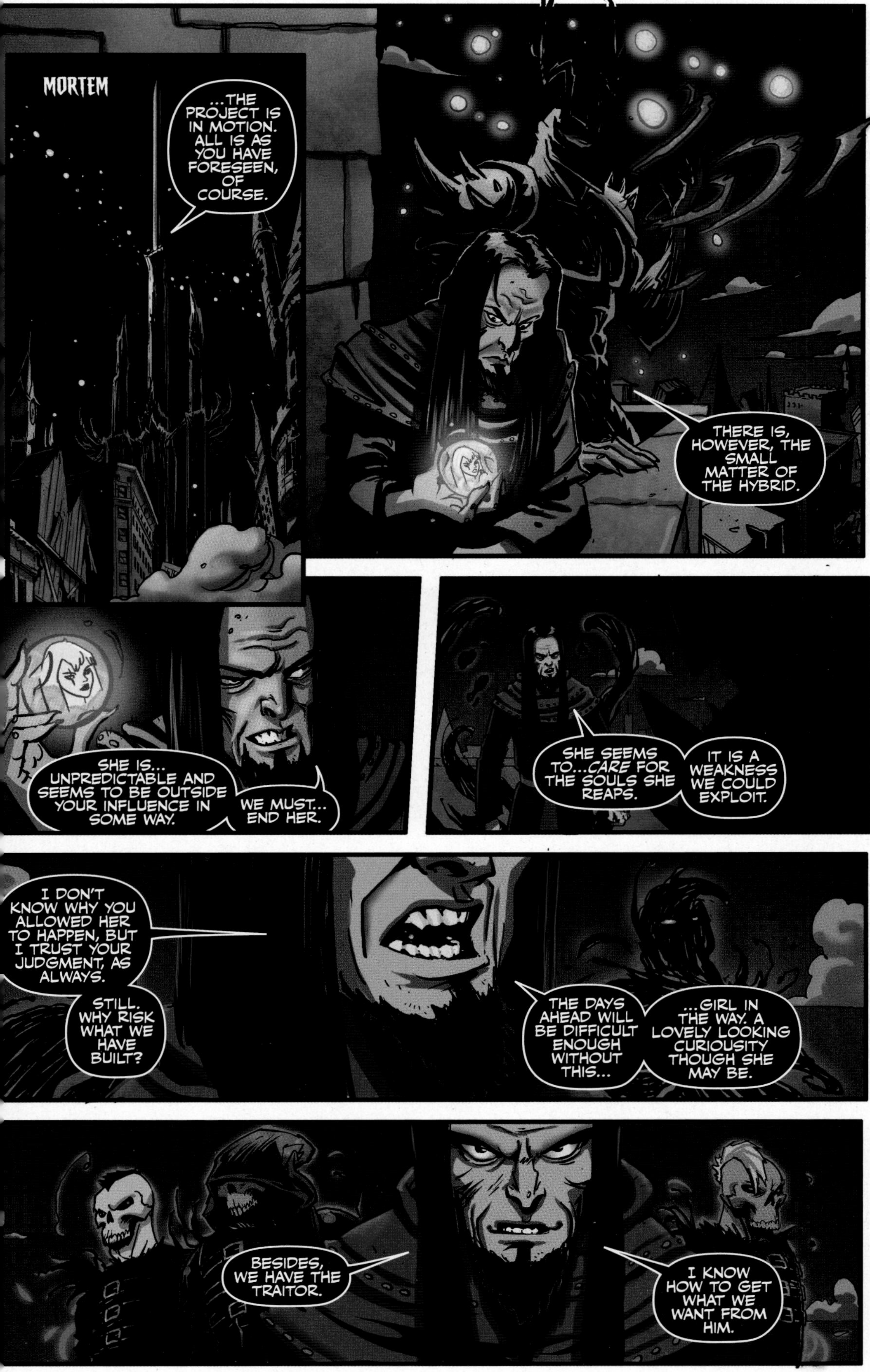
MORTEM
...THE PROJECT IS IN MOTION. ALL IS AS YOU HAVE FORESEEN, OF COURSE.
THERE IS, HOWEVER, THE SMALL MATTER OF THE HYBRID.
SHE IS... UNPREDICTABLE AND SEEMS TO BE OUTSIDE YOUR INFLUENCE IN SOME WAY.
WE MUST... END HER.
SHE SEEMS TO...*CARE* FOR THE SOULS SHE REAPS.
IT IS A WEAKNESS WE COULD EXPLOIT.
I DON'T KNOW WHY YOU ALLOWED HER TO HAPPEN, BUT I TRUST YOUR JUDGMENT, AS ALWAYS.
STILL. WHY RISK WHAT WE HAVE BUILT?
THE DAYS AHEAD WILL BE DIFFICULT ENOUGH WITHOUT THIS...
...GIRL IN THE WAY. A LOVELY LOOKING CURIOUSITY THOUGH SHE MAY BE.
BESIDES, WE HAVE THE TRAITOR.
I KNOW HOW TO GET WHAT WE WANT FROM HIM.

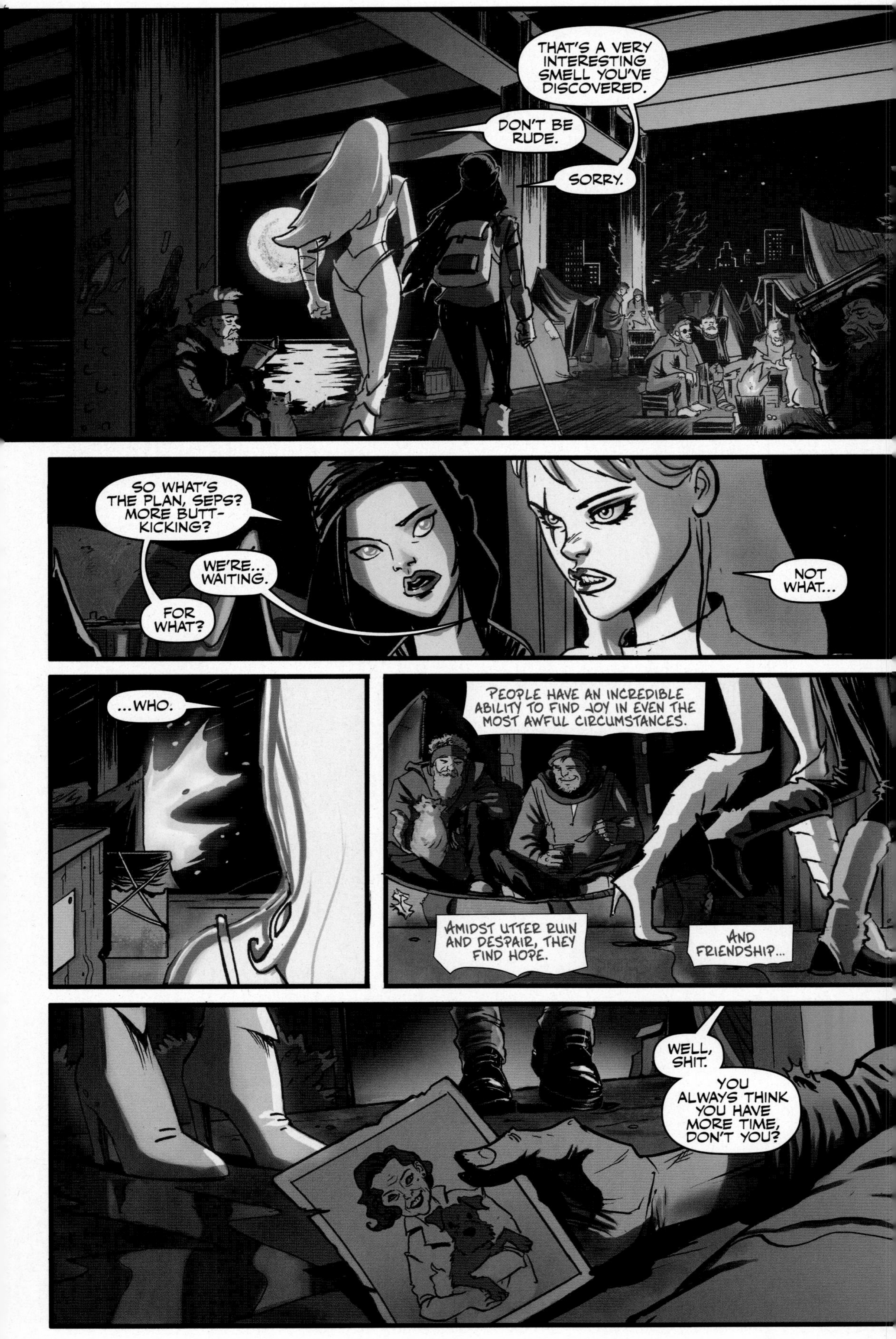
THAT'S A VERY INTERESTING SMELL YOU'VE DISCOVERED.
DON'T BE RUDE.
SORRY.
SO WHAT'S THE PLAN, SEPS? MORE BUTT-KICKING?
WE'RE... WAITING.
FOR WHAT?
NOT WHAT...
...WHO.
PEOPLE HAVE AN INCREDIBLE ABILITY TO FIND JOY IN EVEN THE MOST AWFUL CIRCUMSTANCES.
AMIDST UTTER RUIN AND DESPAIR, THEY FIND HOPE.
AND FRIENDSHIP...
WELL, SHIT.
YOU ALWAYS THINK YOU HAVE MORE TIME, DON'T YOU?

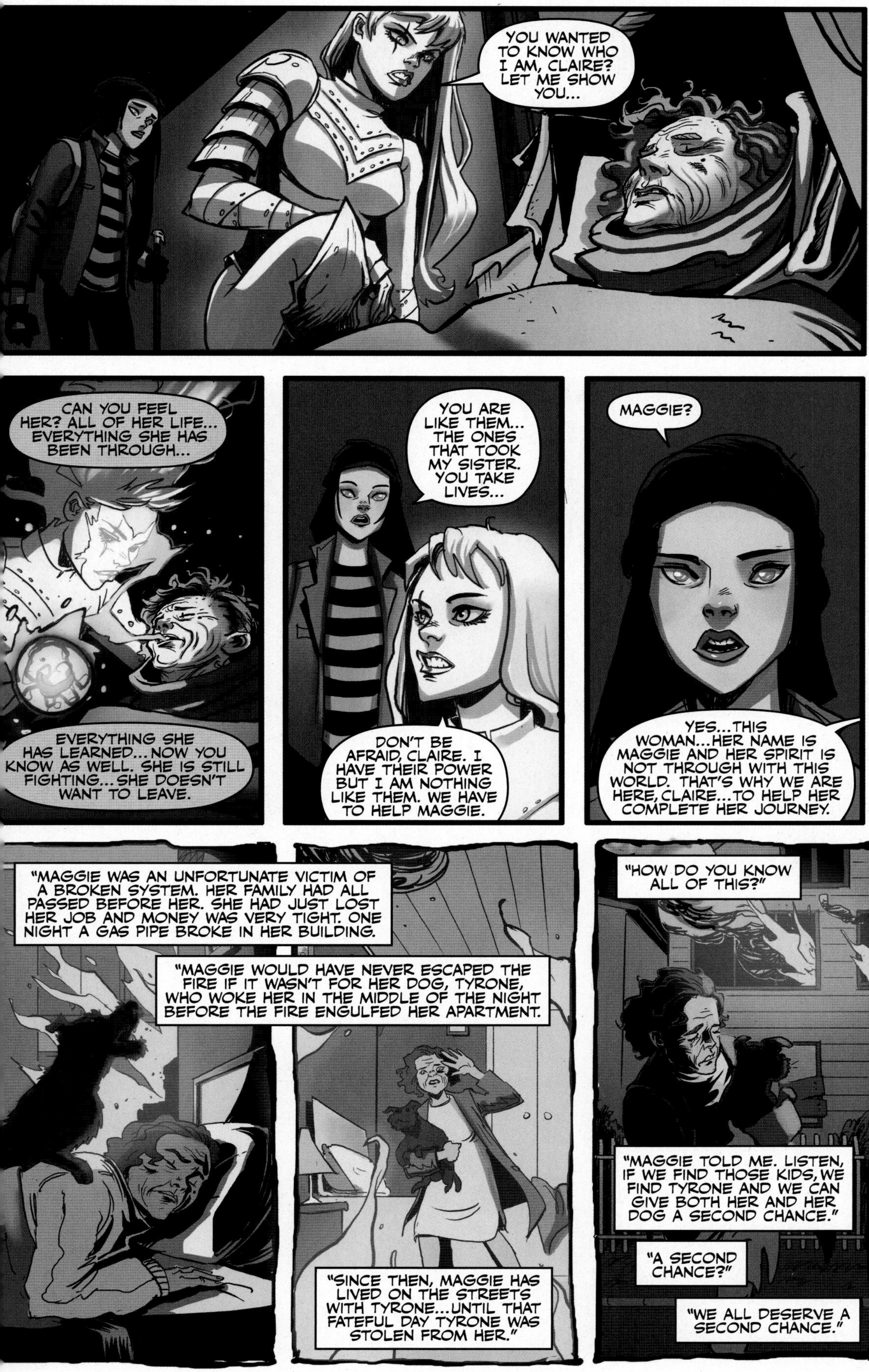
YOU WANTED TO KNOW WHO I AM, CLAIRE? LET ME SHOW YOU...
CAN YOU FEEL HER? ALL OF HER LIFE... EVERYTHING SHE HAS BEEN THROUGH...
EVERYTHING SHE HAS LEARNED... NOW YOU KNOW AS WELL. SHE IS STILL FIGHTING... SHE DOESN'T WANT TO LEAVE.
YOU ARE LIKE THEM... THE ONES THAT TOOK MY SISTER. YOU TAKE LIVES...
DON'T BE AFRAID, CLAIRE. I HAVE THEIR POWER BUT I AM NOTHING LIKE THEM. WE HAVE TO HELP MAGGIE.
MAGGIE?
YES... THIS WOMAN... HER NAME IS MAGGIE AND HER SPIRIT IS NOT THROUGH WITH THIS WORLD. THAT'S WHY WE ARE HERE, CLAIRE... TO HELP HER COMPLETE HER JOURNEY.
"MAGGIE WAS AN UNFORTUNATE VICTIM OF A BROKEN SYSTEM. HER FAMILY HAD ALL PASSED BEFORE HER. SHE HAD JUST LOST HER JOB AND MONEY WAS VERY TIGHT. ONE NIGHT A GAS PIPE BROKE IN HER BUILDING.
"MAGGIE WOULD HAVE NEVER ESCAPED THE FIRE IF IT WASN'T FOR HER DOG, TYRONE, WHO WOKE HER IN THE MIDDLE OF THE NIGHT BEFORE THE FIRE ENGULFED HER APARTMENT.
"SINCE THEN, MAGGIE HAS LIVED ON THE STREETS WITH TYRONE... UNTIL THAT FATEFUL DAY TYRONE WAS STOLEN FROM HER."
"HOW DO YOU KNOW ALL OF THIS?"
"MAGGIE TOLD ME. LISTEN, IF WE FIND THOSE KIDS, WE FIND TYRONE AND WE CAN GIVE BOTH HER AND HER DOG A SECOND CHANCE."
"A SECOND CHANCE?"
"WE ALL DESERVE A SECOND CHANCE."

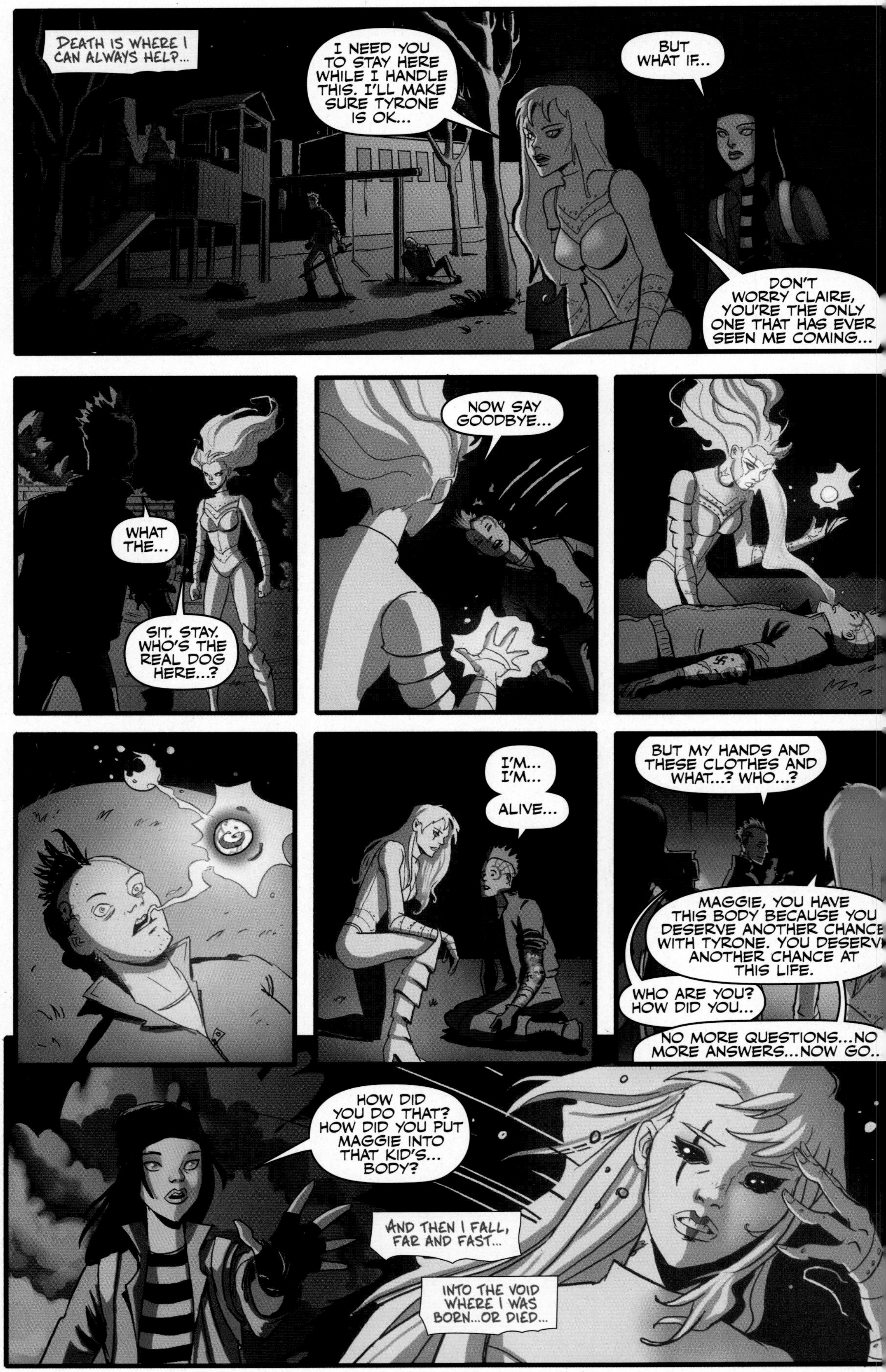
DEATH IS WHERE I CAN ALWAYS HELP...
I NEED YOU TO STAY HERE WHILE I HANDLE THIS. I'LL MAKE SURE TYRONE IS OK...
BUT WHAT IF...
DON'T WORRY CLAIRE, YOU'RE THE ONLY ONE THAT HAS EVER SEEN ME COMING...
WHAT THE...
SIT. STAY. WHO'S THE REAL DOG HERE...?
NOW SAY GOODBYE...
I'M... I'M...
ALIVE...
BUT MY HANDS AND THESE CLOTHES AND WHAT...? WHO...?
MAGGIE, YOU HAVE THIS BODY BECAUSE YOU DESERVE ANOTHER CHANCE WITH TYRONE. YOU DESERVE ANOTHER CHANCE AT THIS LIFE.
WHO ARE YOU? HOW DID YOU...
NO MORE QUESTIONS...NO MORE ANSWERS...NOW GO...
HOW DID YOU DO THAT? HOW DID YOU PUT MAGGIE INTO THAT KID'S... BODY?
AND THEN I FALL, FAR AND FAST...
INTO THE VOID WHERE I WAS BORN...OR DIED...

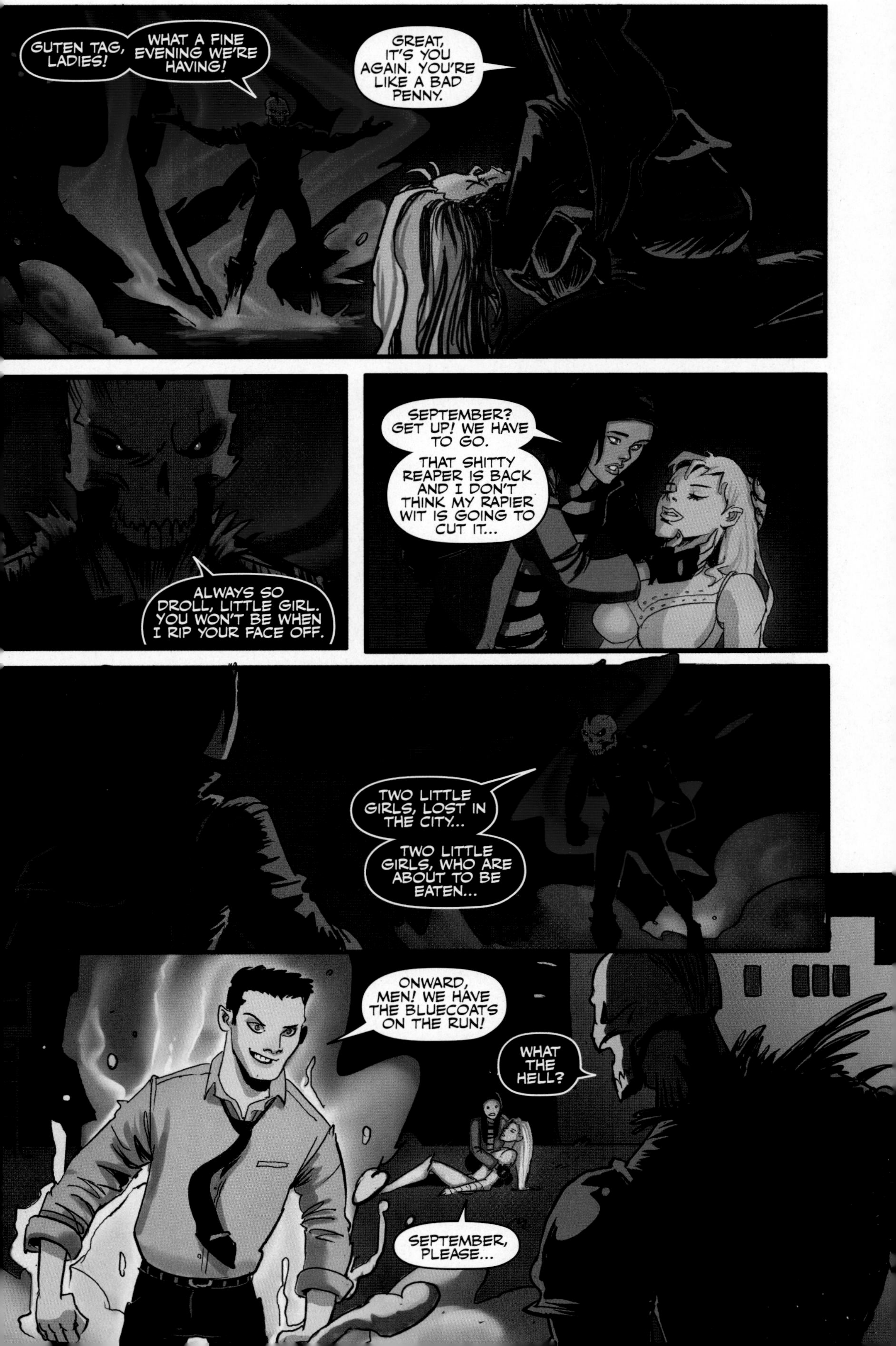
GUTEN TAG, LADIES!
WHAT A FINE EVENING WE'RE HAVING!
GREAT, IT'S YOU AGAIN. YOU'RE LIKE A BAD PENNY.
ALWAYS SO DROLL, LITTLE GIRL. YOU WON'T BE WHEN I RIP YOUR FACE OFF.
SEPTEMBER? GET UP! WE HAVE TO GO.
THAT SHITTY REAPER IS BACK AND I DON'T THINK MY RAPIER WIT IS GOING TO CUT IT...
TWO LITTLE GIRLS, LOST IN THE CITY...
TWO LITTLE GIRLS, WHO ARE ABOUT TO BE EATEN...
ONWARD, MEN! WE HAVE THE BLUECOATS ON THE RUN!
WHAT THE HELL?
SEPTEMBER, PLEASE...

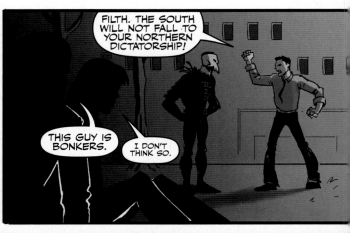

OH, IT'S YOU! MY OLD PAL PAT, THE CONFEDERATE SOLDIER WHO DIED NOBLY FIGHTING FOR THE RIGHT TO OWN PEOPLE?

IT SEEMS YOU HAVE JUMPED YET AGAIN INTO ANOTHER MORTAL...

THIS ONE FAR LESS PRETTY AND DEFINITELY MORE STUFFY...I GUESS YOU WORE OUT THAT OTHER BODY HUH? WHAT A SHAME HEHEHE....

FILTH. THE SOUTH WILL NOT FALL TO YOUR NORTHERN DICTATORSHIP!

THIS GUY IS BONKERS.

I DON'T THINK SO.

YEAH, YEAH. THE SOUTH WILL RISE AGAIN. RIGHT.

ARE YOU OKAY?

NO, BUT I FEEL A LITTLE STRONGER...

JUST HOLD ON, AND TRUST ME.

WAIT, HOW DID YOU GET OVER THE--?

SWASSSSH

I BEG YOUR PARDON, SIR, BUT I MUST BE GOING NOW...

THANK YOU FOR THE CHAT, BUT I HAVE A WAR TO FIGHT.

I AM SO DEAD...

SLWIP

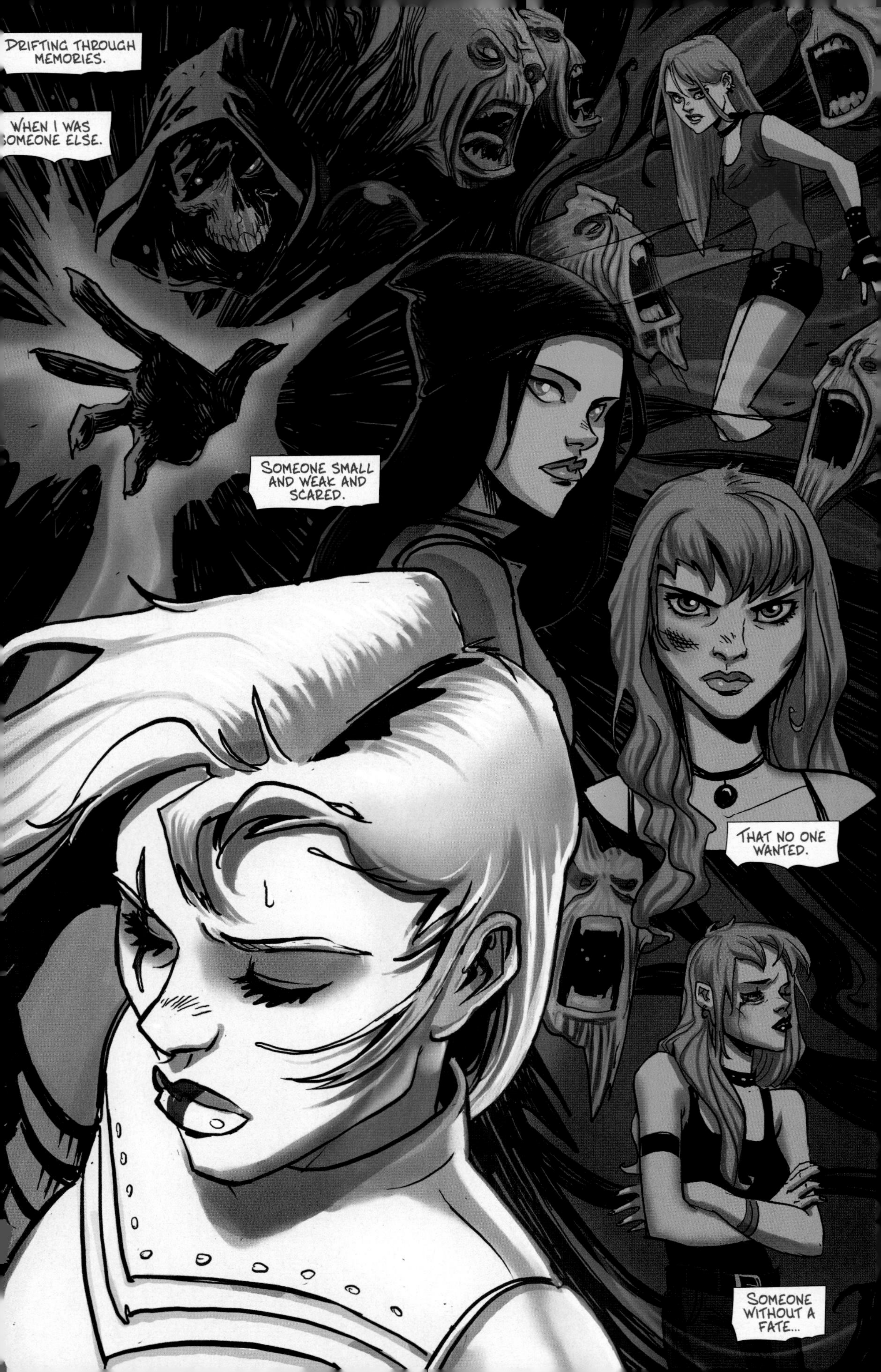
DRIFTING THROUGH MEMORIES.
WHEN I WAS SOMEONE ELSE.
SOMEONE SMALL AND WEAK AND SCARED.
THAT NO ONE WANTED.
SOMEONE WITHOUT A FATE...

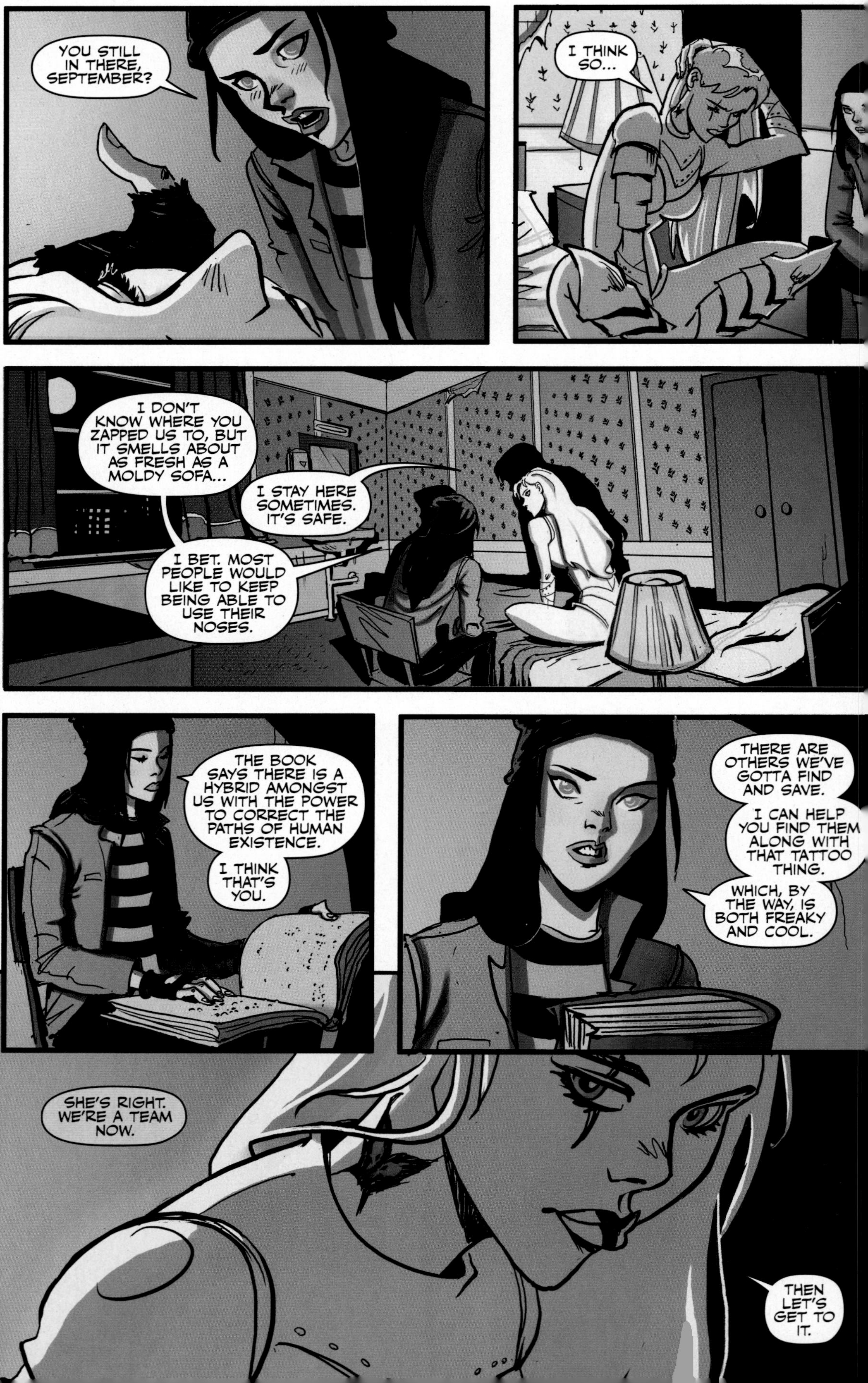

YOU STILL IN THERE, SEPTEMBER?
I THINK SO...
I DON'T KNOW WHERE YOU ZAPPED US TO, BUT IT SMELLS ABOUT AS FRESH AS A MOLDY SOFA...
I STAY HERE SOMETIMES. IT'S SAFE.
I BET. MOST PEOPLE WOULD LIKE TO KEEP BEING ABLE TO USE THEIR NOSES.
THE BOOK SAYS THERE IS A HYBRID AMONGST US WITH THE POWER TO CORRECT THE PATHS OF HUMAN EXISTENCE.
I THINK THAT'S YOU.
THERE ARE OTHERS WE'VE GOTTA FIND AND SAVE.
I CAN HELP YOU FIND THEM ALONG WITH THAT TATTOO THING.
WHICH, BY THE WAY, IS BOTH FREAKY AND COOL.
SHE'S RIGHT. WE'RE A TEAM NOW.
THEN LET'S GET TO IT.

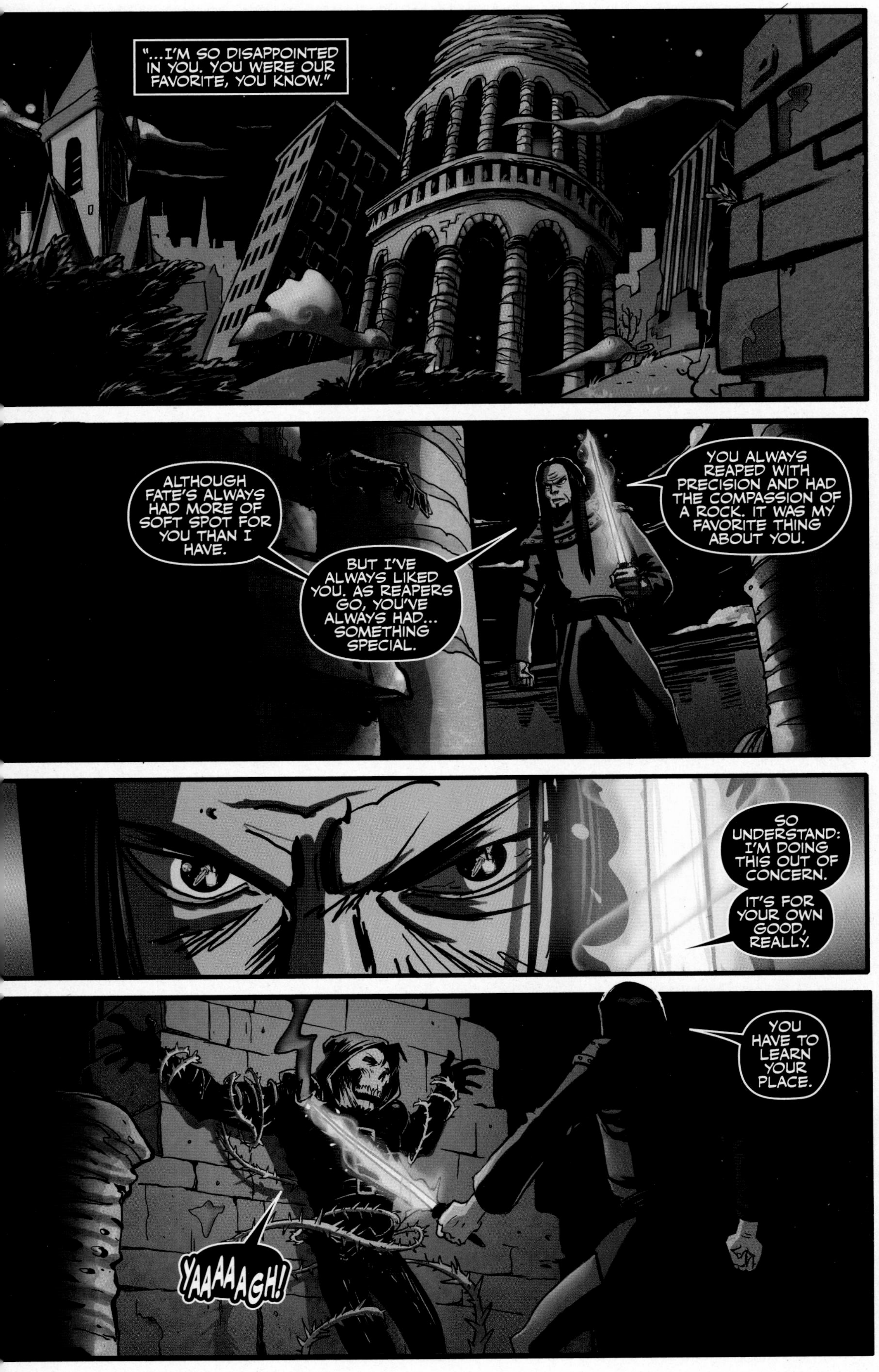
"...I'M SO DISAPPOINTED IN YOU. YOU WERE OUR FAVORITE, YOU KNOW."
ALTHOUGH FATE'S ALWAYS HAD MORE OF SOFT SPOT FOR YOU THAN I HAVE.
BUT I'VE ALWAYS LIKED YOU. AS REAPERS GO, YOU'VE ALWAYS HAD... SOMETHING SPECIAL.
YOU ALWAYS REAPED WITH PRECISION AND HAD THE COMPASSION OF A ROCK. IT WAS MY FAVORITE THING ABOUT YOU.
SO UNDERSTAND: I'M DOING THIS OUT OF CONCERN.
IT'S FOR YOUR OWN GOOD, REALLY.
YOU HAVE TO LEARN YOUR PLACE.
YAAAAAGH!

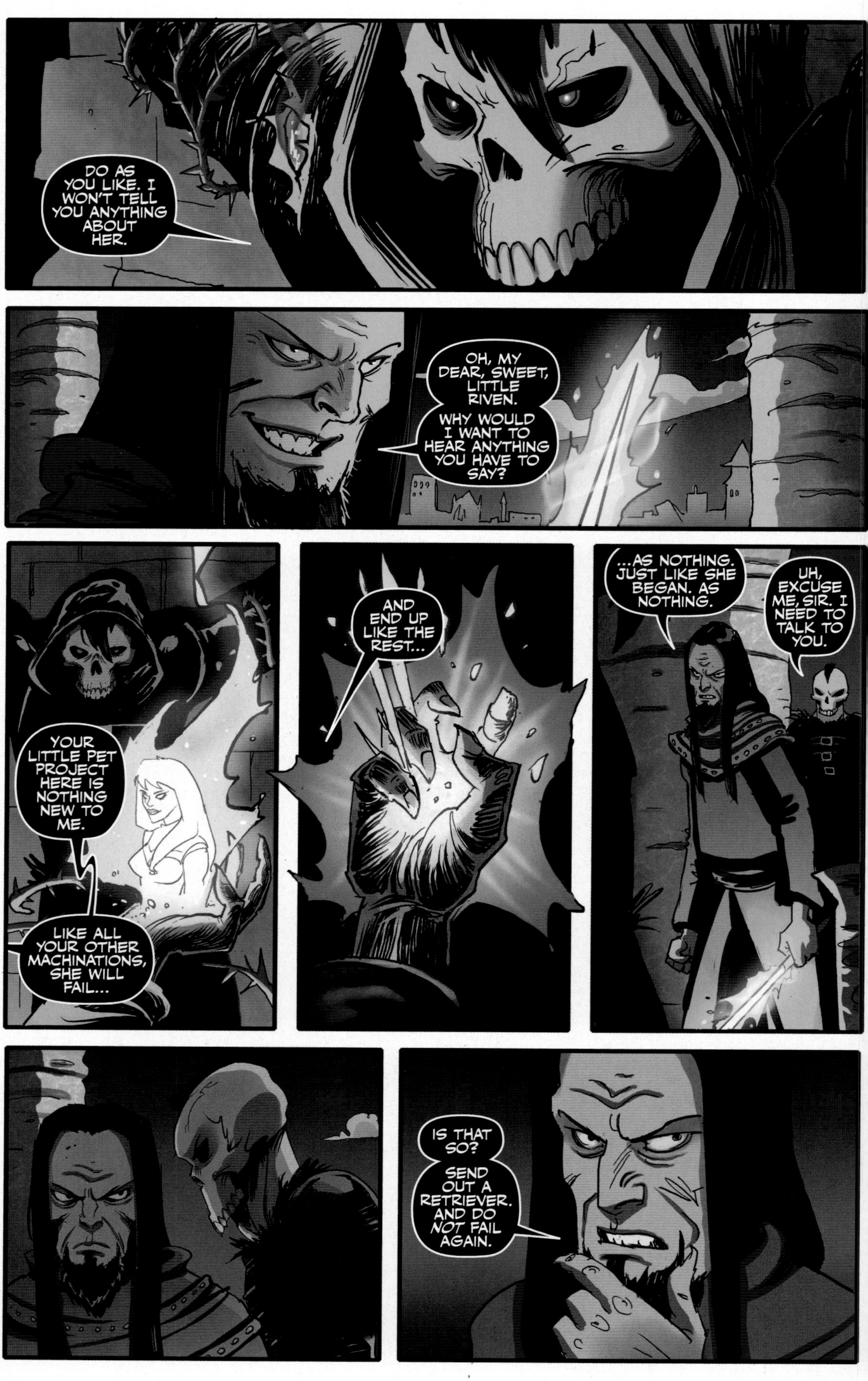
DO AS YOU LIKE. I WON'T TELL YOU ANYTHING ABOUT HER.
OH, MY DEAR, SWEET, LITTLE RIVEN.
WHY WOULD I WANT TO HEAR ANYTHING YOU HAVE TO SAY?
YOUR LITTLE PET PROJECT HERE IS NOTHING NEW TO ME.
LIKE ALL YOUR OTHER MACHINATIONS, SHE WILL FAIL...
AND END UP LIKE THE REST...
...AS NOTHING. JUST LIKE SHE BEGAN. AS NOTHING.
UH, EXCUSE ME, SIR. I NEED TO TALK TO YOU.
IS THAT SO?
SEND OUT A RETRIEVER. AND DO *NOT* FAIL AGAIN.

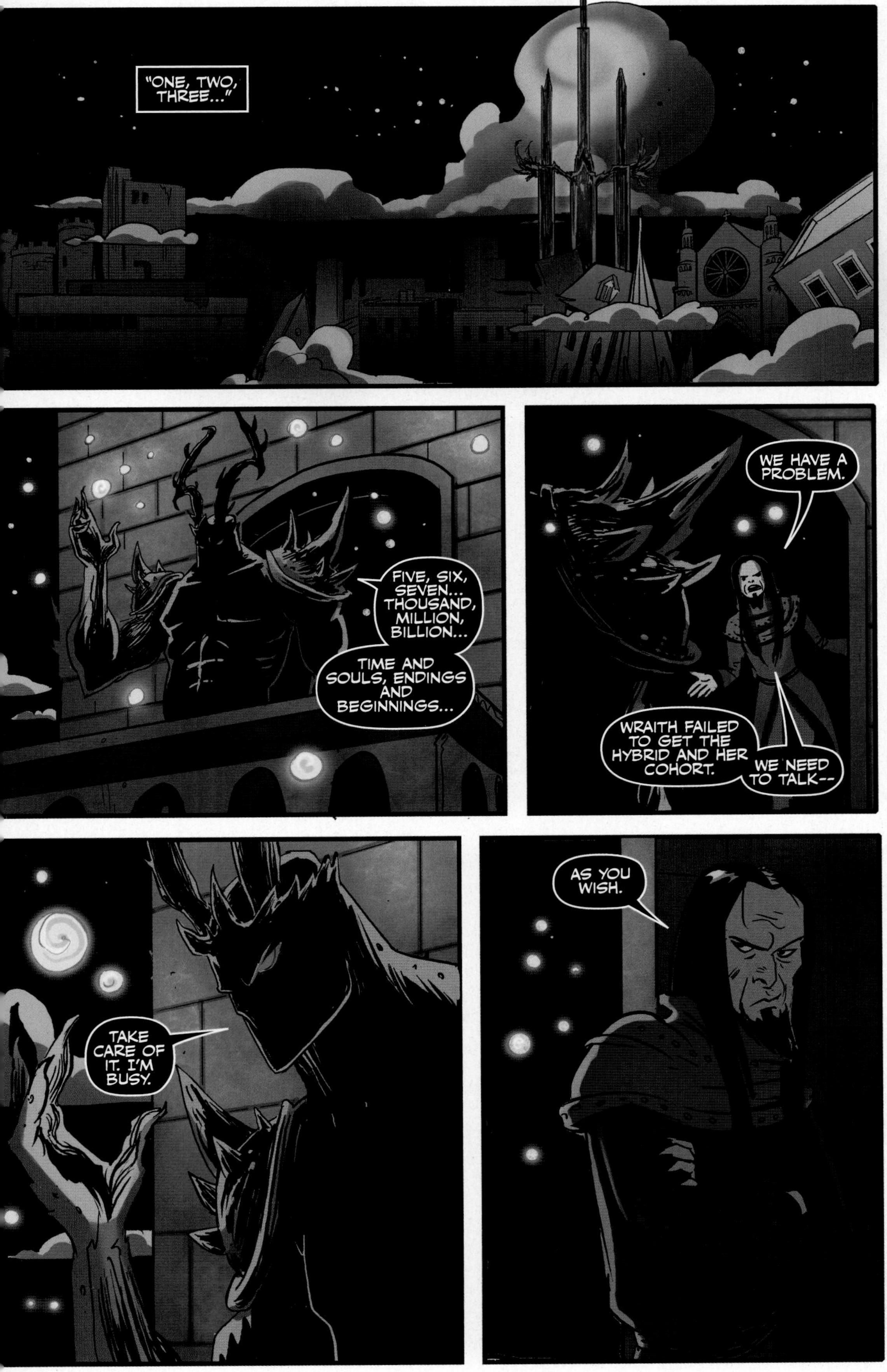
"ONE, TWO, THREE..."
FIVE, SIX, SEVEN... THOUSAND, MILLION, BILLION...
TIME AND SOULS, ENDINGS AND BEGINNINGS...
WE HAVE A PROBLEM.
WRAITH FAILED TO GET THE HYBRID AND HER COHORT.
WE NEED TO TALK--
TAKE CARE OF IT. I'M BUSY.
AS YOU WISH.

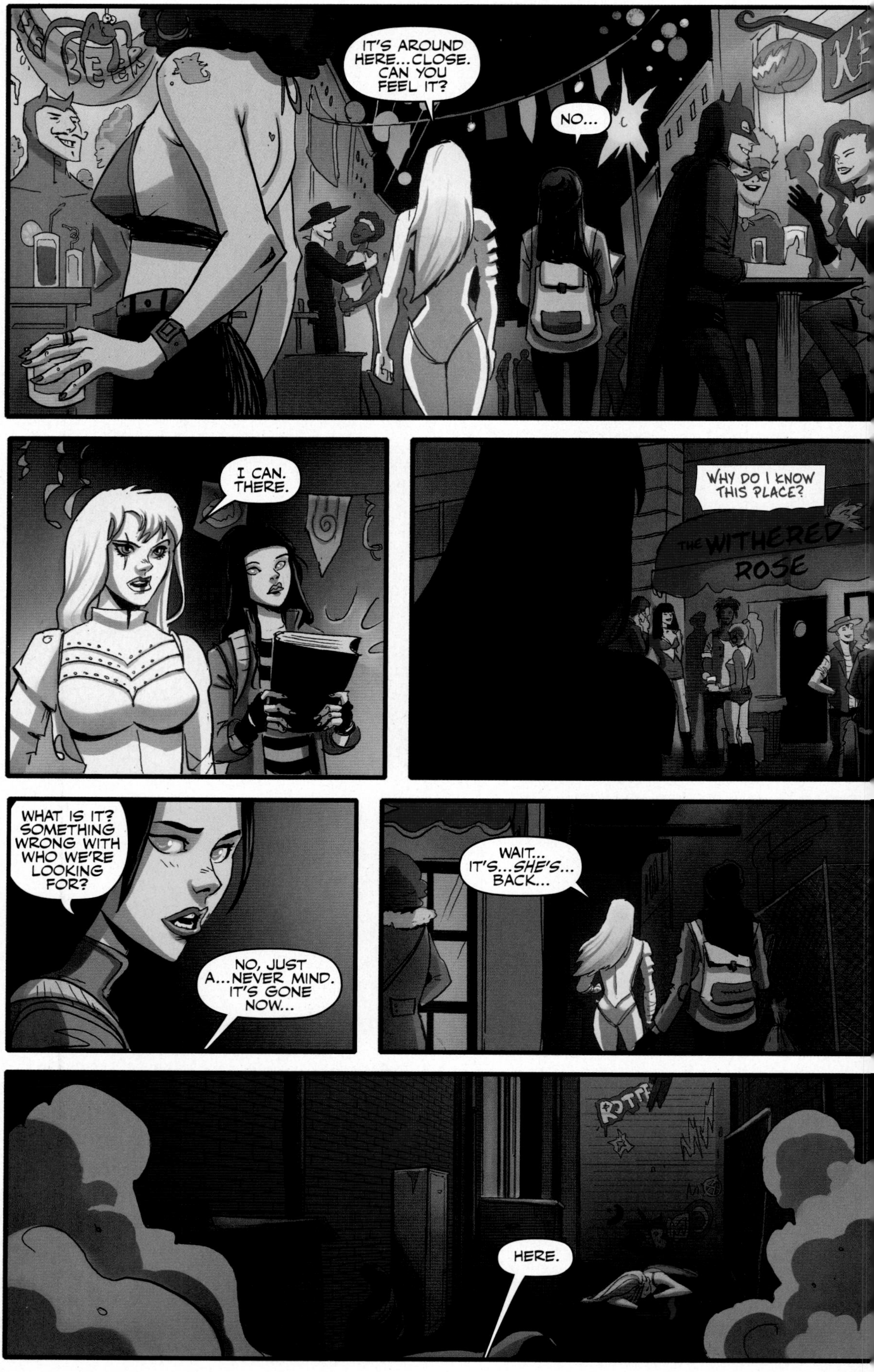
IT'S AROUND HERE...CLOSE. CAN YOU FEEL IT?
NO...
I CAN. THERE.
WHY DO I KNOW THIS PLACE?
THE WITHERED ROSE
WHAT IS IT? SOMETHING WRONG WITH WHO WE'RE LOOKING FOR?
NO, JUST A...NEVER MIND. IT'S GONE NOW...
WAIT... IT'S...SHE'S... BACK...
HERE.

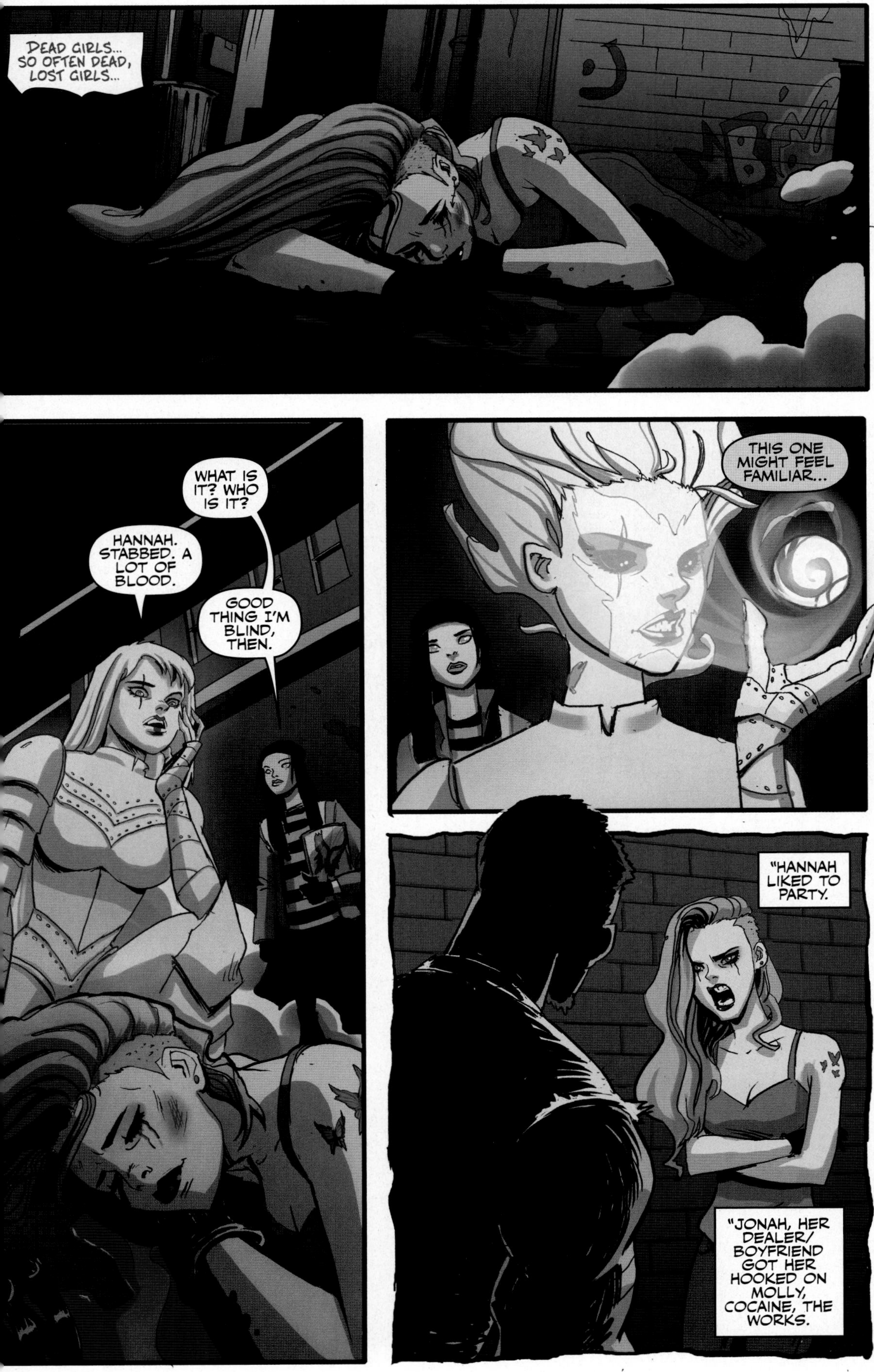
DEAD GIRLS... SO OFTEN DEAD, LOST GIRLS...
WHAT IS IT? WHO IS IT?
HANNAH. STABBED. A LOT OF BLOOD.
GOOD THING I'M BLIND, THEN.
THIS ONE MIGHT FEEL FAMILIAR...
"HANNAH LIKED TO PARTY.
"JONAH, HER DEALER/ BOYFRIEND GOT HER HOOKED ON MOLLY, COCAINE, THE WORKS.

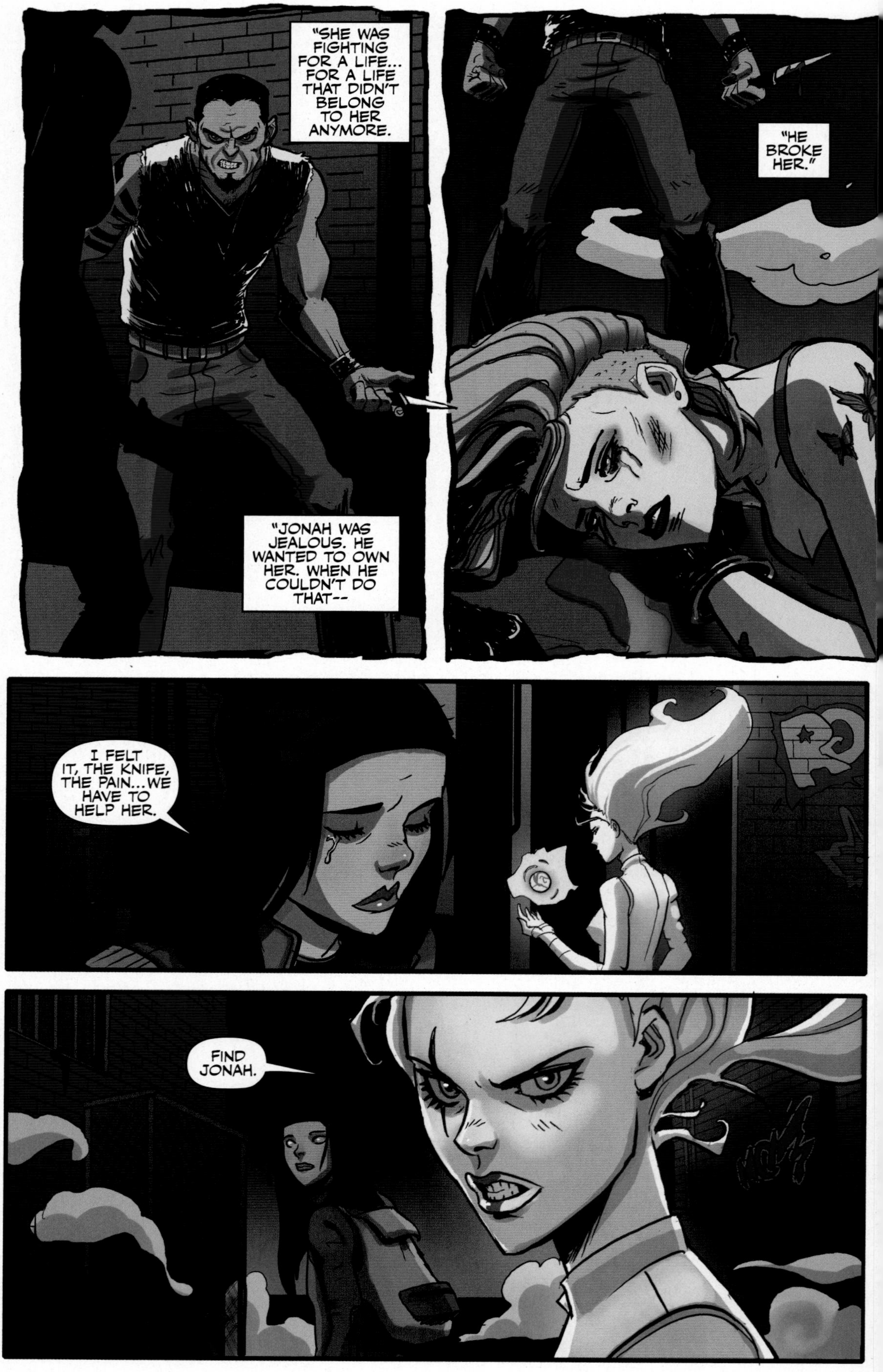
"SHE WAS FIGHTING FOR A LIFE... FOR A LIFE THAT DIDN'T BELONG TO HER ANYMORE.
"JONAH WAS JEALOUS. HE WANTED TO OWN HER. WHEN HE COULDN'T DO THAT--
"HE BROKE HER."
I FELT IT, THE KNIFE, THE PAIN...WE HAVE TO HELP HER.
FIND JONAH.

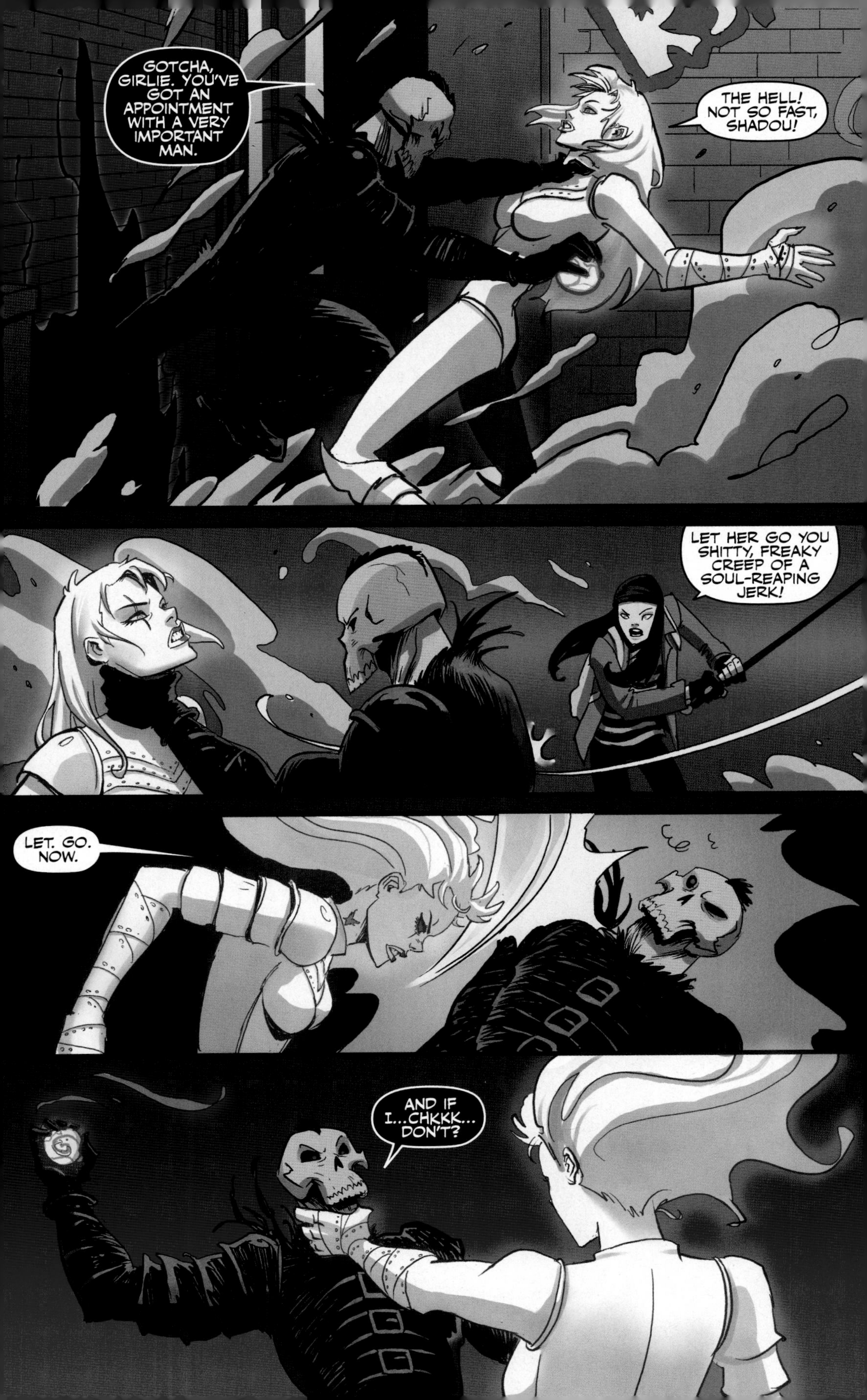
GOTCHA, GIRLIE. YOU'VE GOT AN APPOINTMENT WITH A VERY IMPORTANT MAN.
THE HELL! NOT SO FAST, SHADOU!
LET HER GO YOU SHITTY, FREAKY CREEP OF A SOUL-REAPING JERK!
LET. GO. NOW.
AND IF I...CHKKK... DON'T?

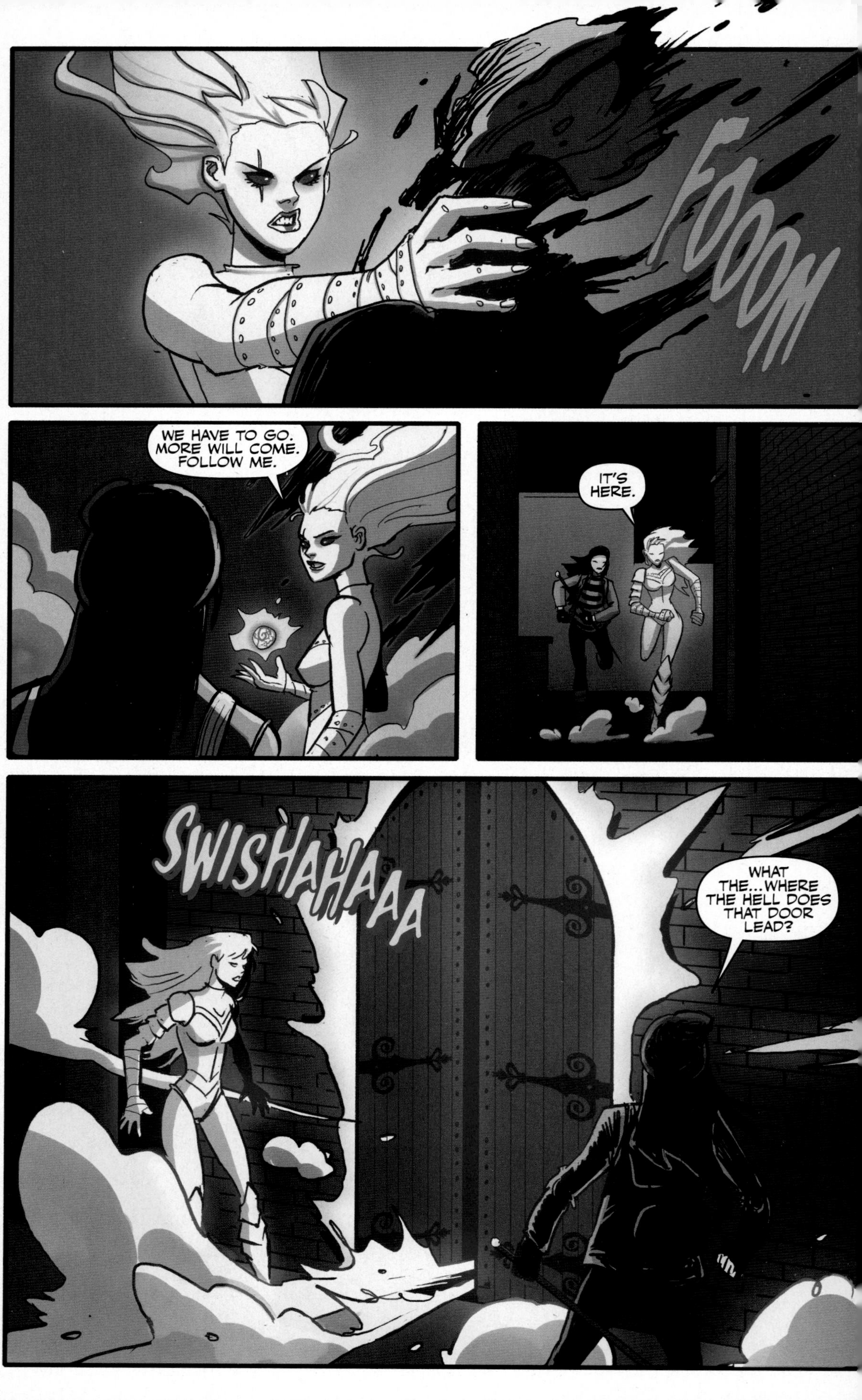
FOOOM
WE HAVE TO GO. MORE WILL COME. FOLLOW ME.
IT'S HERE.
SWISHAHAAAA
WHAT THE...WHERE THE HELL DOES THAT DOOR LEAD?

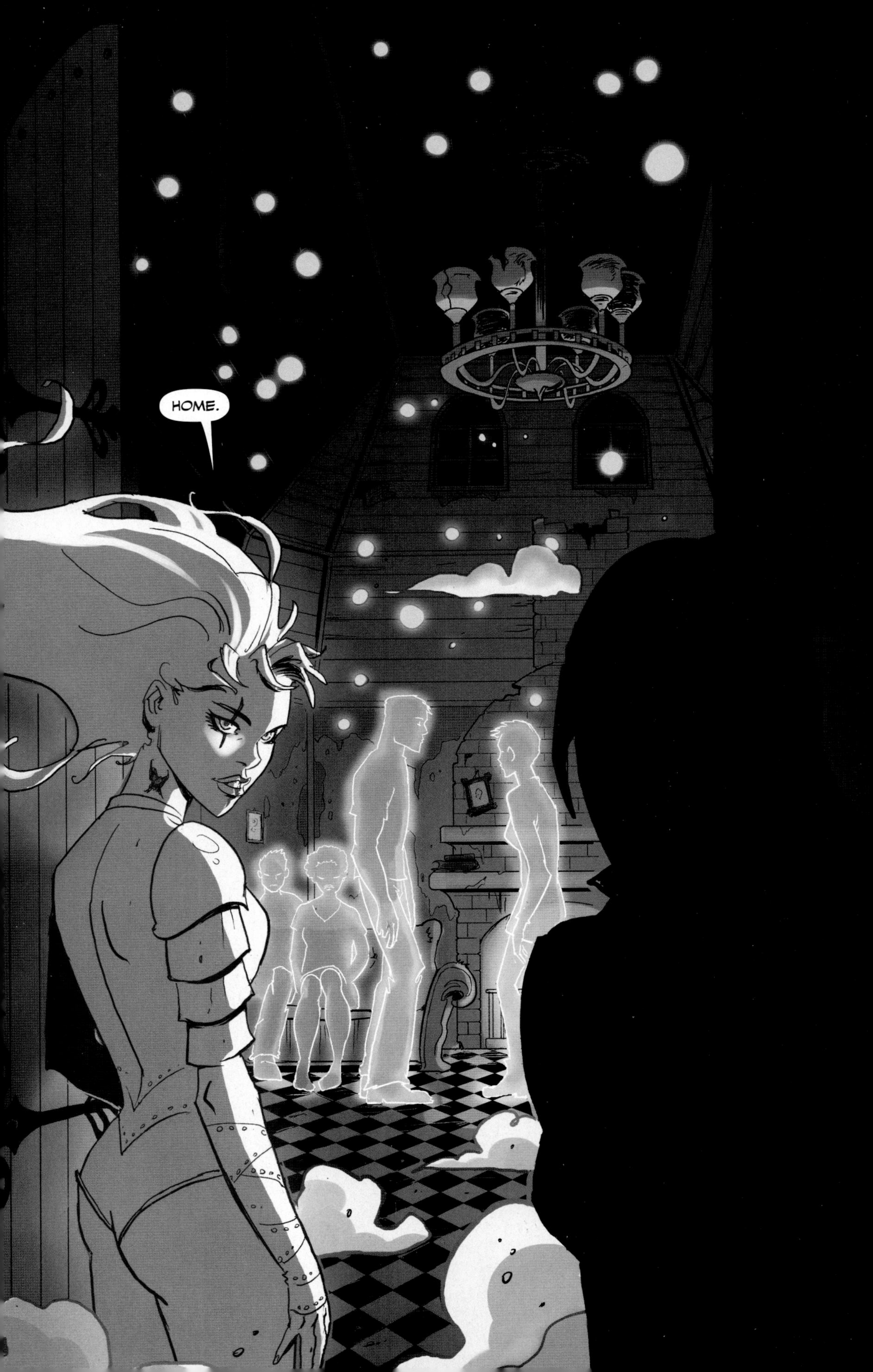
HOME.

To our Kickstarter Children of Fate
THANK YOU!

Aaron Alexovich, Aaron Seipel, Aimee Hurst, AJ, Alan Candler, Alexander Strindberg, Amalia Helene Menna, Amanda, Amber M Holcomb, Amelia Constance Laughlan, Andres Plaza, Andrew E. C. Head, Andy Gould, Angeline Burton, Anthony Pierce, Anthony Rivera, Antonio Couzo, Arthur Washburne IV, Ashley Hill, Astria Starwynd, Aurelia, Ben Kahn, Beth, Blaine Hodge III, Bob Salley, bobby kirchner, Bradley Bradley, Brian, Brian Fox, Brian Steadman, Brian Swinburne, Bryan Greiner, Callum Wood, Cam Mezé, CanerŞahin, Carmen Ryan, Carolina Panero, Casey, CatherineHG, Cathy Schwartz, Chadwick Torseth, Charles Boyung, Charles j. Carroll, Chastity Ashley, Chimaera, Chris Dresden, Chris Mamitag, Christa Brolley, CK Russell, Claire Findley, Claire Murray, Clare Mothershaw-Henney, Claus Nielsen, clydene nee, Cole Coleman, colin65, creekstone, Cristiana, D Kelly, Dakota Horbaczek, Damon English, dan, Dana, Danny Occhipinti, Darren Vellnagel, David Berck, David Brewer, David Cechini, David Cole, David Duritsky, David Edwards Jr., David Golbitz, David Lizewski, David Mayo, dee, Derek Freeman, Devon Zoccole, Donald Ferris, Donna Poole Watson, Edgarín Ulrico, Elaine Cassell, Ellen Douglas, Emily Felt, Emily Maret, Emily Swan, Ethan Belanger, Eva Jarkiewicz, Everett Criswell, Feirbrand, Fernando Del Bosque, Gaëlle Muavaka, Gary Bloom, Gary Strysick, Gavin K-Y, geoff mcneill, Glaring Mistake, Grant Nelson, Greg Scott Bailey, Haley Williams, hanksfan, Harrison, Heather Palmer, Heidi, Hendrik Blom, Howard Benson, Independent Comic Book Review, Isaac 'Will It Work' Dansicker, Ivy A. Nightmare, J.R. Riedel, Jacob "Ryoku" Walker, James Ferguson, James Goodwin, James Renger, Jaquilyn Mackey, Jason Barton Smith, Jason Chesley, Jason Langenkamp, Jason Leung, Jason Robinson, Jay Bandoy, Jay Magnum, Jean-Francois Larochelle, Jeffrey Bridges, Jen Miller, Jenna Oliver, Jennifer Graevell, Jennifer Wick, Jeremy Wallace, Jerry Walter, Jessica, jester59388, Jim Marion, Joan Dendroff, Joe Martino, Joel Kepler, Joey, John Ashton-Keller, John Grigas, John Idlor, John MacLeod, John Nee, John Neiberger, John Thornburgh, Johnny Kuramoto, Jonathan Bowen, jordan mccabe (dan), Jordan

Colton, Josh C, Josh Morris, Josh Southall, Joshua, Julio A. Ayala Angulo, Justin Agin, Kai Norcross, Kali, Kallen, Karolien Kathryn Kramer, Katy Rex, Keith Brady, Keith Shimabukuro, Kelly Cassidy, Ken Dare, Kevin Magill, kevin matzel, Kevin McCormick, Kristof Mar, Kyle Fleishman, Kyle Rupert, Lance J Graham, Lance Seifert, LateToTheParty7, Lewis Kajune, Lilavati, Lindsay Garside, Lori Klepper, Luc Rivard, Lucas Patterson, Luis Salgado, Maggie Phoenix, Maggie Wright, Marc Pipitone, MarcelŠtefánik, Marcos A. Davila, Mark Myers, Mark Patterson, Mark Sugiyama, mark williams, Mason "Cheeser" Williams, Mats W, Matt DeVoe, Matt Grisdela, Matt M McElroy, Matt McCue, Matt Murphy, Matthew Edwards, matthew mihalko, Mauro, Mayer Turkin, Michael, Michael Grafton, Michael Mariano, Michael Woodson, Michel McCammon, Mike Beck, Mike Earl, Mike Ohsfeldt, Millie Fi Mayfield, Miriam Ramsey, Morgan Szufnarowski, nabil, Naser, Nathaniel Mohr, Ndras, Nicholas Vieth, Nikki DeHaven, Nissa Day, oooohzones, oscar m baez, PantherPage, Patrick Webster, Paul Moskowitz, Paul Yeates, Phil, Phil Ogden, Philip Butler-Lee, plueschkissen, Preston Propes, Quanah Otto, R. Matthews, R.Soares, Rame, Rocket-Man Hill, Raúl Treviño, Ray Boone, RayK, rckrafft, Rebecca Fraser, Reizak, Revenant, Rhiannon Raphael, Richard, Richard Hartwig, Richard Petty, Richard Schwartz, Rick Ernst, Rob, Rob Al, Rob Ryan, Rob Soto, Robert Dyche, Robert Jan de Vries, robin smith, Ron Peterson, Royce Viso, Ryan Lenig, Ryan Quint, Samba Krueger, Sarey Martin McIvor, Savanna Valdez, scott mitchell rosenberg, Scott Sullivan, Sean McConnell, Sean Millott, Sebastian Matthews, Sergio Talavera, Shadow, Shahria, Fouladi, Shanna Maria Hayward, Shannon, Sharon Wells, Shaun Bezold, Shawn Hill, Shoshana Sternlicht, Slamfist Media, Step Wallace, Stephanie, Stephen Byrnes, Stephen Di Palma, Stephen Loiaconi, Steven Clark, Steven Hoveke, Stone Chin, Stu Copland, SwordFire, Takashi Oguchi, TAKEHIKO AMANO, Tamarra Leigh Phillips, Tara Krueger, Tess, Tessa Riley, Thomas Zilling, Tormented WoOS of OOoE, Thorsten, Timmi Dennis, tina turner, Tom Akel, Tom Mandrake/ John Ostrander, Trent Knouse, Trinere, TwistedMusicLover, Tyler Sex son, Tymothy, Vicki, Wade Parsons, Wayne Melvin, William McMillan II, William Mix, Xandy Barry, You Can Sleep When You're Dead, Yusuf Artun, Zach Crawford

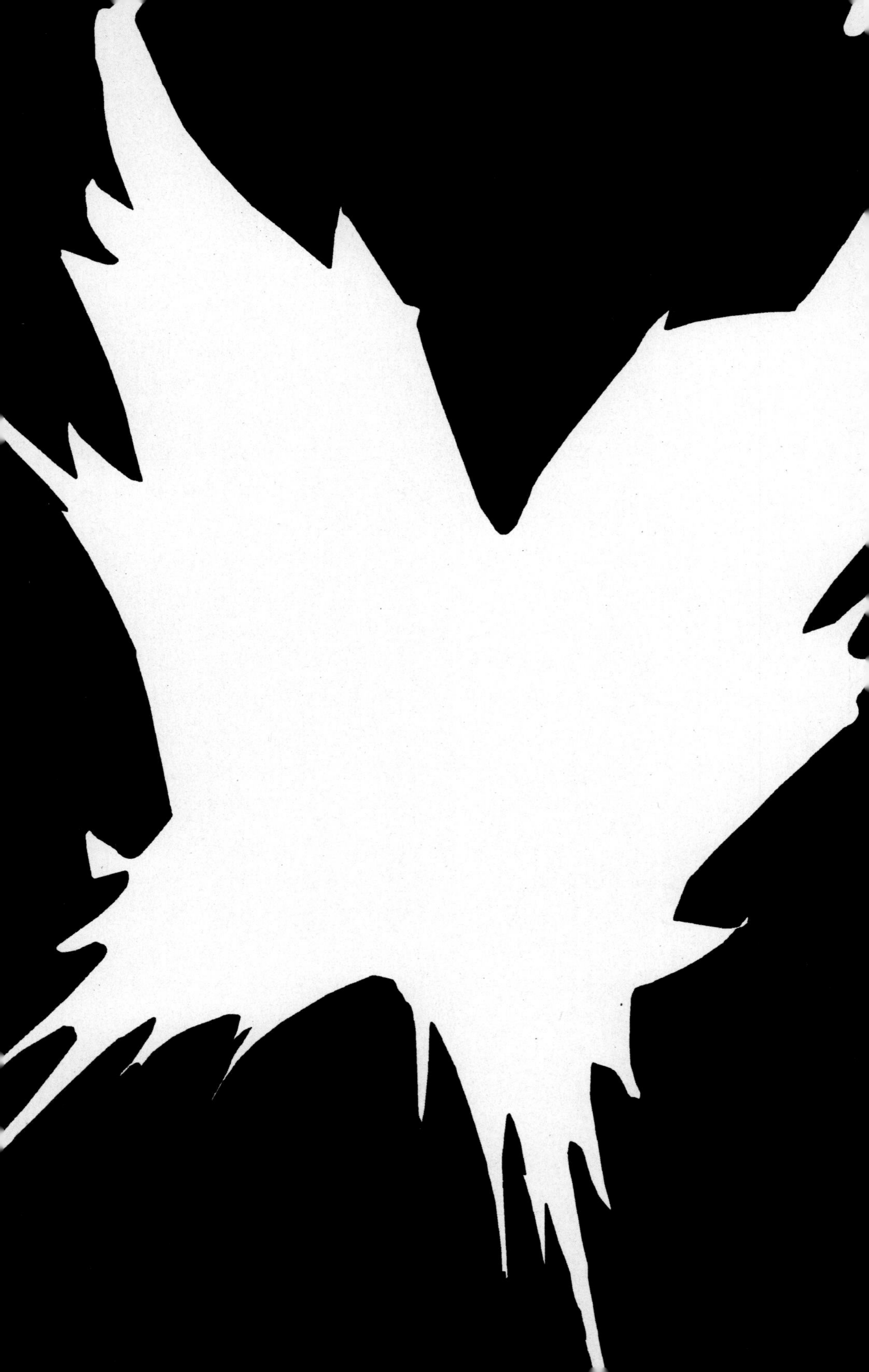

CHAPTER 3
TRINITY

DAVID HINE
Writer

ELENA SALCEDO
Editor

TINA VALENTINO
Artist

VINCENT VALENTINE
Production Art & Design

KATARINA DEVIC
Colorist

TINA VALENTINO
Cover Art

TROY PETERI
Letterer

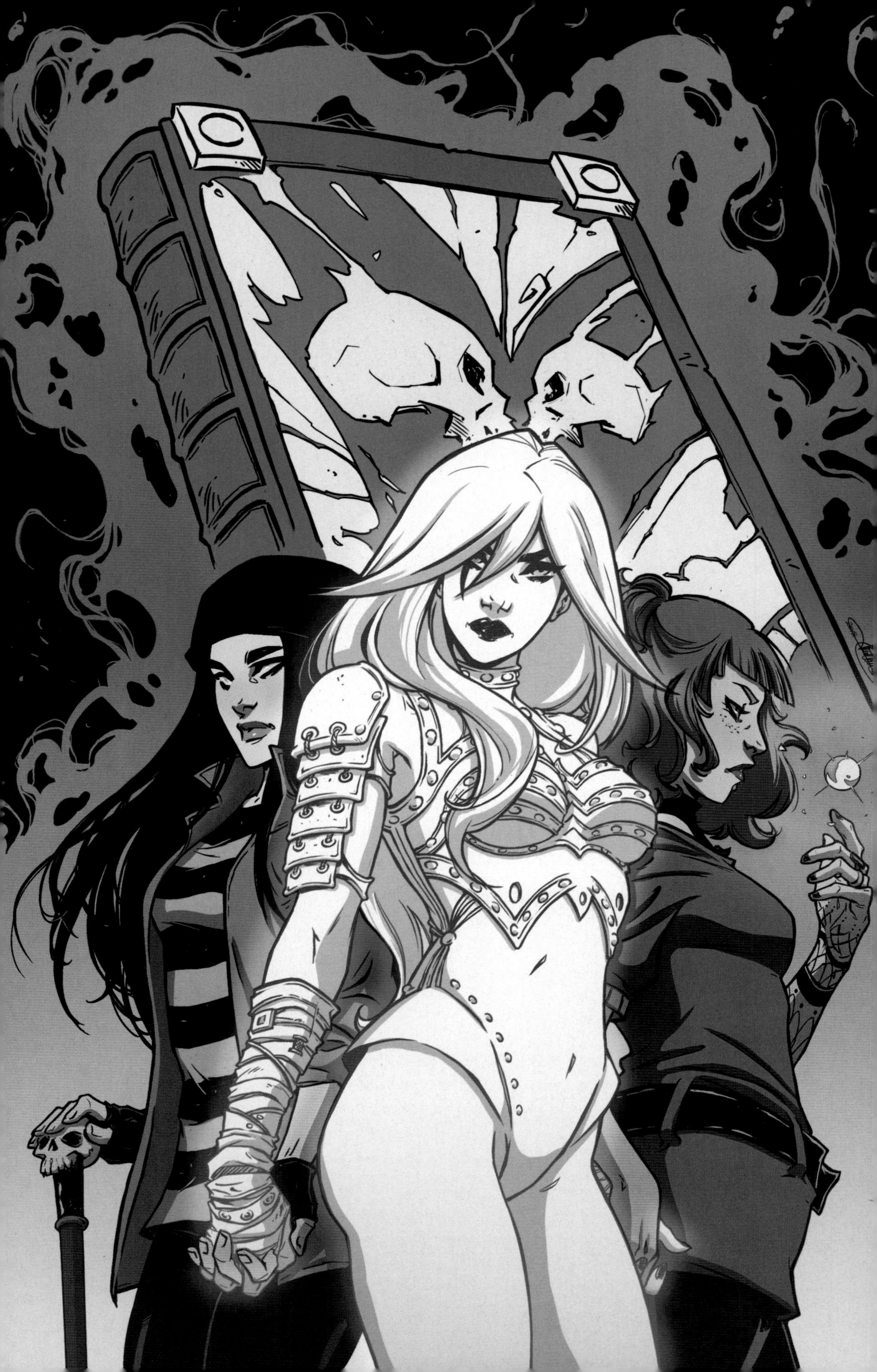

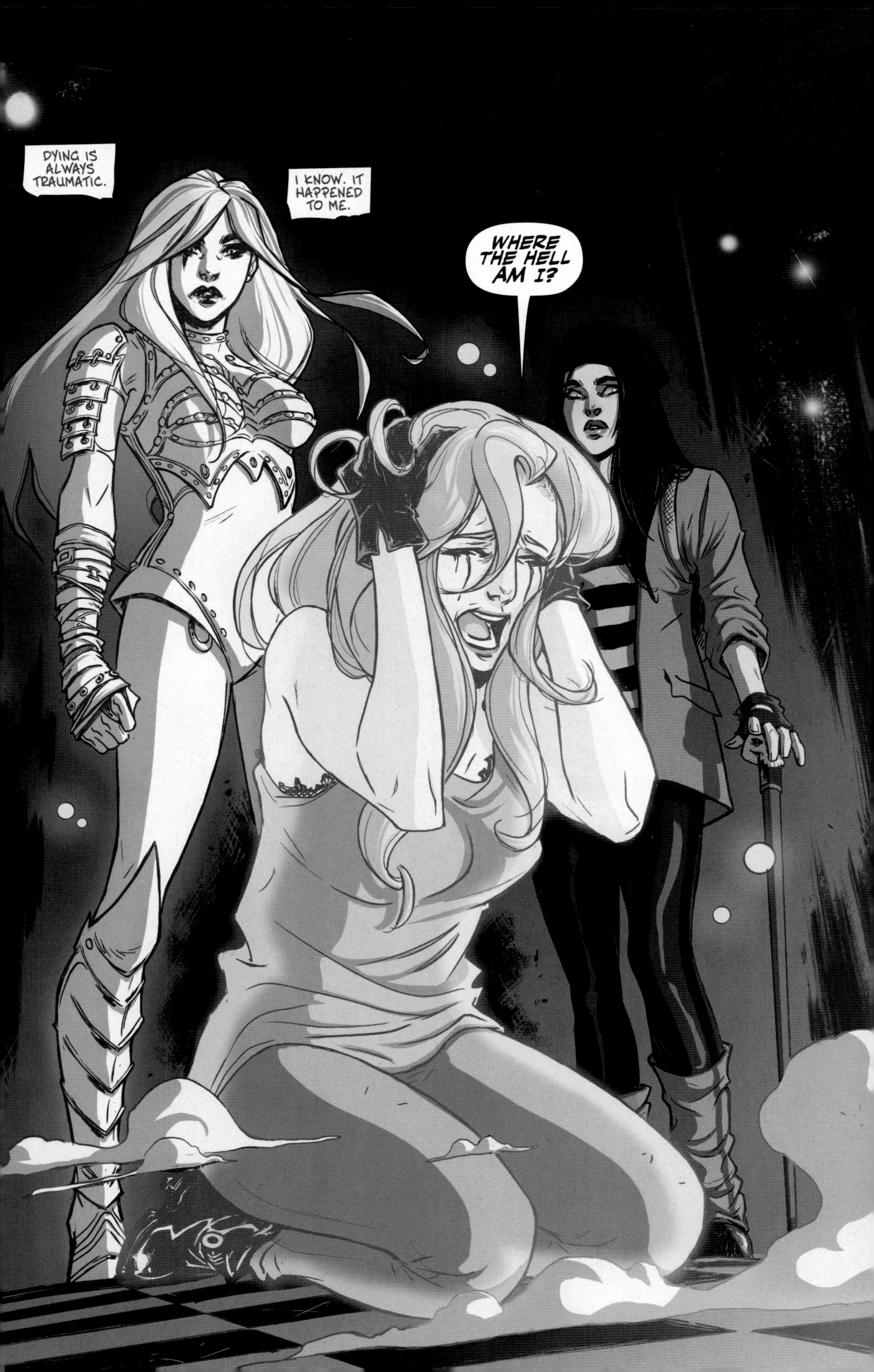
DYING IS ALWAYS TRAUMATIC.
I KNOW. IT HAPPENED TO ME.
WHERE THE HELL AM I?

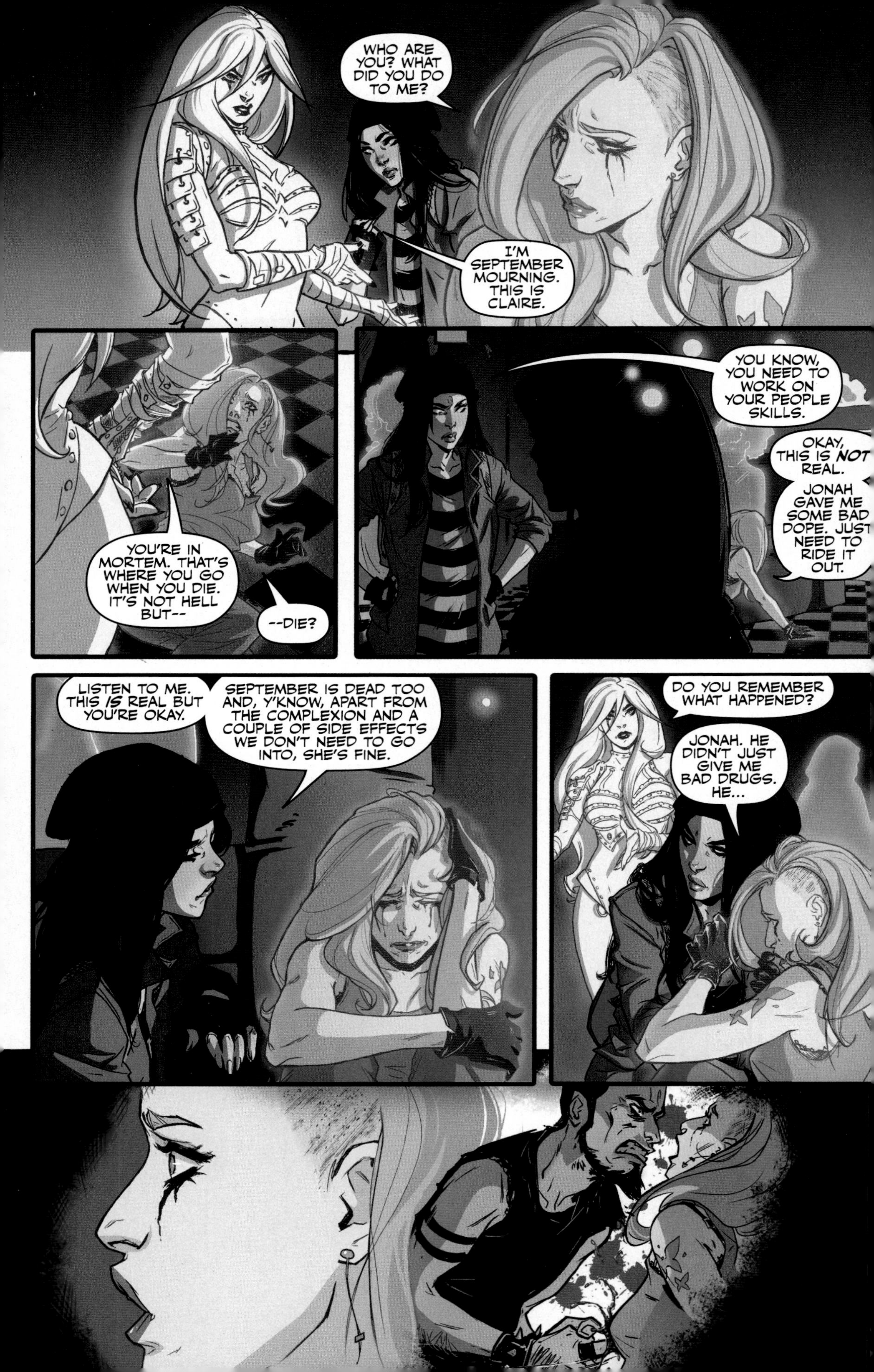
WHO ARE YOU? WHAT DID YOU DO TO ME?
I'M SEPTEMBER MOURNING. THIS IS CLAIRE.
YOU'RE IN MORTEM. THAT'S WHERE YOU GO WHEN YOU DIE. IT'S NOT HELL BUT--
--DIE?
YOU KNOW, YOU NEED TO WORK ON YOUR PEOPLE SKILLS.
OKAY, THIS IS *NOT* REAL.
JONAH GAVE ME SOME BAD DOPE. JUST NEED TO RIDE IT OUT.
LISTEN TO ME. THIS *IS* REAL BUT YOU'RE OKAY.
SEPTEMBER IS DEAD TOO AND, Y'KNOW, APART FROM THE COMPLEXION AND A COUPLE OF SIDE EFFECTS WE DON'T NEED TO GO INTO, SHE'S FINE.
DO YOU REMEMBER WHAT HAPPENED?
JONAH. HE DIDN'T JUST GIVE ME BAD DRUGS. HE...

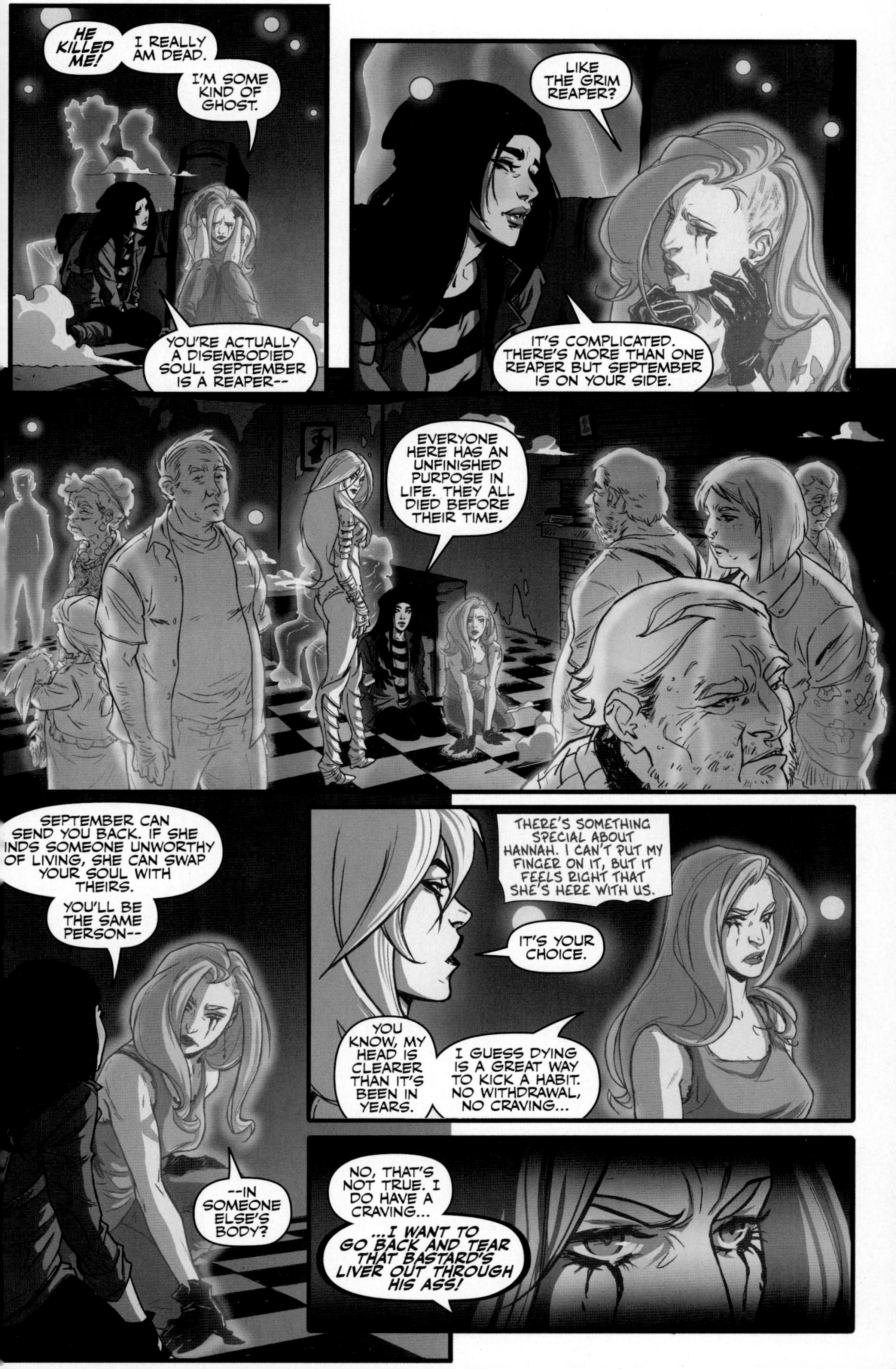
HE KILLED ME!
I REALLY AM DEAD.
I'M SOME KIND OF GHOST.
YOU'RE ACTUALLY A DISEMBODIED SOUL. SEPTEMBER IS A REAPER--
LIKE THE GRIM REAPER?
IT'S COMPLICATED. THERE'S MORE THAN ONE REAPER BUT SEPTEMBER IS ON YOUR SIDE.
EVERYONE HERE HAS AN UNFINISHED PURPOSE IN LIFE. THEY ALL DIED BEFORE THEIR TIME.
SEPTEMBER CAN SEND YOU BACK. IF SHE INDS SOMEONE UNWORTHY OF LIVING, SHE CAN SWAP YOUR SOUL WITH THEIRS.
YOU'LL BE THE SAME PERSON--
--IN SOMEONE ELSE'S BODY?
THERE'S SOMETHING SPECIAL ABOUT HANNAH. I CAN'T PUT MY FINGER ON IT, BUT IT FEELS RIGHT THAT SHE'S HERE WITH US.
IT'S YOUR CHOICE.
YOU KNOW, MY HEAD IS CLEARER THAN IT'S BEEN IN YEARS.
I GUESS DYING IS A GREAT WAY TO KICK A HABIT. NO WITHDRAWAL, NO CRAVING...
NO, THAT'S NOT TRUE. I DO HAVE A CRAVING...
...I WANT TO GO BACK AND TEAR THAT BASTARD'S LIVER OUT THROUGH HIS ASS!

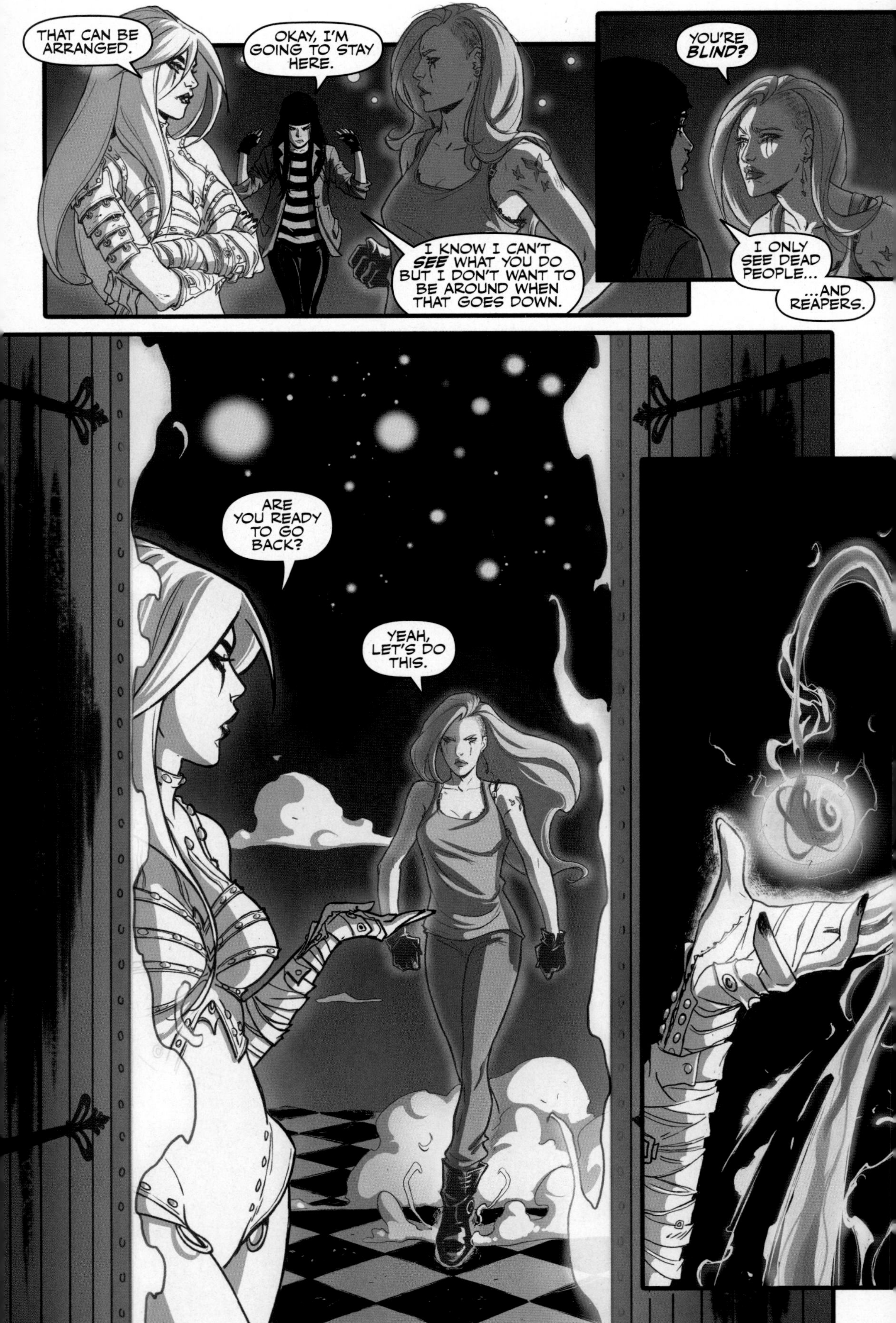
THAT CAN BE ARRANGED.
OKAY, I'M GOING TO STAY HERE.
I KNOW I CAN'T SEE WHAT YOU DO BUT I DON'T WANT TO BE AROUND WHEN THAT GOES DOWN.
YOU'RE BLIND?
I ONLY SEE DEAD PEOPLE...
...AND REAPERS.
ARE YOU READY TO GO BACK?
YEAH, LET'S DO THIS.

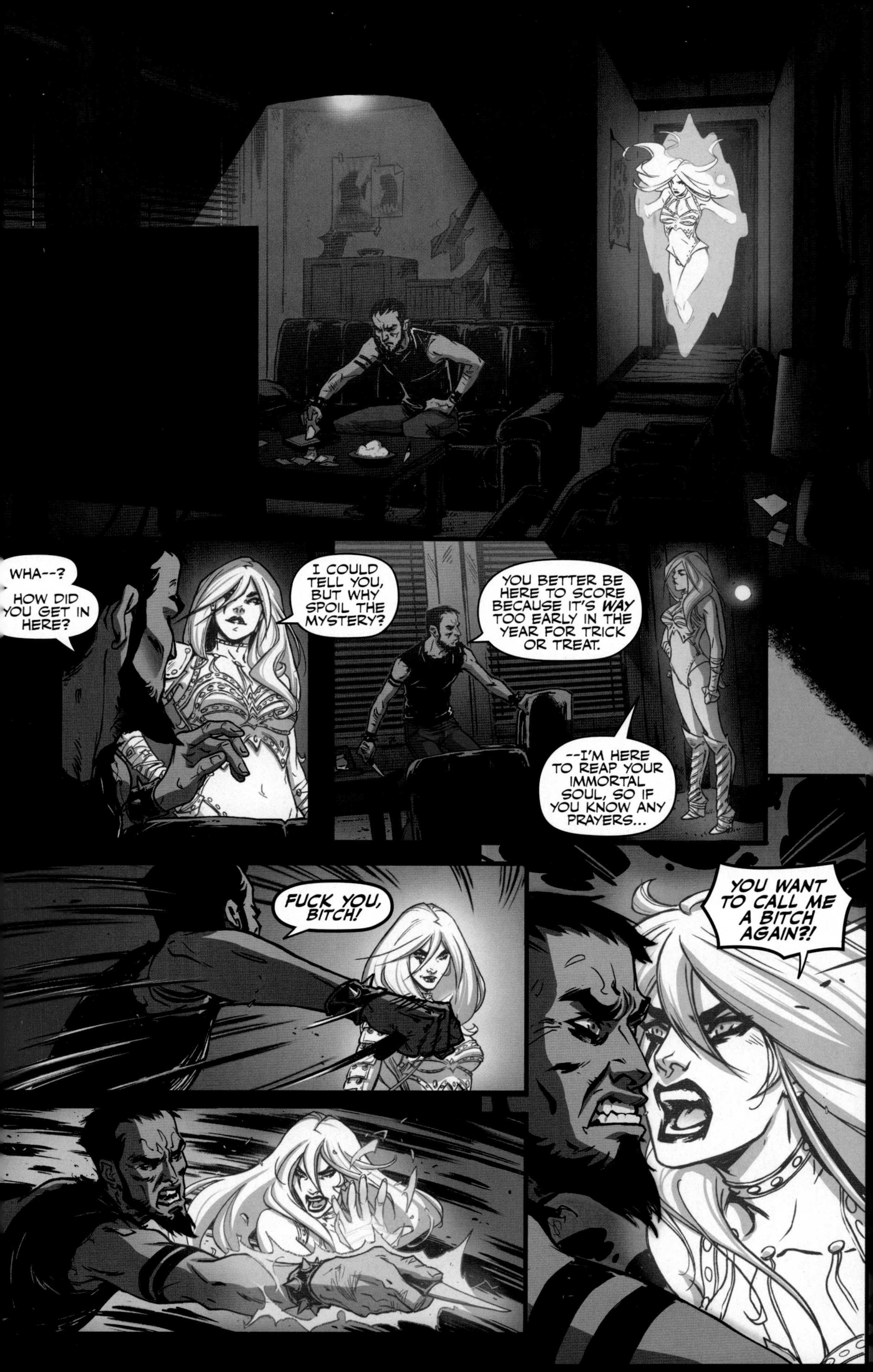
WHA--?
HOW DID YOU GET IN HERE?
I COULD TELL YOU, BUT WHY SPOIL THE MYSTERY?
YOU BETTER BE HERE TO SCORE BECAUSE IT'S *WAY* TOO EARLY IN THE YEAR FOR TRICK OR TREAT.
--I'M HERE TO REAP YOUR IMMORTAL SOUL, SO IF YOU KNOW ANY PRAYERS...
FUCK YOU, BITCH!
YOU WANT TO CALL ME A BITCH AGAIN?!

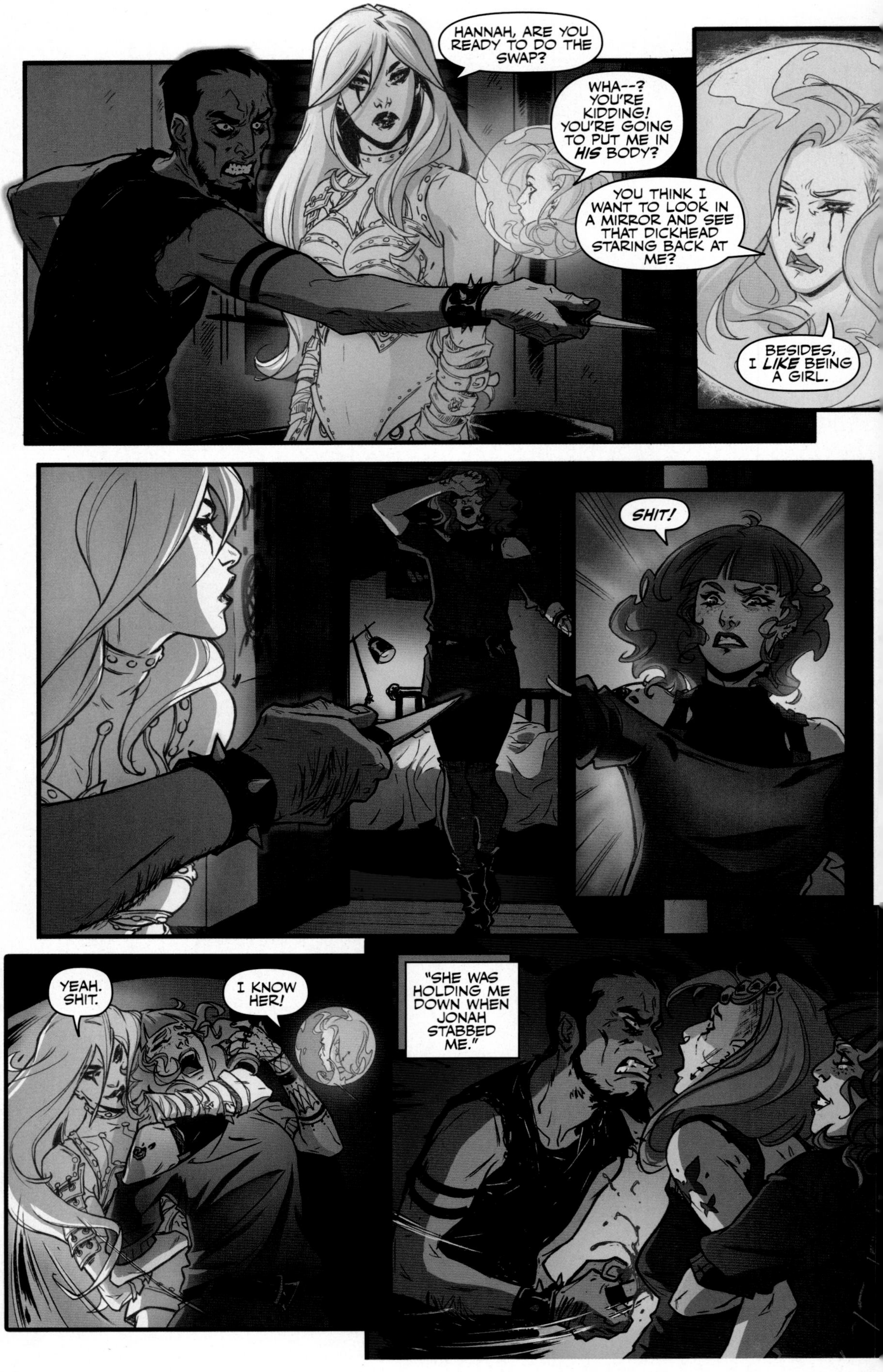
HANNAH, ARE YOU READY TO DO THE SWAP?
WHA--? YOU'RE KIDDING! YOU'RE GOING TO PUT ME IN *HIS* BODY?
YOU THINK I WANT TO LOOK IN A MIRROR AND SEE THAT DICKHEAD STARING BACK AT ME?
BESIDES, I *LIKE* BEING A GIRL.
SHIT!
YEAH. SHIT.
I KNOW HER!
"SHE WAS HOLDING ME DOWN WHEN JONAH STABBED ME."

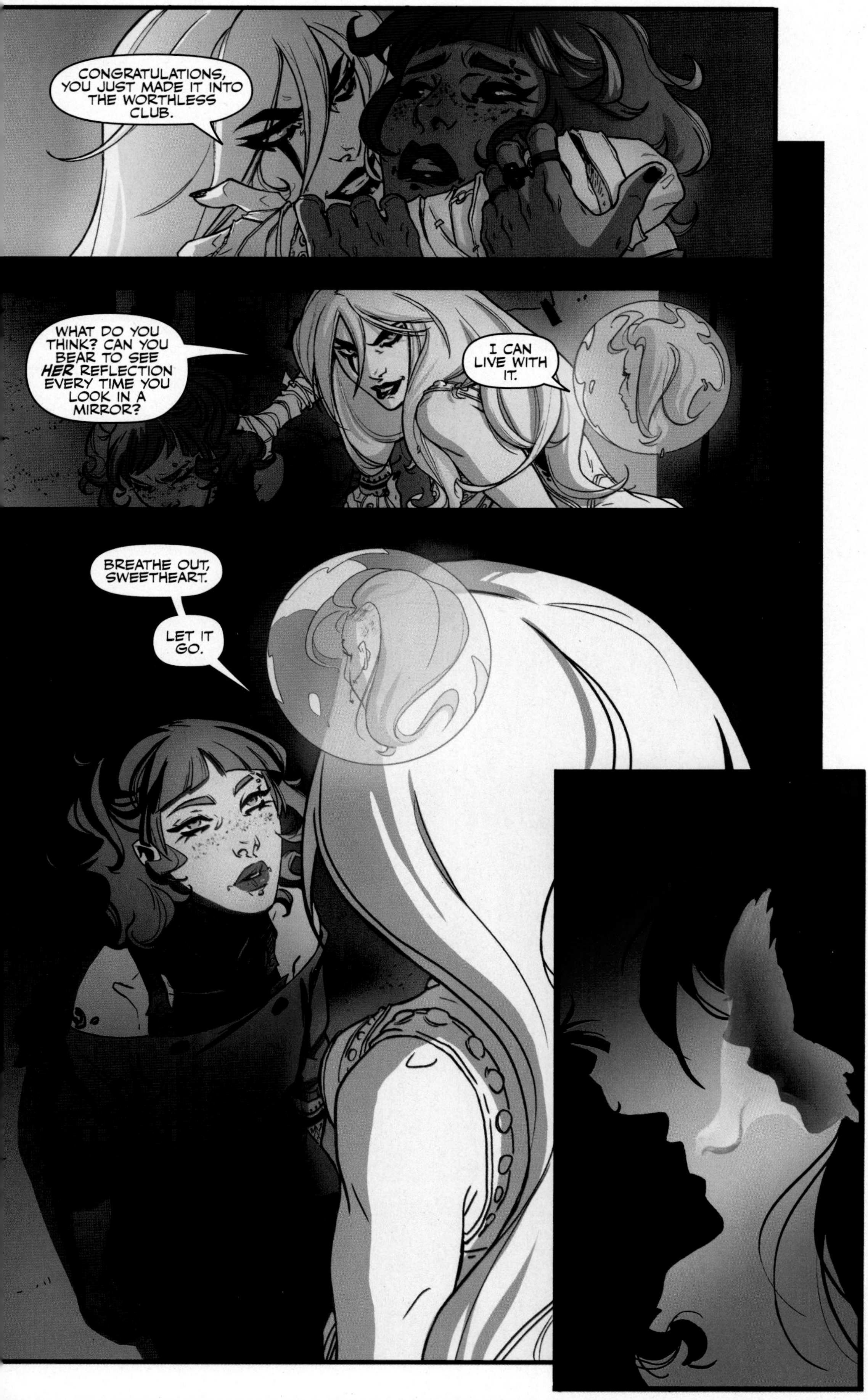
CONGRATULATIONS, YOU JUST MADE IT INTO THE WORTHLESS CLUB.
WHAT DO YOU THINK? CAN YOU BEAR TO SEE HER REFLECTION EVERY TIME YOU LOOK IN A MIRROR?
I CAN LIVE WITH IT.
BREATHE OUT, SWEETHEART.
LET IT GO.

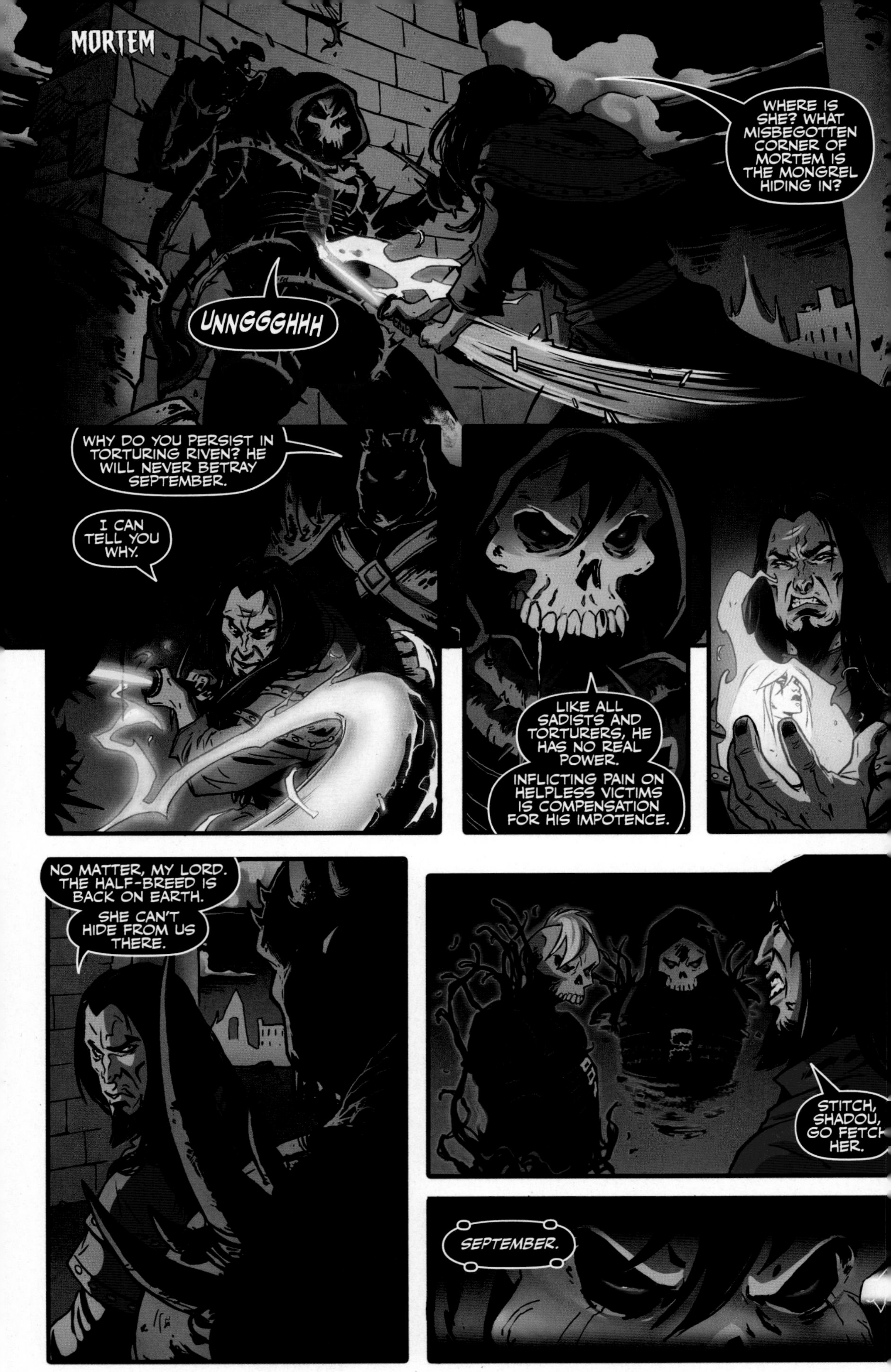
MORTEM
WHERE IS SHE? WHAT MISBEGOTTEN CORNER OF MORTEM IS THE MONGREL HIDING IN?
UNNGGGHHH
WHY DO YOU PERSIST IN TORTURING RIVEN? HE WILL NEVER BETRAY SEPTEMBER.
I CAN TELL YOU WHY.
LIKE ALL SADISTS AND TORTURERS, HE HAS NO REAL POWER.
INFLICTING PAIN ON HELPLESS VICTIMS IS COMPENSATION FOR HIS IMPOTENCE.
NO MATTER, MY LORD. THE HALF-BREED IS BACK ON EARTH.
SHE CAN'T HIDE FROM US THERE.
STITCH, SHADOU, GO FETCH HER.
SEPTEMBER.

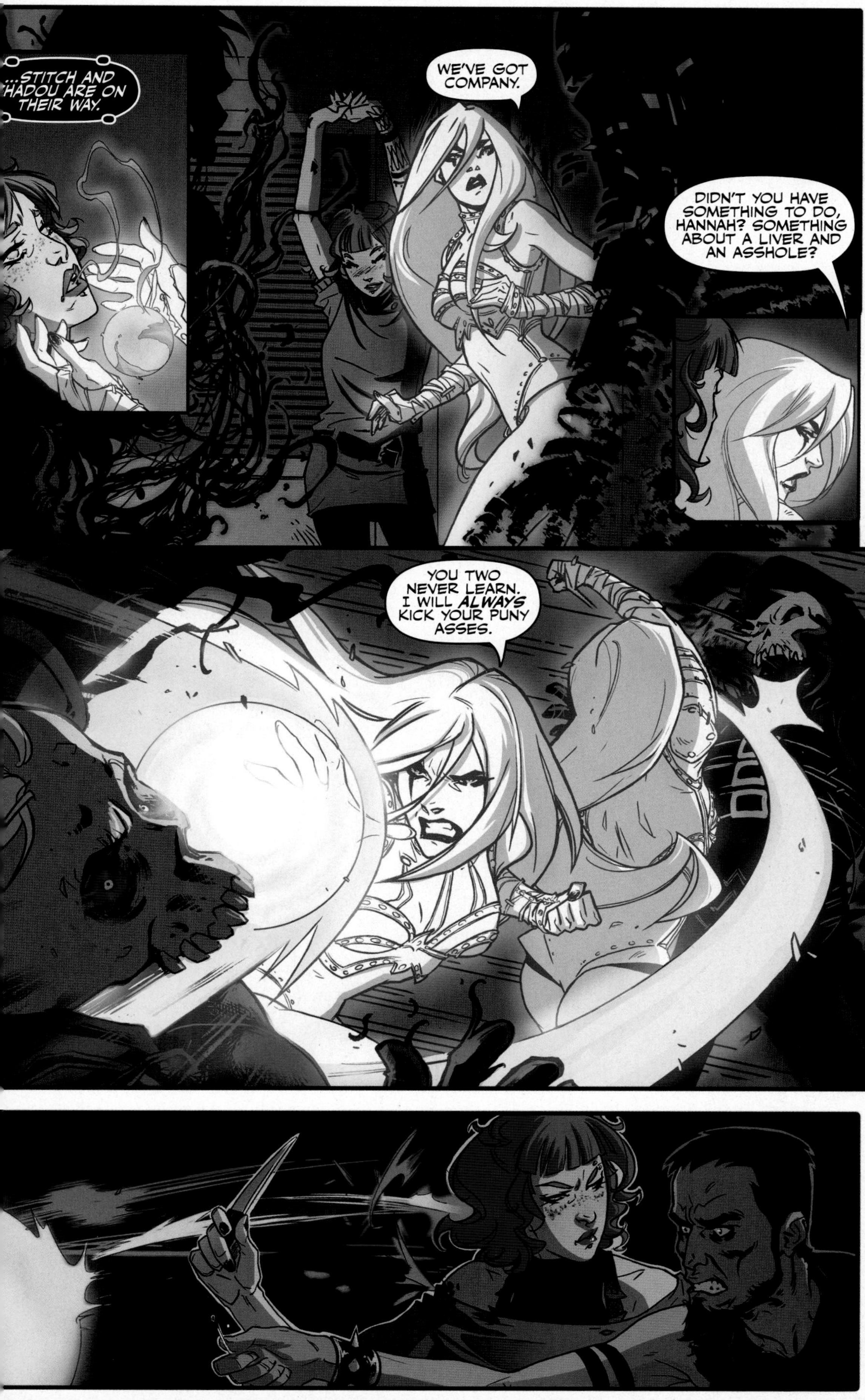
...STITCH AND SHADOU ARE ON THEIR WAY.
WE'VE GOT COMPANY.
DIDN'T YOU HAVE SOMETHING TO DO, HANNAH? SOMETHING ABOUT A LIVER AND AN ASSHOLE?
YOU TWO NEVER LEARN. I WILL ALWAYS KICK YOUR PUNY ASSES.

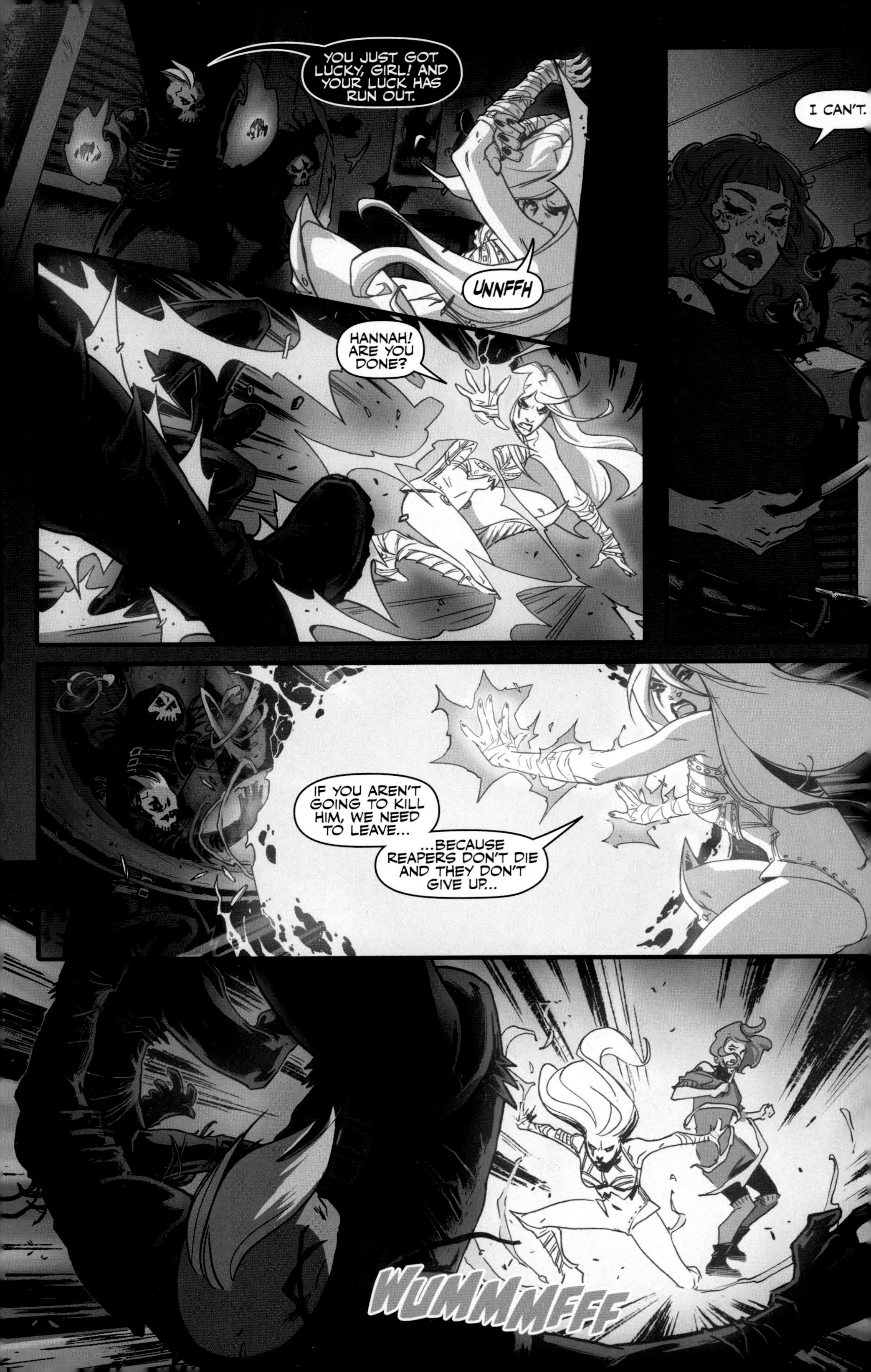
YOU JUST GOT LUCKY, GIRL! AND YOUR LUCK HAS RUN OUT.
UNNFFH
I CAN'T.
HANNAH! ARE YOU DONE?
IF YOU AREN'T GOING TO KILL HIM, WE NEED TO LEAVE...
...BECAUSE REAPERS DON'T DIE AND THEY DON'T GIVE UP...
WUMMMFFF

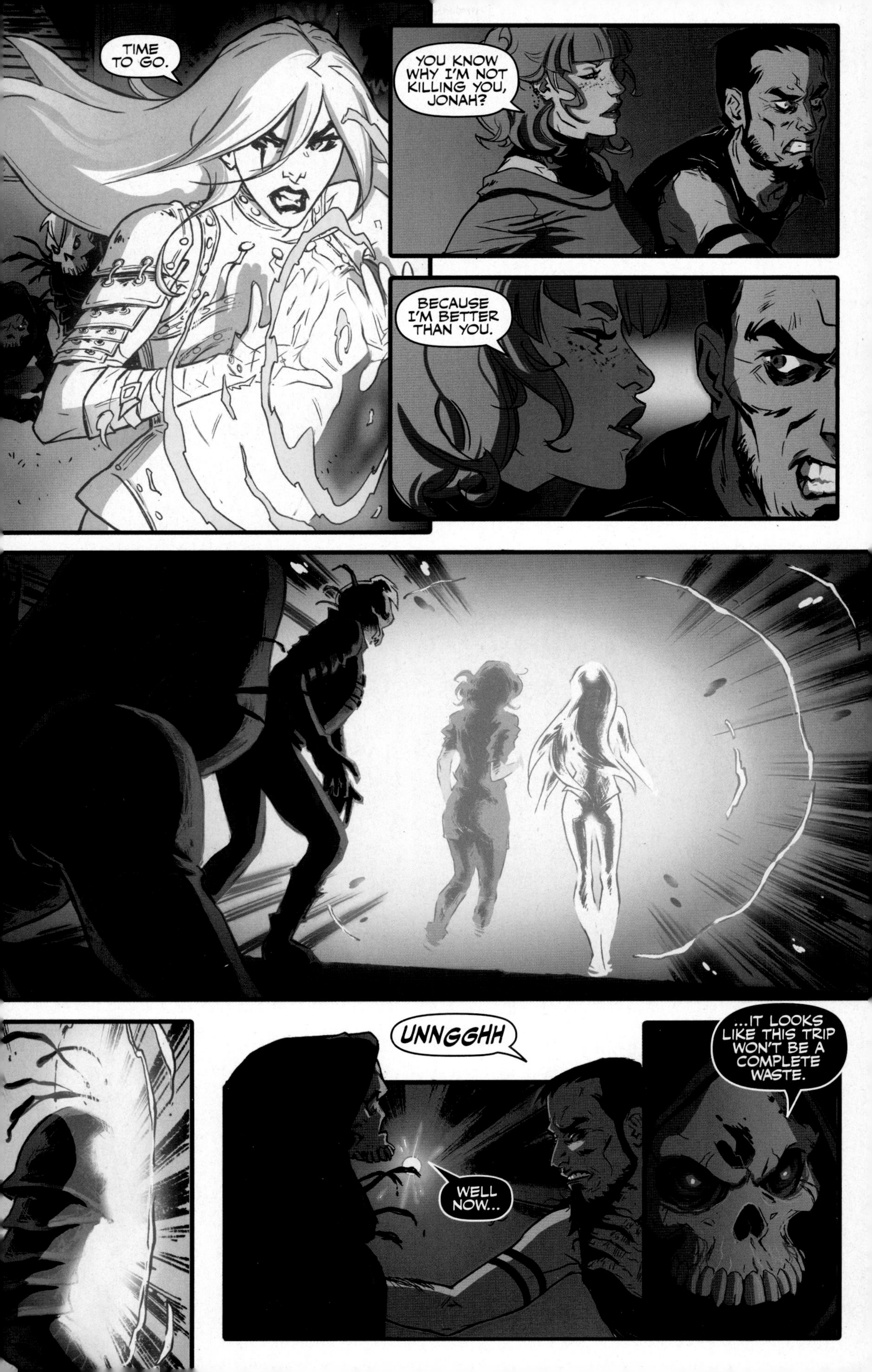
TIME TO GO.
YOU KNOW WHY I'M NOT KILLING YOU, JONAH?
BECAUSE I'M BETTER THAN YOU.
UNNGGHH
WELL NOW...
...IT LOOKS LIKE THIS TRIP WON'T BE A COMPLETE WASTE.

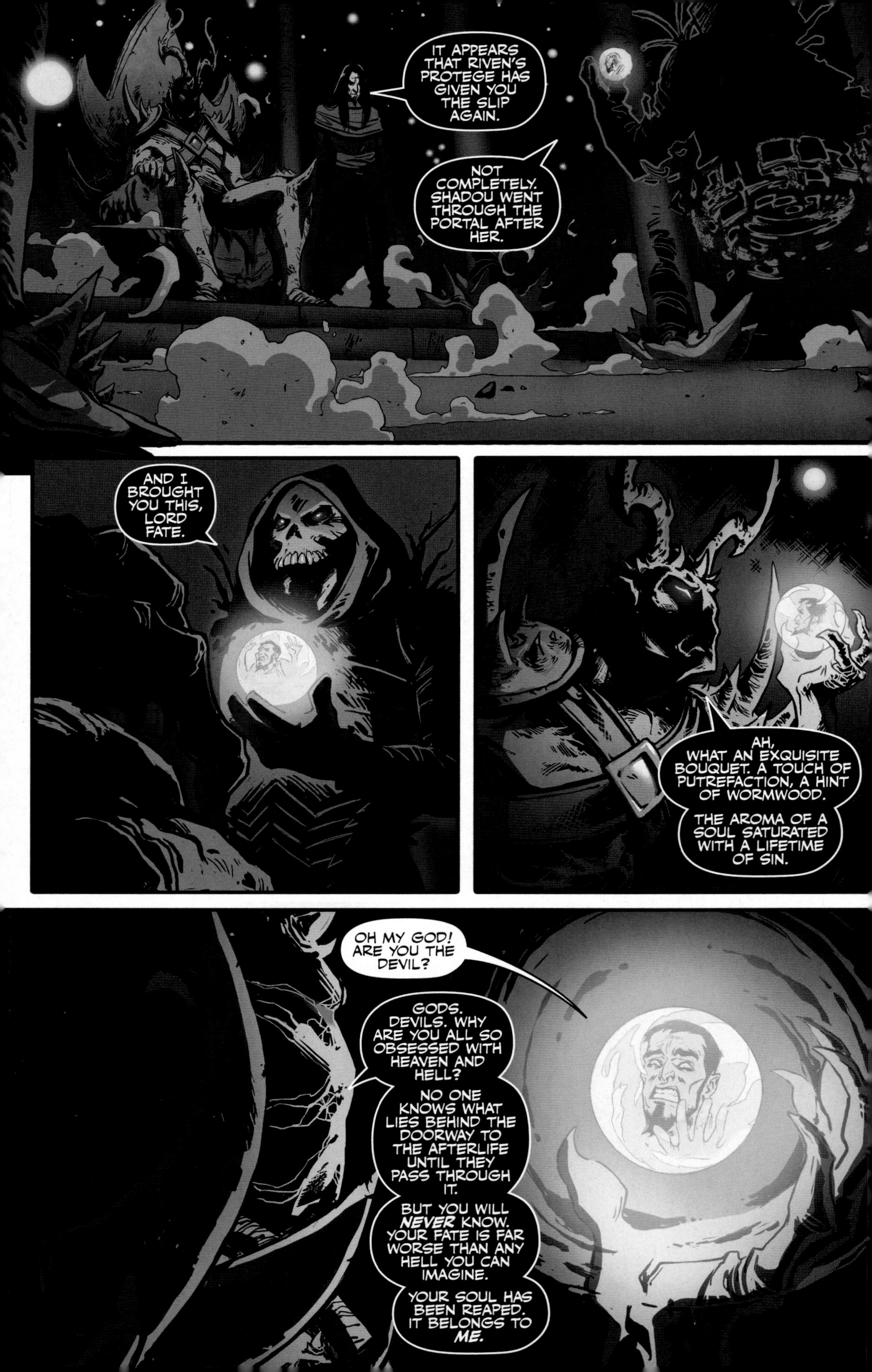
IT APPEARS THAT RIVEN'S PROTEGE HAS GIVEN YOU THE SLIP AGAIN.
NOT COMPLETELY. SHADOU WENT THROUGH THE PORTAL AFTER HER.
AND I BROUGHT YOU THIS, LORD FATE.
AH, WHAT AN EXQUISITE BOUQUET. A TOUCH OF PUTREFACTION, A HINT OF WORMWOOD.
THE AROMA OF A SOUL SATURATED WITH A LIFETIME OF SIN.
OH MY GOD! ARE YOU THE DEVIL?
GODS. DEVILS. WHY ARE YOU ALL SO OBSESSED WITH HEAVEN AND HELL?
NO ONE KNOWS WHAT LIES BEHIND THE DOORWAY TO THE AFTERLIFE UNTIL THEY PASS THROUGH IT.
BUT YOU WILL ***NEVER*** KNOW. YOUR FATE IS FAR WORSE THAN ANY HELL YOU CAN IMAGINE.
YOUR SOUL HAS BEEN REAPED. IT BELONGS TO ***ME.***

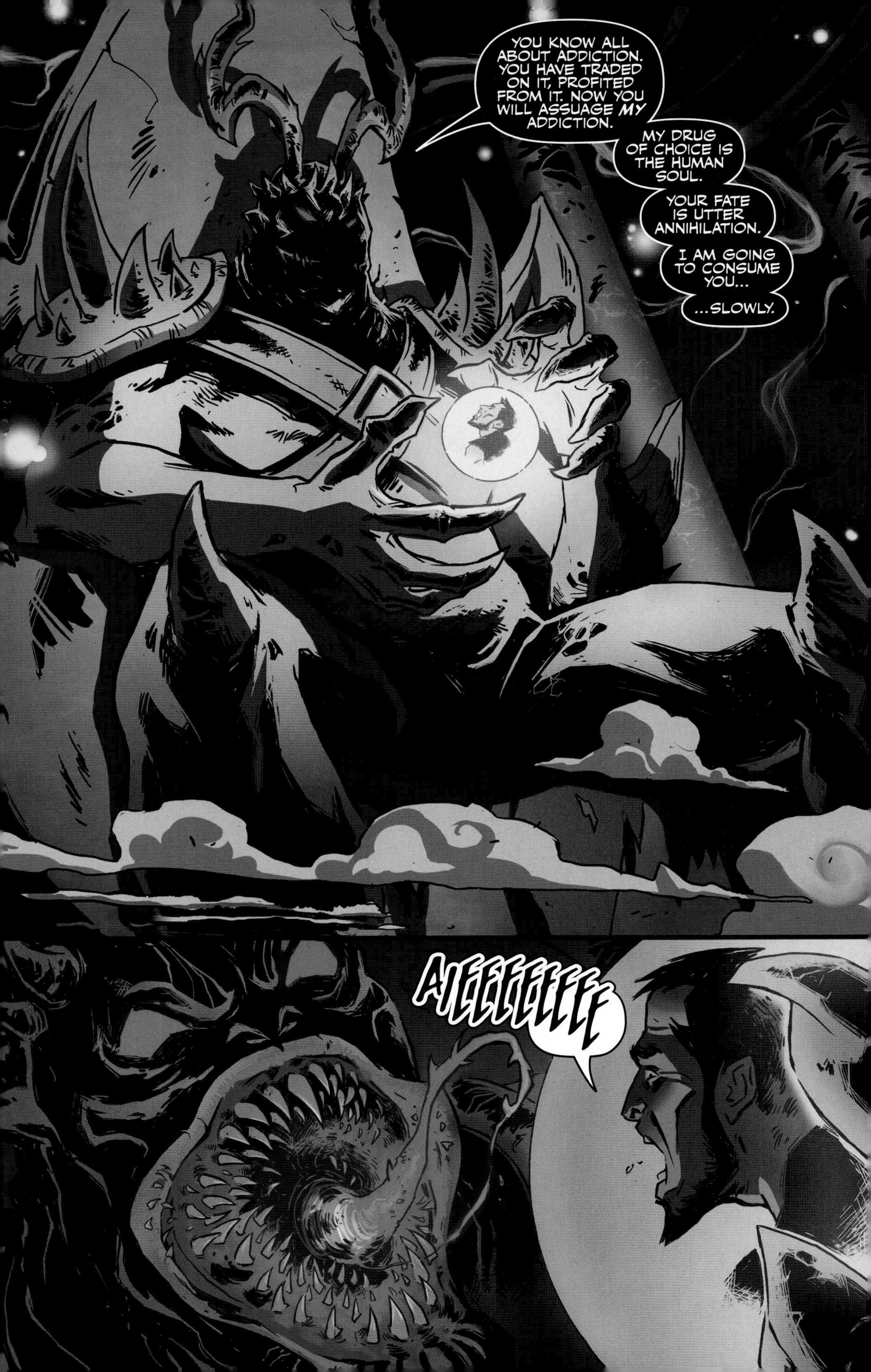
YOU KNOW ALL ABOUT ADDICTION. YOU HAVE TRADED ON IT, PROFITED FROM IT. NOW YOU WILL ASSUAGE *MY* ADDICTION.
MY DRUG OF CHOICE IS THE HUMAN SOUL.
YOUR FATE IS UTTER ANNIHILATION.
I AM GOING TO CONSUME YOU...
...SLOWLY.
AIEEEEEEEE

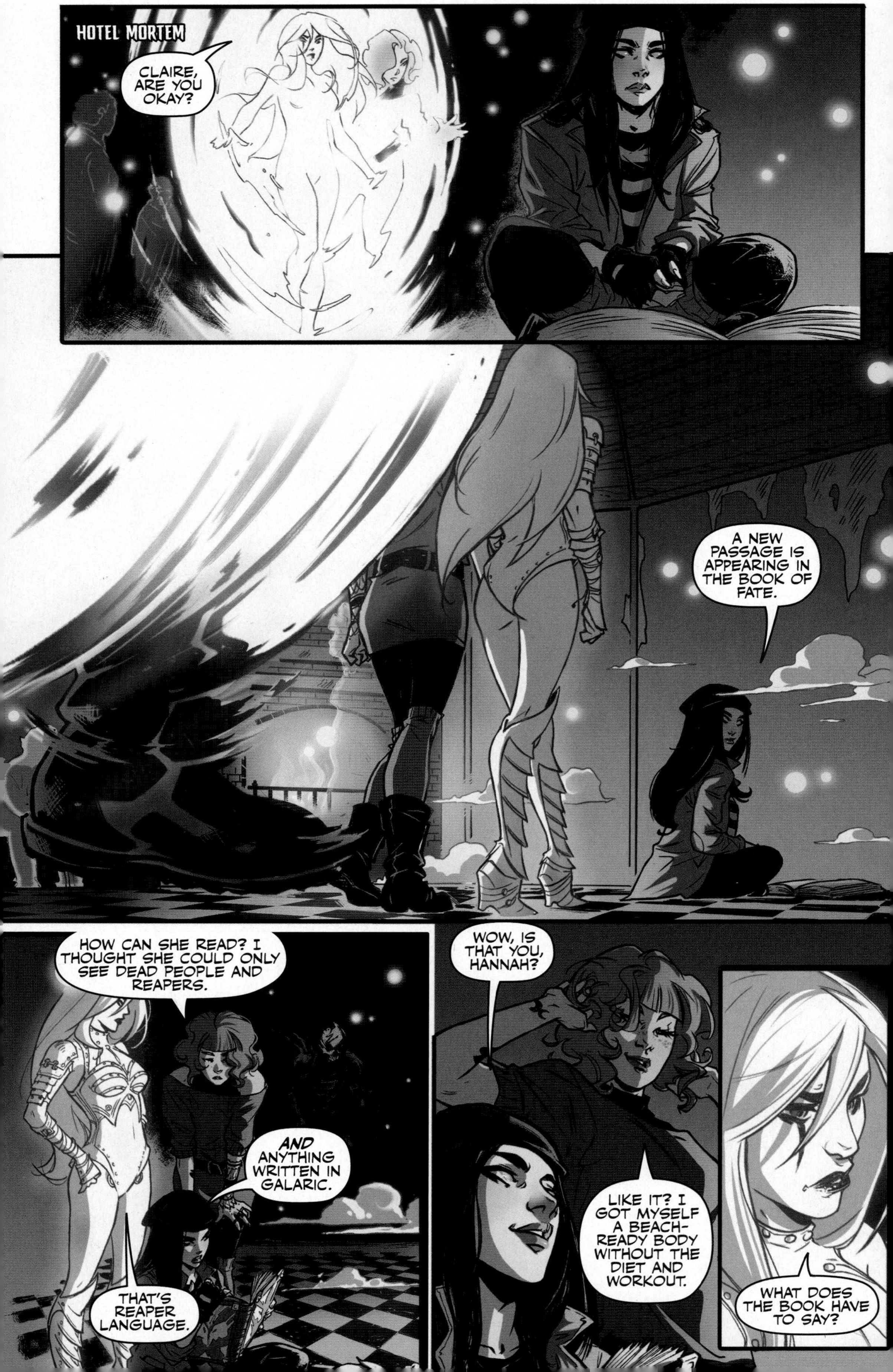
HOTEL MORTEM
CLAIRE, ARE YOU OKAY?
A NEW PASSAGE IS APPEARING IN THE BOOK OF FATE.
HOW CAN SHE READ? I THOUGHT SHE COULD ONLY SEE DEAD PEOPLE AND REAPERS.
AND ANYTHING WRITTEN IN GALARIC.
THAT'S REAPER LANGUAGE.
WOW, IS THAT YOU, HANNAH?
LIKE IT? I GOT MYSELF A BEACH-READY BODY WITHOUT THE DIET AND WORKOUT.
WHAT DOES THE BOOK HAVE TO SAY?

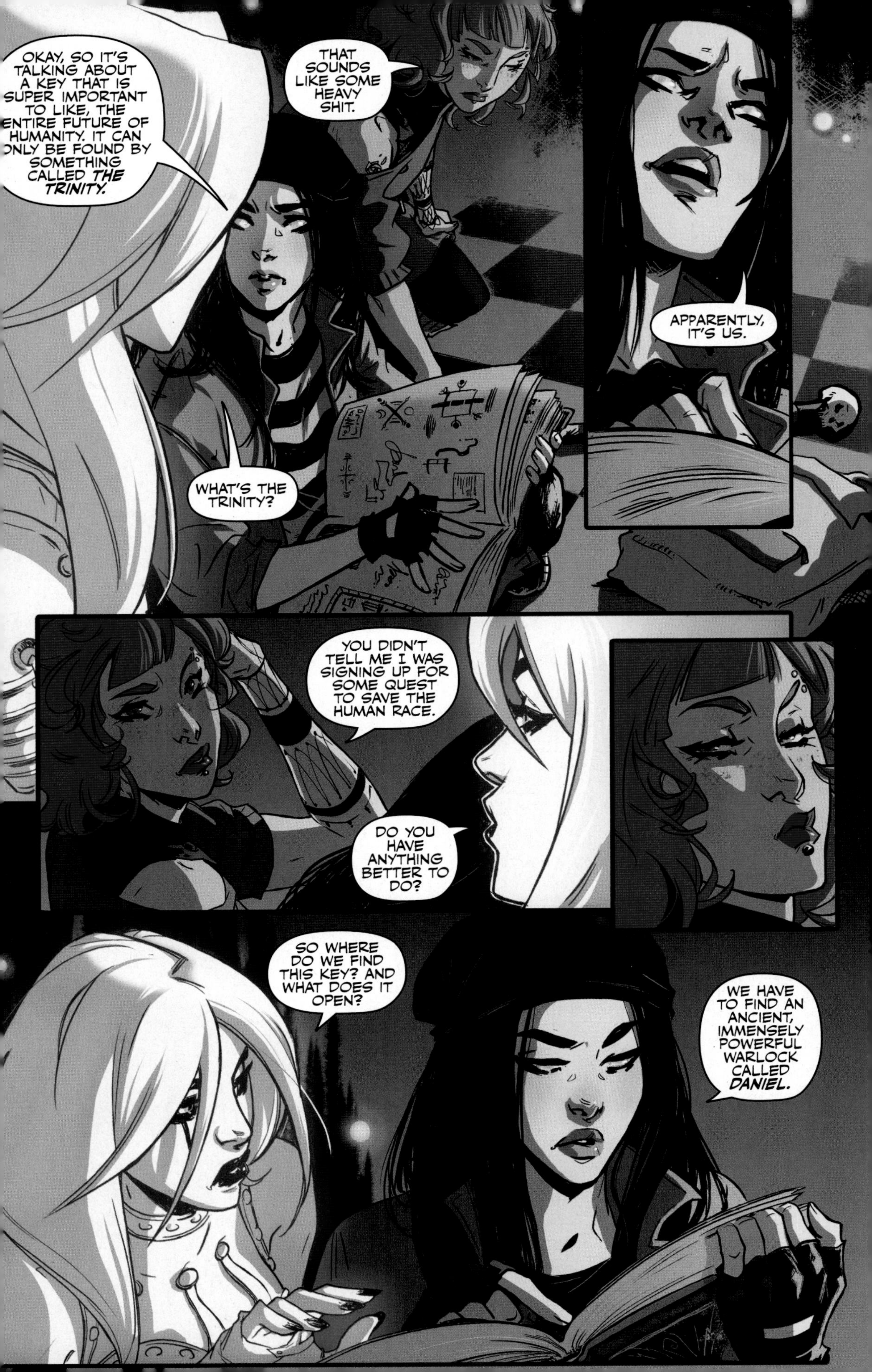
OKAY, SO IT'S TALKING ABOUT A KEY THAT IS SUPER IMPORTANT TO LIKE, THE ENTIRE FUTURE OF HUMANITY. IT CAN ONLY BE FOUND BY SOMETHING CALLED *THE TRINITY.*
THAT SOUNDS LIKE SOME HEAVY SHIT.
WHAT'S THE TRINITY?
APPARENTLY, IT'S US.
YOU DIDN'T TELL ME I WAS SIGNING UP FOR SOME QUEST TO SAVE THE HUMAN RACE.
DO YOU HAVE ANYTHING BETTER TO DO?
SO WHERE DO WE FIND THIS KEY? AND WHAT DOES IT OPEN?
WE HAVE TO FIND AN ANCIENT, IMMENSELY POWERFUL WARLOCK CALLED *DANIEL.*

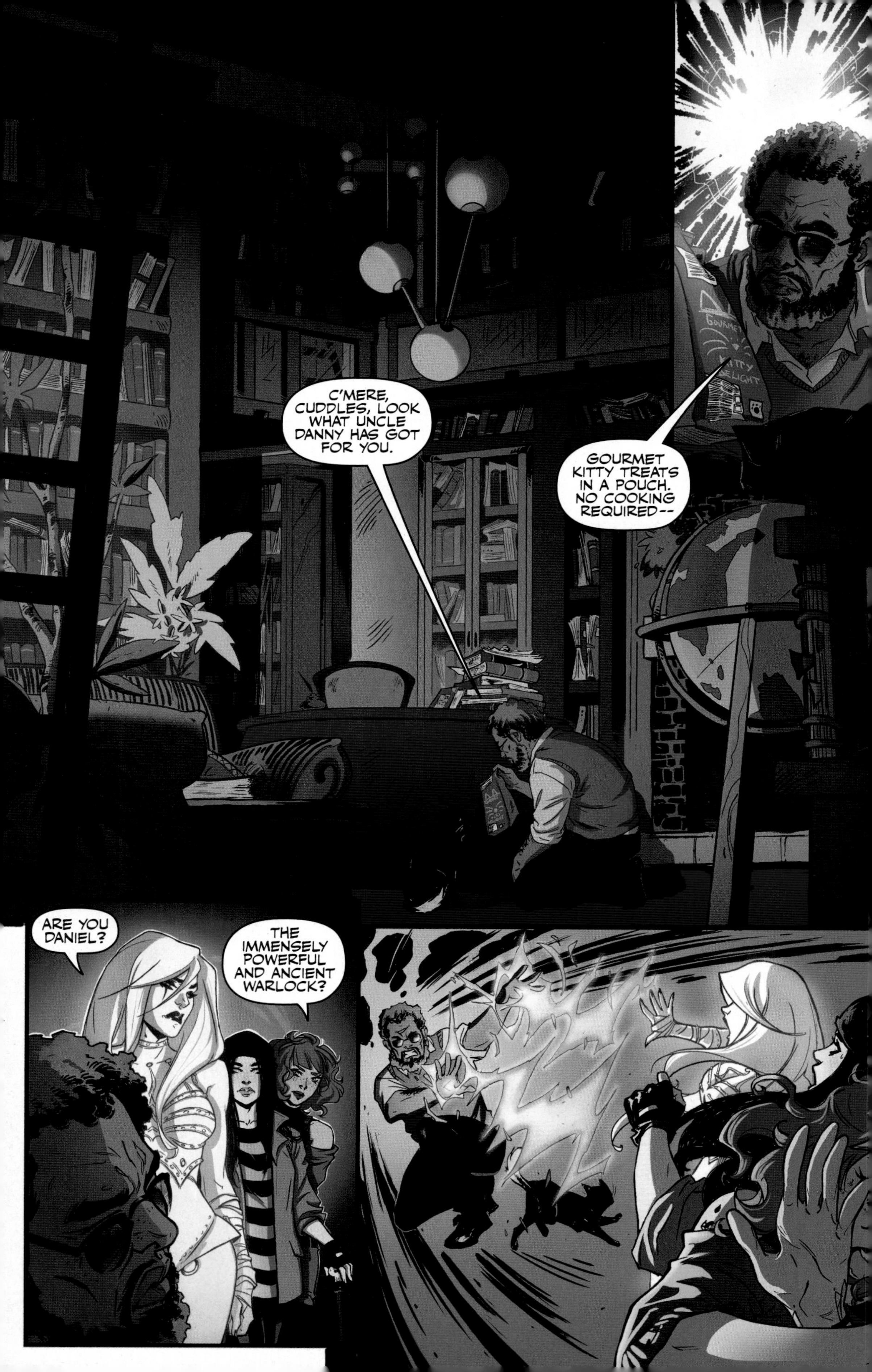
C'MERE, CUDDLES, LOOK WHAT UNCLE DANNY HAS GOT FOR YOU.
GOURMET KITTY TREATS IN A POUCH. NO COOKING REQUIRED--
ARE YOU DANIEL?
THE IMMENSELY POWERFUL AND ANCIENT WARLOCK?

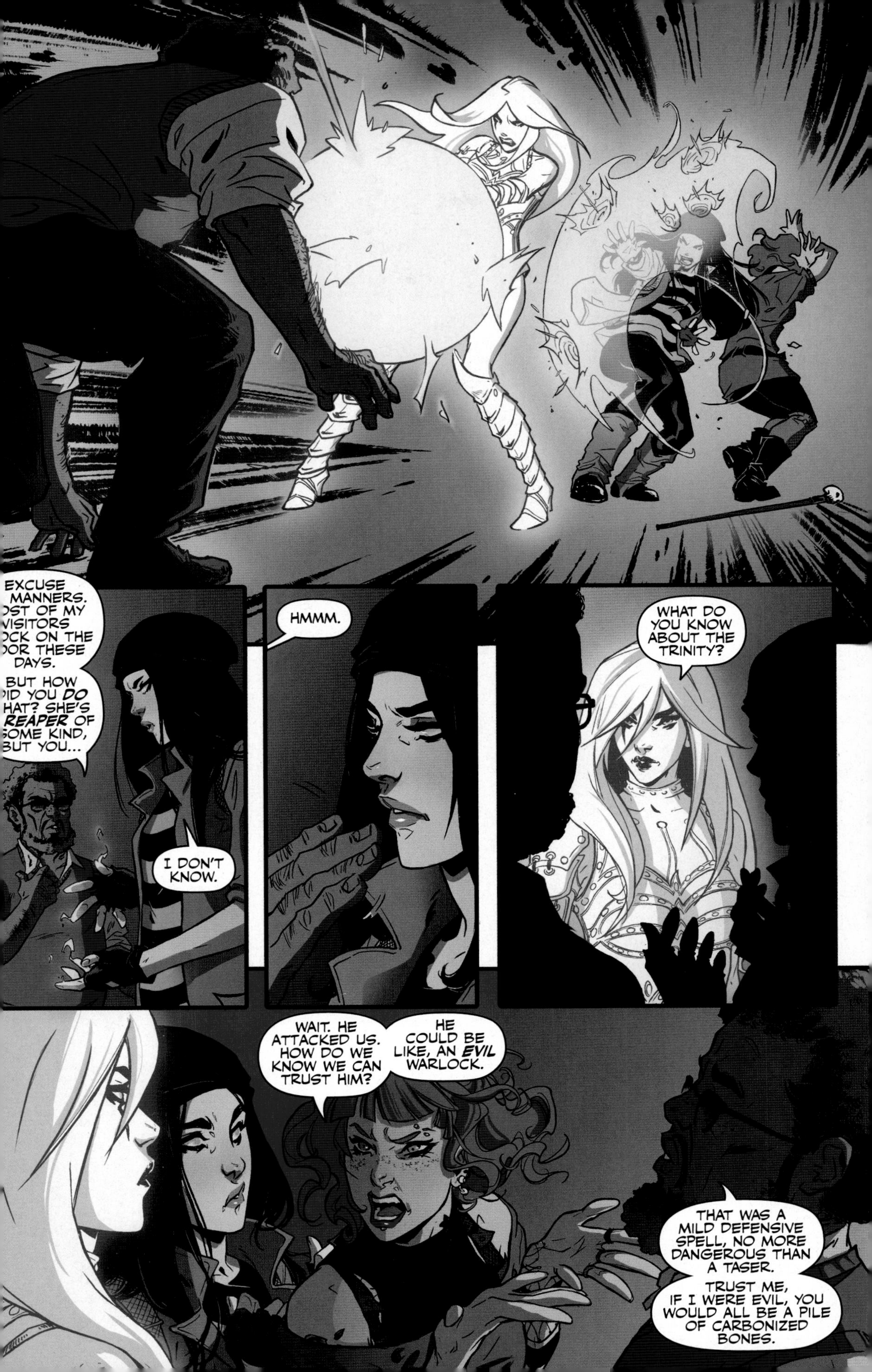

EXCUSE MANNERS. OST OF MY VISITORS OCK ON THE OOR THESE DAYS.
BUT HOW DID YOU DO HAT? SHE'S REAPER OF SOME KIND, BUT YOU...
I DON'T KNOW.
HMMM.
WHAT DO YOU KNOW ABOUT THE TRINITY?
WAIT. HE ATTACKED US. HOW DO WE KNOW WE CAN TRUST HIM?
HE COULD BE LIKE, AN EVIL WARLOCK.
THAT WAS A MILD DEFENSIVE SPELL, NO MORE DANGEROUS THAN A TASER.
TRUST ME, IF I WERE EVIL, YOU WOULD ALL BE A PILE OF CARBONIZED BONES.

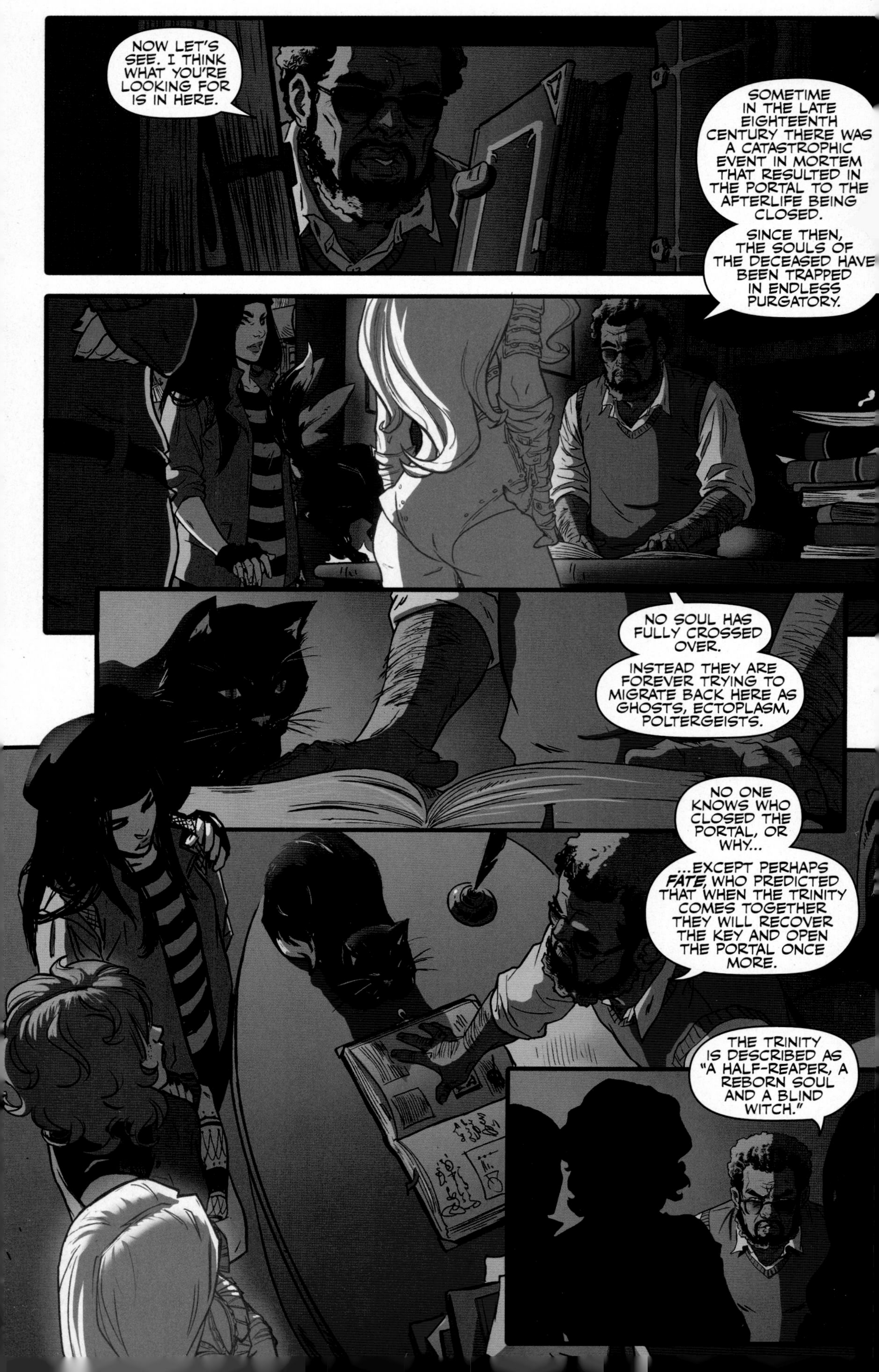
NOW LET'S SEE. I THINK WHAT YOU'RE LOOKING FOR IS IN HERE.
SOMETIME IN THE LATE EIGHTEENTH CENTURY THERE WAS A CATASTROPHIC EVENT IN MORTEM THAT RESULTED IN THE PORTAL TO THE AFTERLIFE BEING CLOSED.
SINCE THEN, THE SOULS OF THE DECEASED HAVE BEEN TRAPPED IN ENDLESS PURGATORY.
NO SOUL HAS FULLY CROSSED OVER.
INSTEAD THEY ARE FOREVER TRYING TO MIGRATE BACK HERE AS GHOSTS, ECTOPLASM, POLTERGEISTS.
NO ONE KNOWS WHO CLOSED THE PORTAL, OR WHY...
...EXCEPT PERHAPS *FATE*, WHO PREDICTED THAT WHEN THE TRINITY COMES TOGETHER THEY WILL RECOVER THE KEY AND OPEN THE PORTAL ONCE MORE.
THE TRINITY IS DESCRIBED AS "A HALF-REAPER, A REBORN SOUL AND A BLIND WITCH."

SO FATE ALWAYS KNEW ABOUT US?

IT GOES WITH THE JOB DESCRIPTION.

WHERE DO WE FIND THE KEY?

ROUGHLY TRANSLATED, "THE DARK CHAMBER AT THE HEART OF THE TOWER."

FATE'S TOWER?

UNFORTUNATELY, YES.

AND DOES IT KNOW WE'RE COMING?

WELL...

DON'T TELL ME...

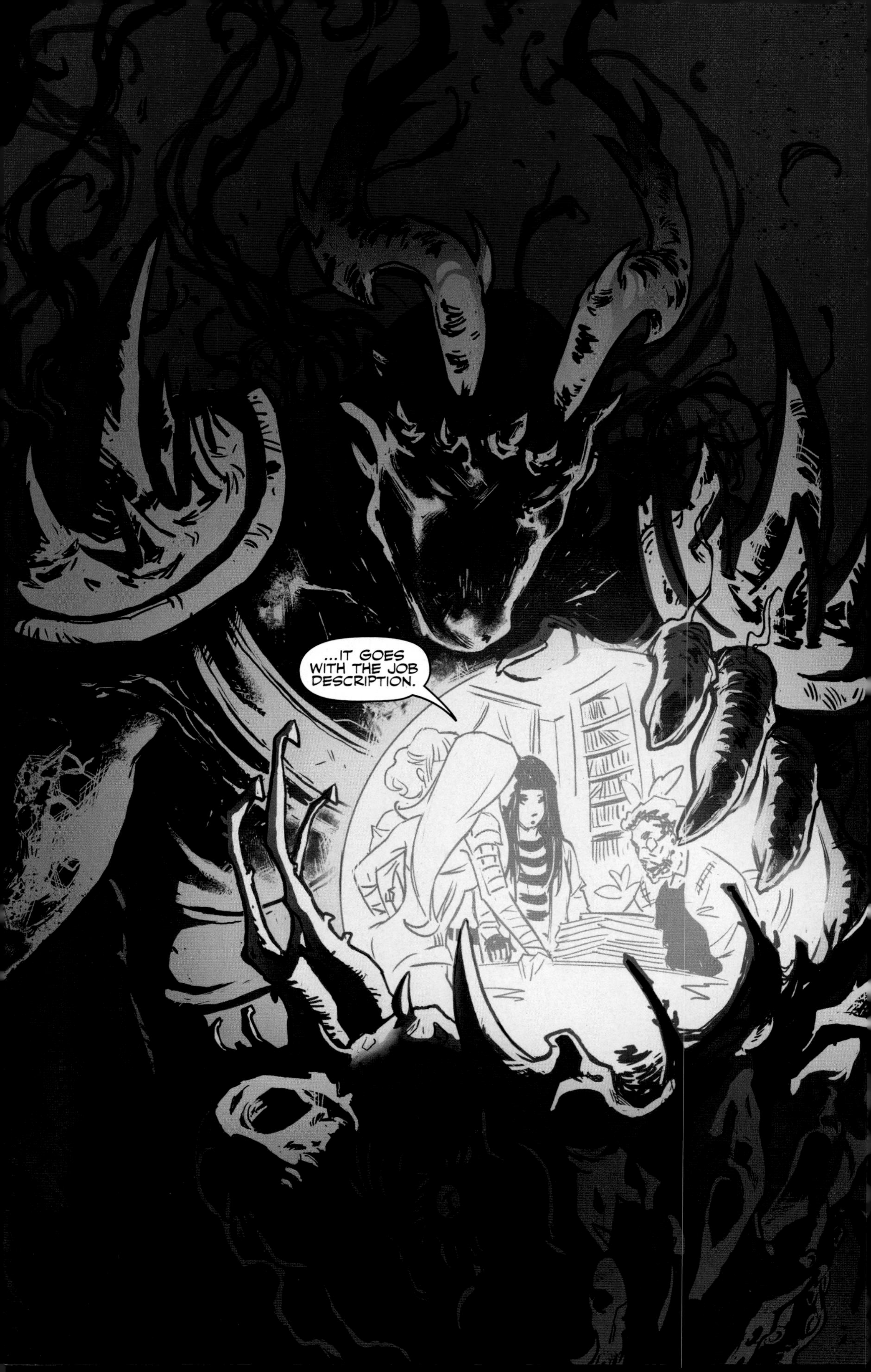
...IT GOES WITH THE JOB DESCRIPTION.

CHAPTER 4
WHEN SEPTEMBER ENDS

DAVID HINE
Writer

TINA VALENTINO
Artist

KATARINA DEVIC
Colorist

TROY PETERI
Letterer

ELENA SALCEDO
Editor

VINCENT VALENTINE
Production Art & Design

MICHAEL BROUSSARD
Cover Art

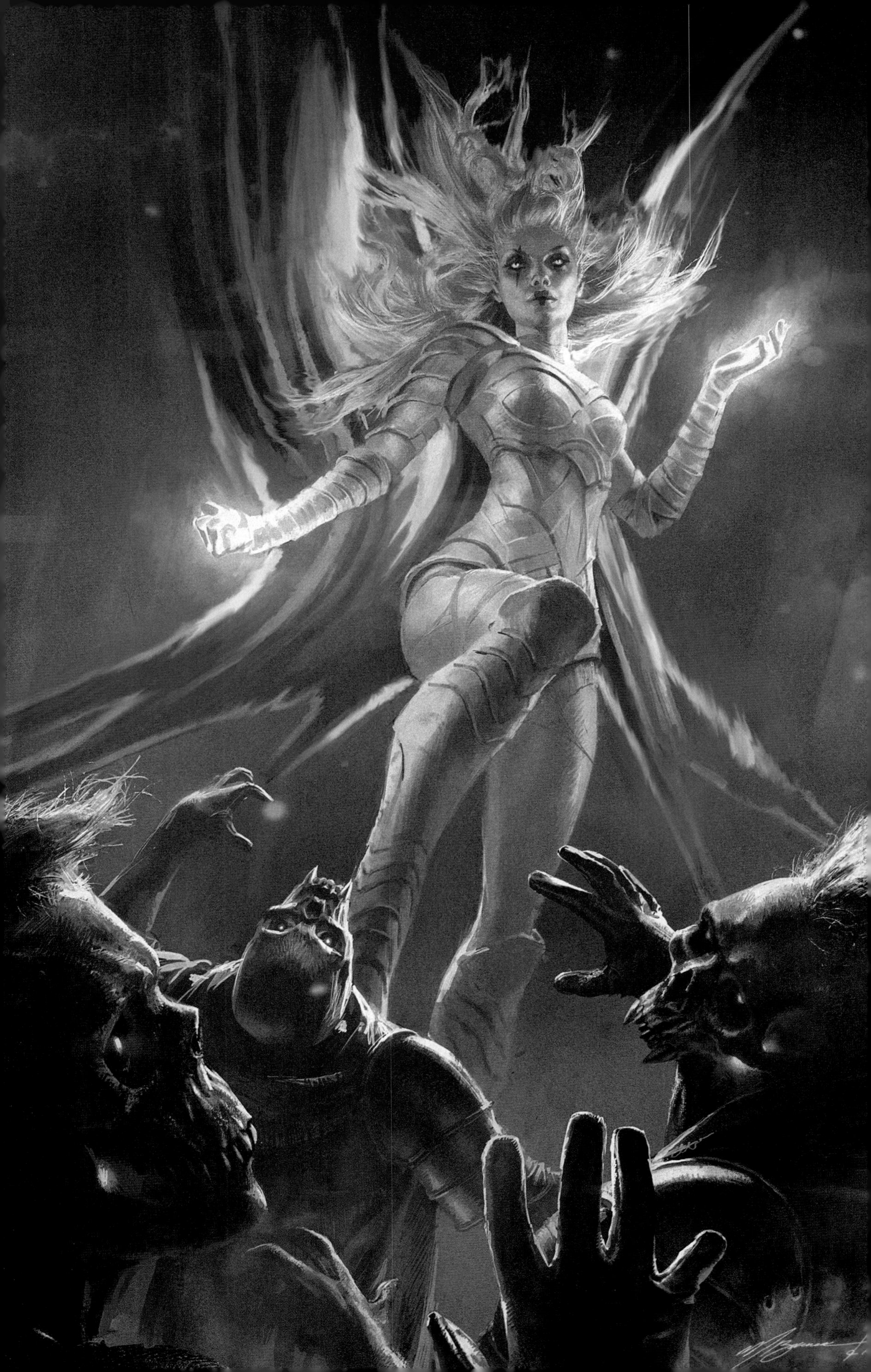

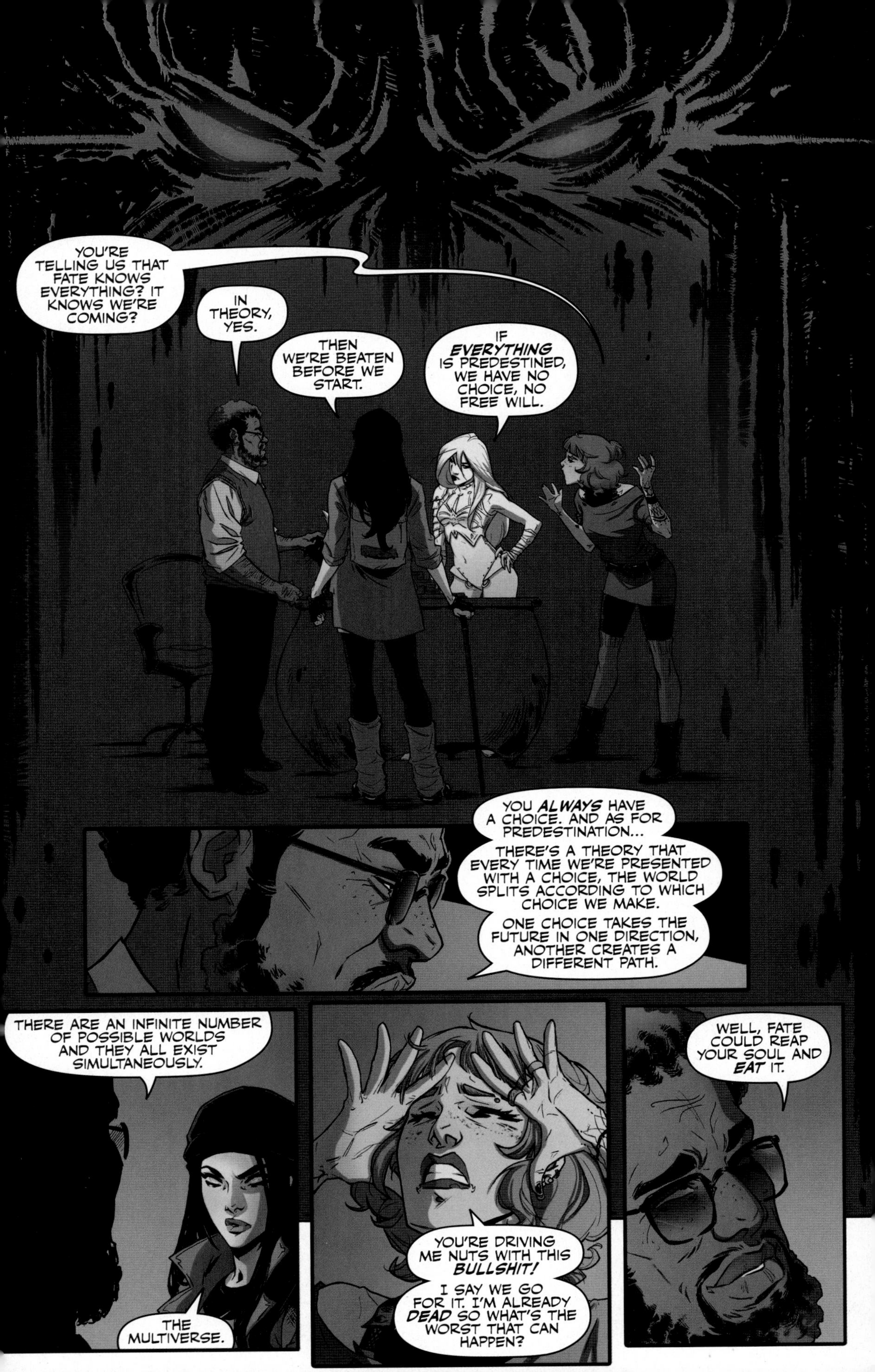

YOU'RE TELLING US THAT FATE KNOWS EVERYTHING? IT KNOWS WE'RE COMING?
IN THEORY, YES.
THEN WE'RE BEATEN BEFORE WE START.
IF *EVERYTHING* IS PREDESTINED, WE HAVE NO CHOICE, NO FREE WILL.
YOU *ALWAYS* HAVE A CHOICE. AND AS FOR PREDESTINATION...
THERE'S A THEORY THAT EVERY TIME WE'RE PRESENTED WITH A CHOICE, THE WORLD SPLITS ACCORDING TO WHICH CHOICE WE MAKE.
ONE CHOICE TAKES THE FUTURE IN ONE DIRECTION, ANOTHER CREATES A DIFFERENT PATH.
THERE ARE AN INFINITE NUMBER OF POSSIBLE WORLDS AND THEY ALL EXIST SIMULTANEOUSLY.
THE MULTIVERSE.
YOU'RE DRIVING ME NUTS WITH THIS *BULLSHIT!*
I SAY WE GO FOR IT. I'M ALREADY *DEAD* SO WHAT'S THE WORST THAT CAN HAPPEN?
WELL, FATE COULD REAP YOUR SOUL AND *EAT* IT.

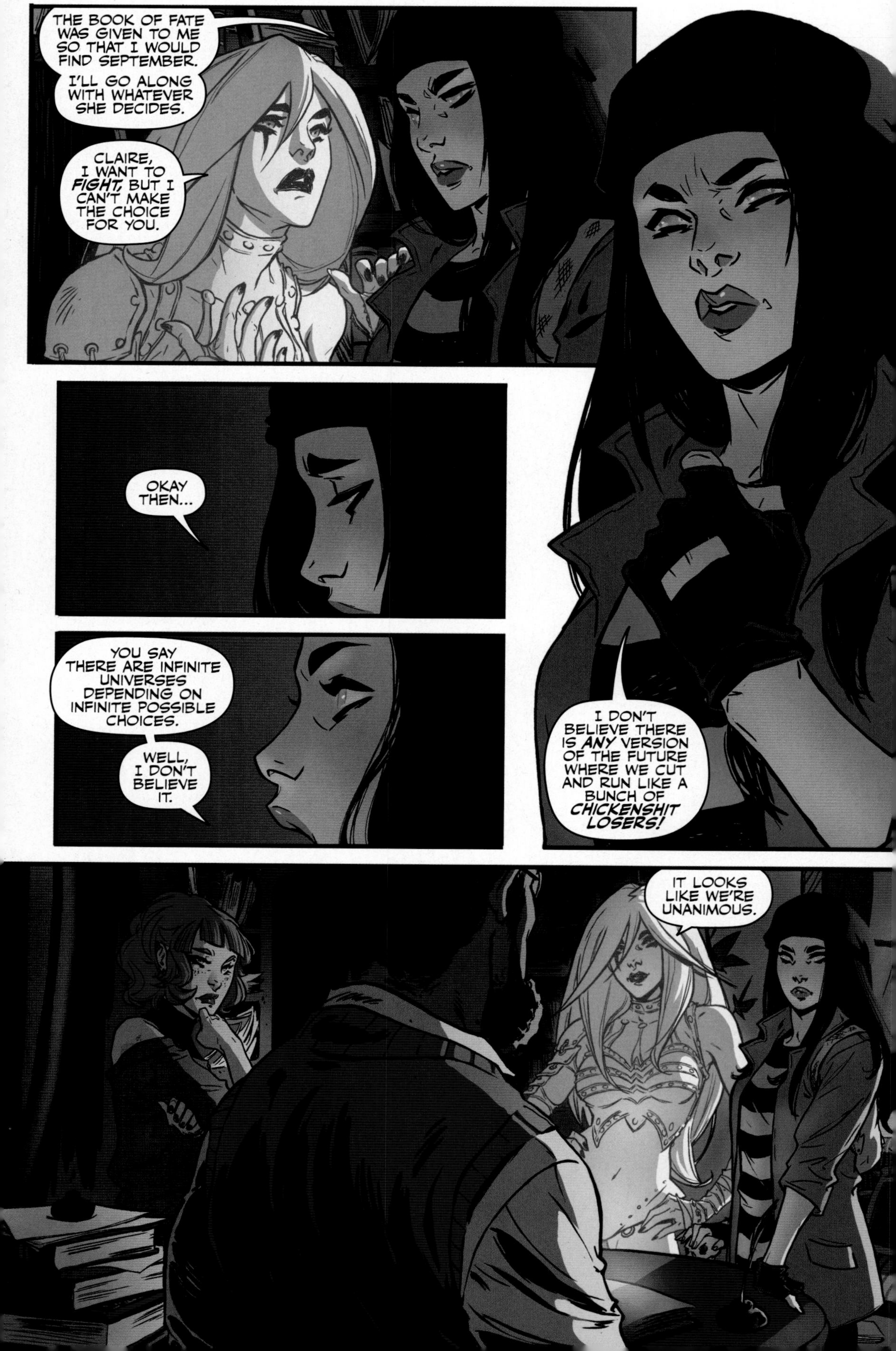
THE BOOK OF FATE WAS GIVEN TO ME SO THAT I WOULD FIND SEPTEMBER.
I'LL GO ALONG WITH WHATEVER SHE DECIDES.
CLAIRE, I WANT TO *FIGHT,* BUT I CAN'T MAKE THE CHOICE FOR YOU.
OKAY THEN...
YOU SAY THERE ARE INFINITE UNIVERSES DEPENDING ON INFINITE POSSIBLE CHOICES.
WELL, I DON'T BELIEVE IT.
I DON'T BELIEVE THERE IS *ANY* VERSION OF THE FUTURE WHERE WE CUT AND RUN LIKE A BUNCH OF *CHICKENSHIT LOSERS!*
IT LOOKS LIKE WE'RE UNANIMOUS.

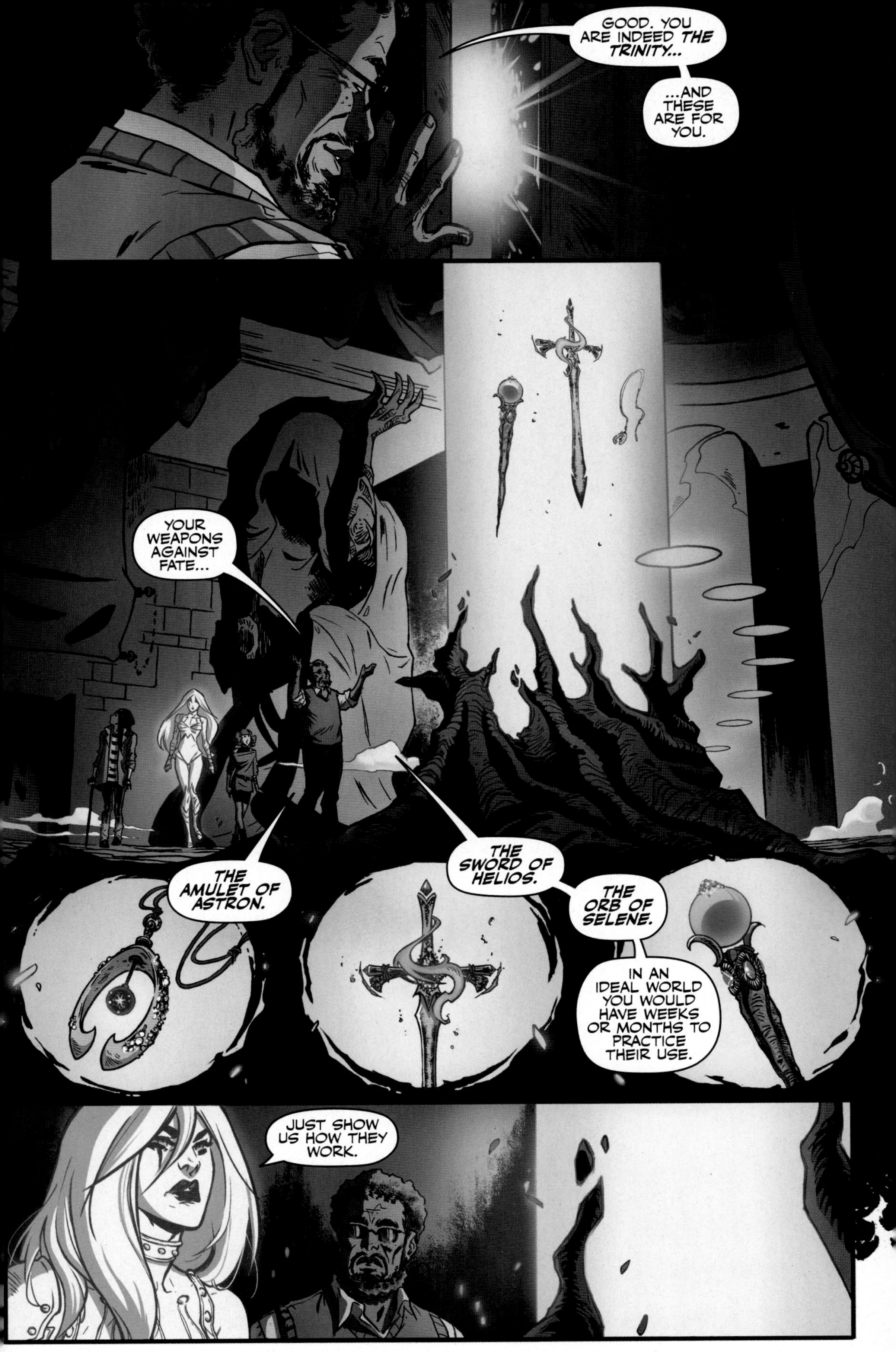
GOOD. YOU ARE INDEED *THE TRINITY...*
...AND THESE ARE FOR YOU.
YOUR WEAPONS AGAINST FATE...
THE AMULET OF ASTRON.
THE SWORD OF HELIOS.
THE ORB OF SELENE.
IN AN IDEAL WORLD YOU WOULD HAVE WEEKS OR MONTHS TO PRACTICE THEIR USE.
JUST SHOW US HOW THEY WORK.

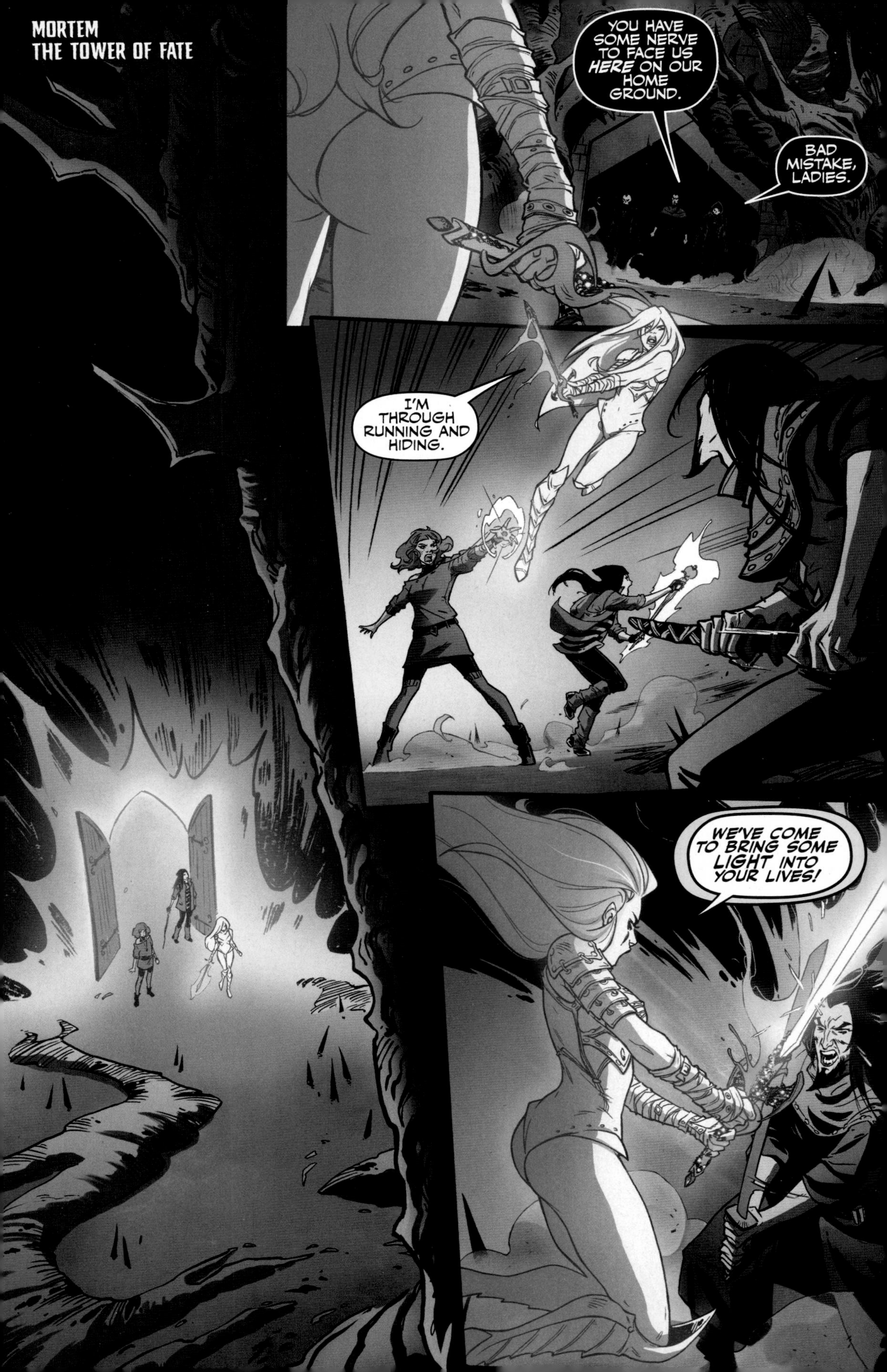
MORTEM
THE TOWER OF FATE
YOU HAVE SOME NERVE TO FACE US HERE ON OUR HOME GROUND.
BAD MISTAKE, LADIES.
I'M THROUGH RUNNING AND HIDING.
WE'VE COME TO BRING SOME LIGHT INTO YOUR LIVES!

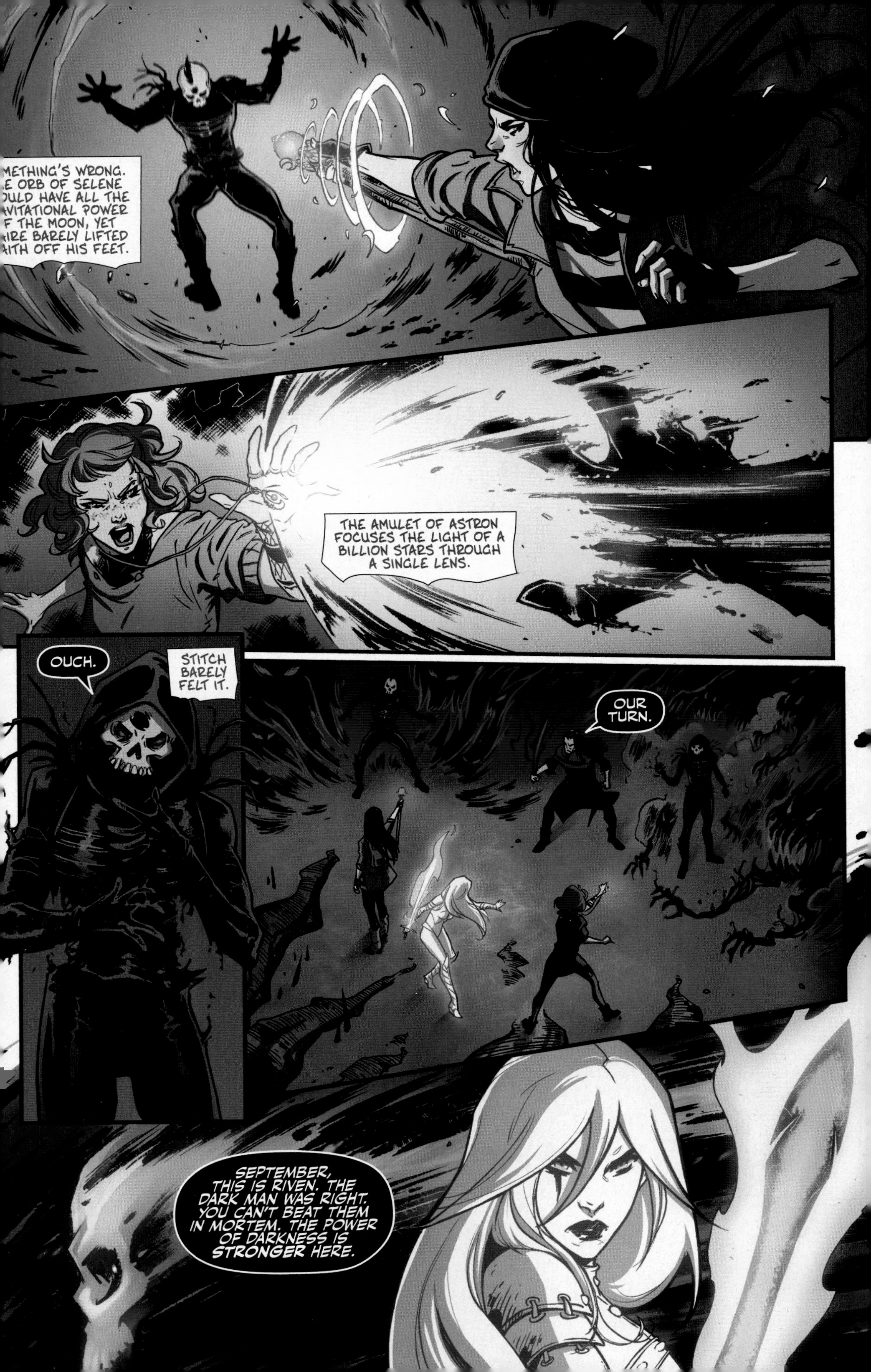
METHING'S WRONG. E ORB OF SELENE OULD HAVE ALL THE AVITATIONAL POWER F THE MOON, YET IRE BARELY LIFTED AITH OFF HIS FEET.
THE AMULET OF ASTRON FOCUSES THE LIGHT OF A BILLION STARS THROUGH A SINGLE LENS.
OUCH.
STITCH BARELY FELT IT.
OUR TURN.
SEPTEMBER, THIS IS RIVEN. THE DARK MAN WAS RIGHT. YOU CAN'T BEAT THEM IN MORTEM. THE POWER OF DARKNESS IS STRONGER HERE.

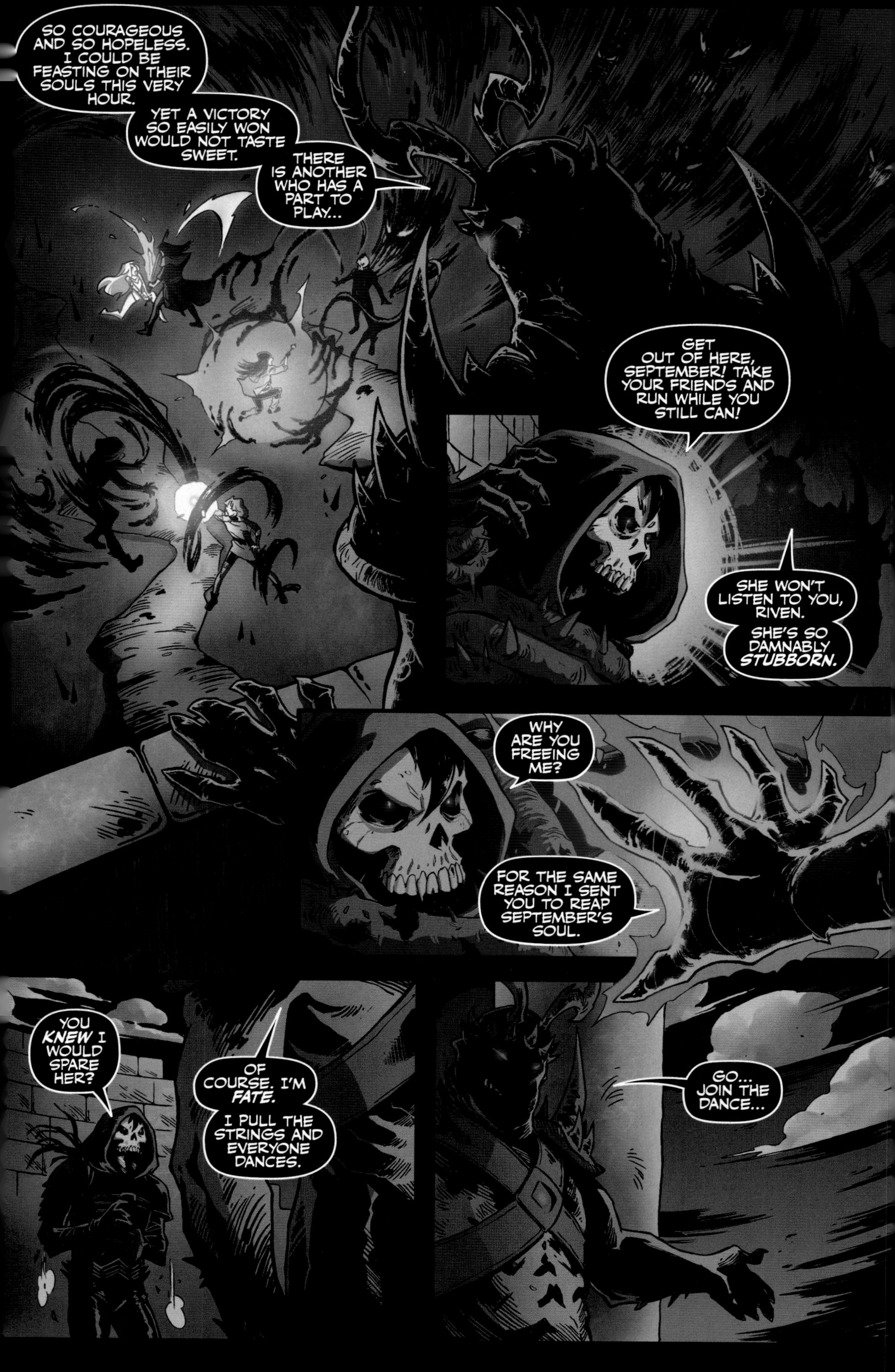
SO COURAGEOUS AND SO HOPELESS. I COULD BE FEASTING ON THEIR SOULS THIS VERY HOUR.
YET A VICTORY SO EASILY WON WOULD NOT TASTE SWEET.
THERE IS ANOTHER WHO HAS A PART TO PLAY...
GET OUT OF HERE, SEPTEMBER! TAKE YOUR FRIENDS AND RUN WHILE YOU STILL CAN!
SHE WON'T LISTEN TO YOU, RIVEN.
SHE'S SO DAMNABLY STUBBORN.
WHY ARE YOU FREEING ME?
FOR THE SAME REASON I SENT YOU TO REAP SEPTEMBER'S SOUL.
YOU KNEW I WOULD SPARE HER?
OF COURSE. I'M FATE.
I PULL THE STRINGS AND EVERYONE DANCES.
GO... JOIN THE DANCE...

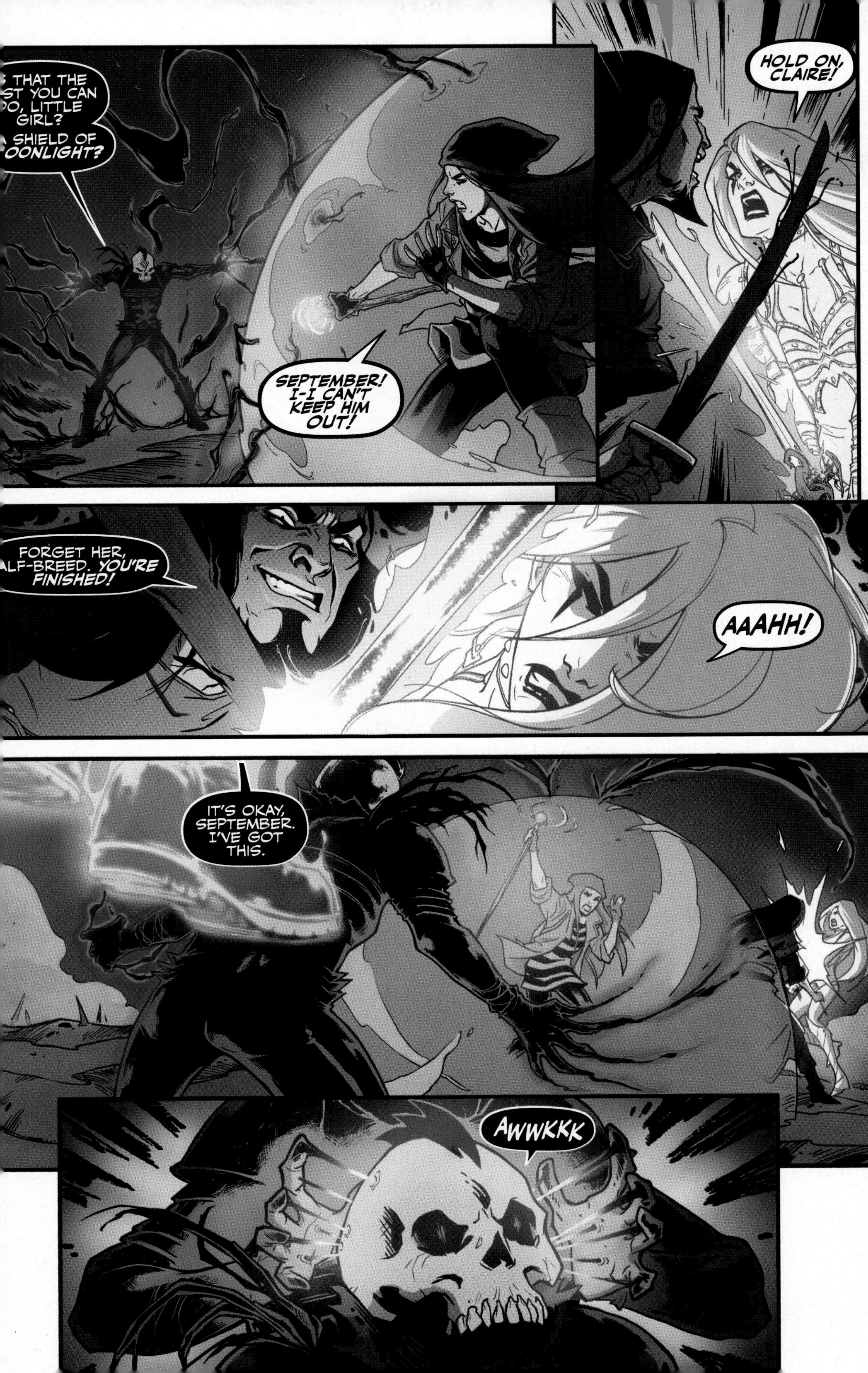
THAT THE ST YOU CAN O, LITTLE GIRL? SHIELD OF OONLIGHT?
SEPTEMBER! I-I CAN'T KEEP HIM OUT!
HOLD ON, CLAIRE!
FORGET HER, ALF-BREED. YOU'RE FINISHED!
AAAHH!
IT'S OKAY, SEPTEMBER. I'VE GOT THIS.
AWWKKK

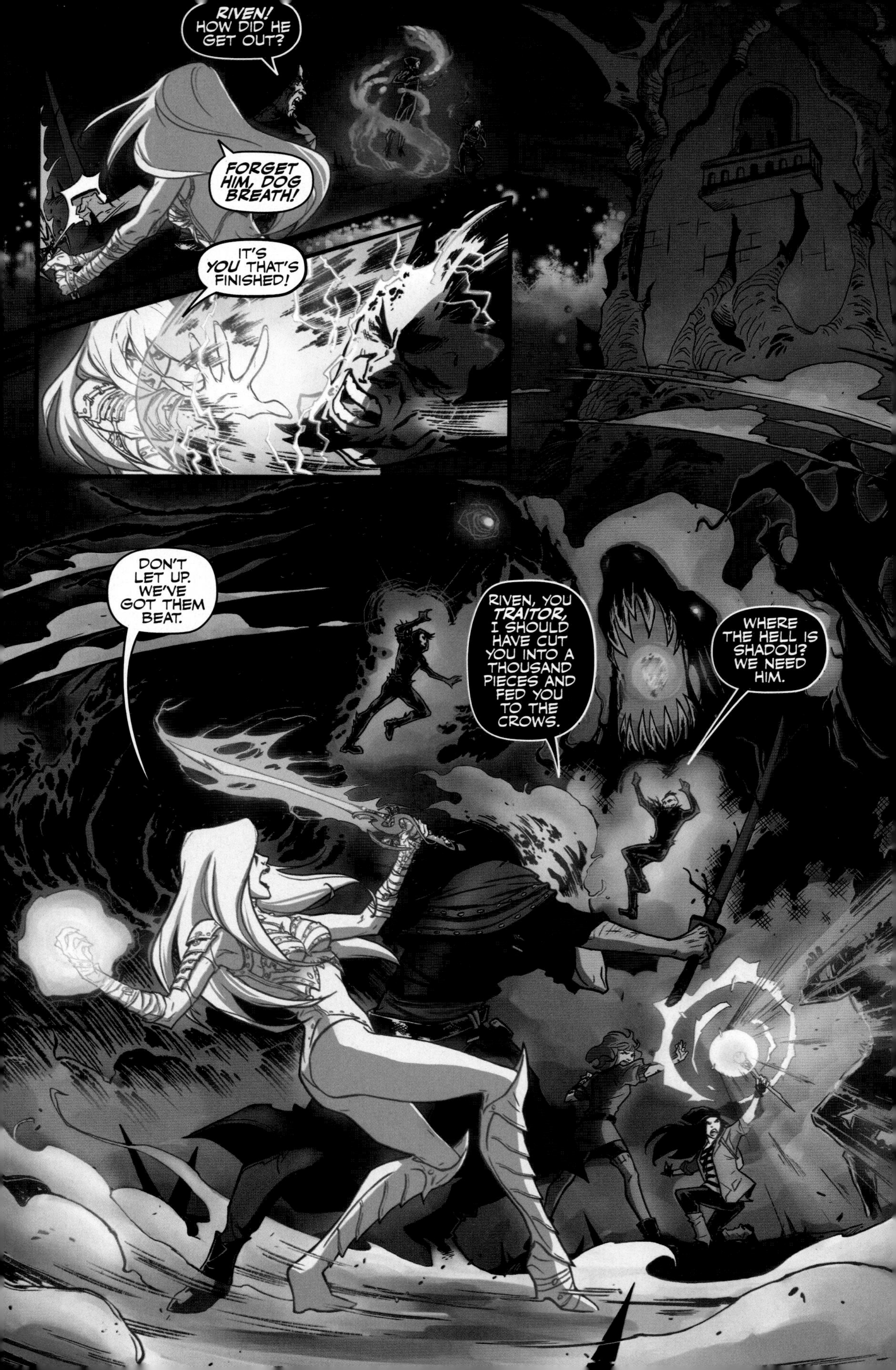
RIVEN! HOW DID HE GET OUT?
FORGET HIM, DOG BREATH!
IT'S YOU THAT'S FINISHED!
DON'T LET UP. WE'VE GOT THEM BEAT.
RIVEN, YOU TRAITOR, I SHOULD HAVE CUT YOU INTO A THOUSAND PIECES AND FED YOU TO THE CROWS.
WHERE THE HELL IS SHADOU? WE NEED HIM.

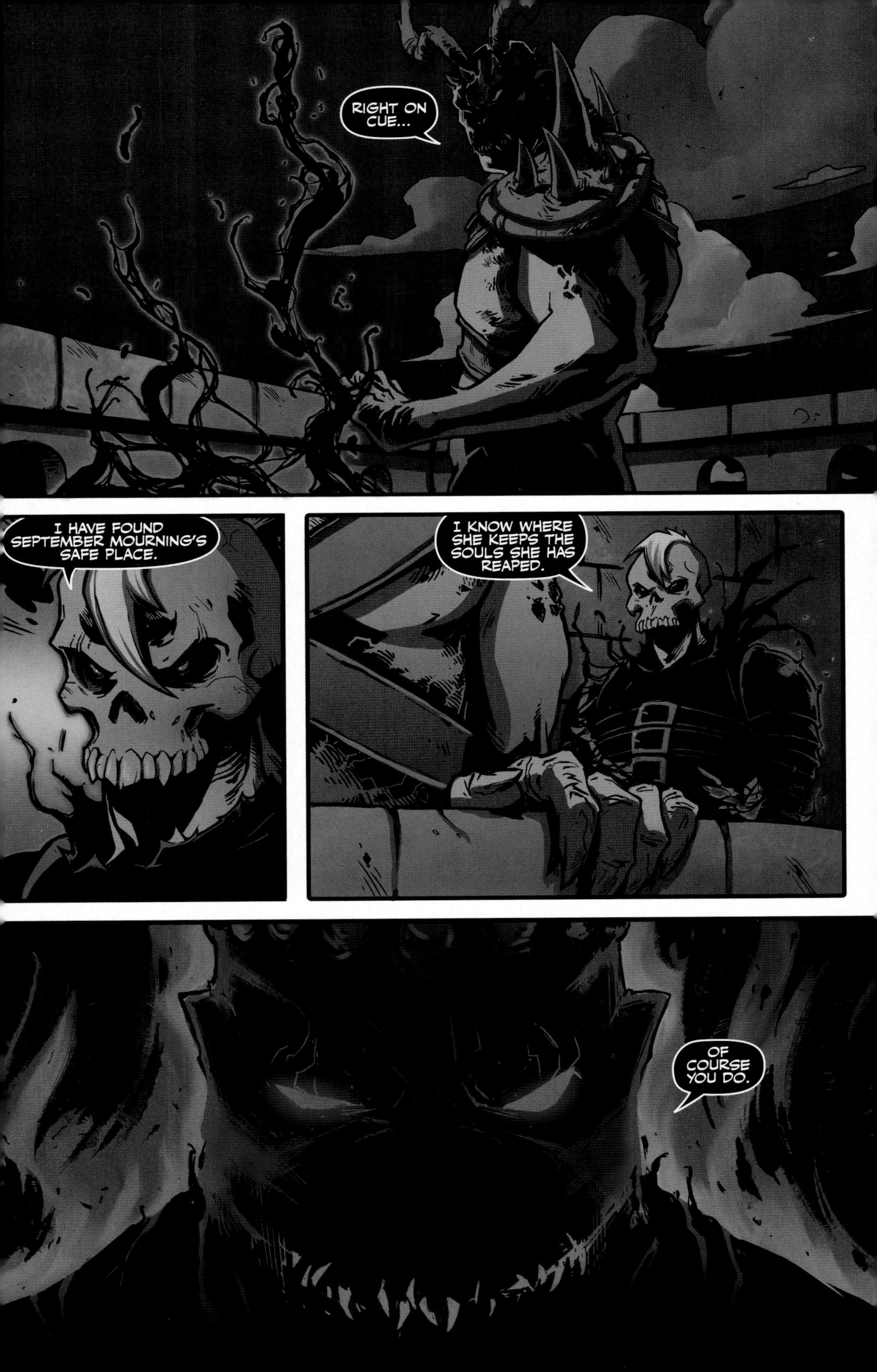
RIGHT ON CUE...
I HAVE FOUND SEPTEMBER MOURNING'S SAFE PLACE.
I KNOW WHERE SHE KEEPS THE SOULS SHE HAS REAPED.
OF COURSE YOU DO.

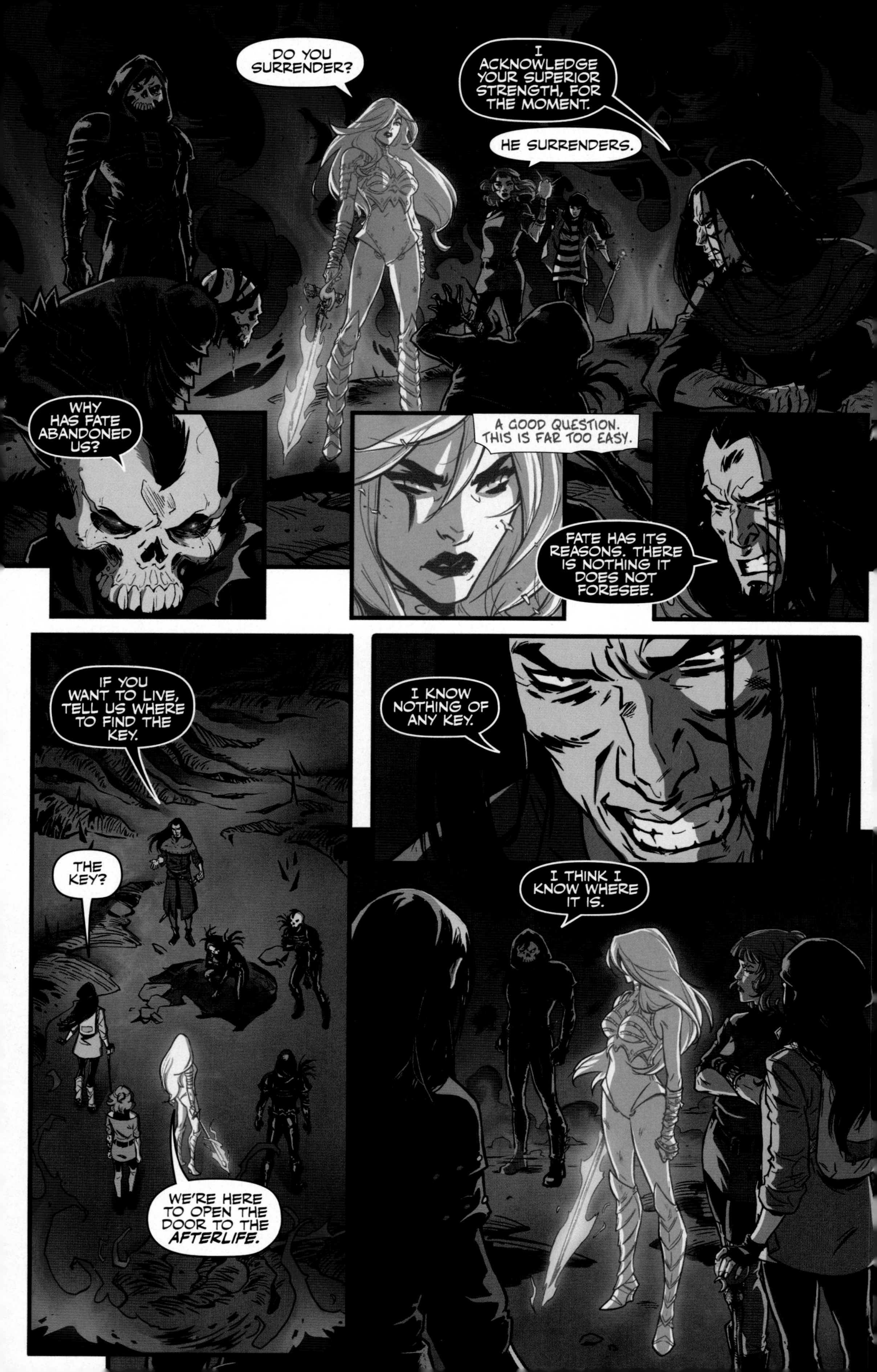
DO YOU SURRENDER?
I ACKNOWLEDGE YOUR SUPERIOR STRENGTH, FOR THE MOMENT.
HE SURRENDERS.
WHY HAS FATE ABANDONED US?
A GOOD QUESTION. THIS IS FAR TOO EASY.
FATE HAS ITS REASONS. THERE IS NOTHING IT DOES NOT FORESEE.
IF YOU WANT TO LIVE, TELL US WHERE TO FIND THE KEY.
THE KEY?
WE'RE HERE TO OPEN THE DOOR TO THE *AFTERLIFE.*
I KNOW NOTHING OF ANY KEY.
I THINK I KNOW WHERE IT IS.

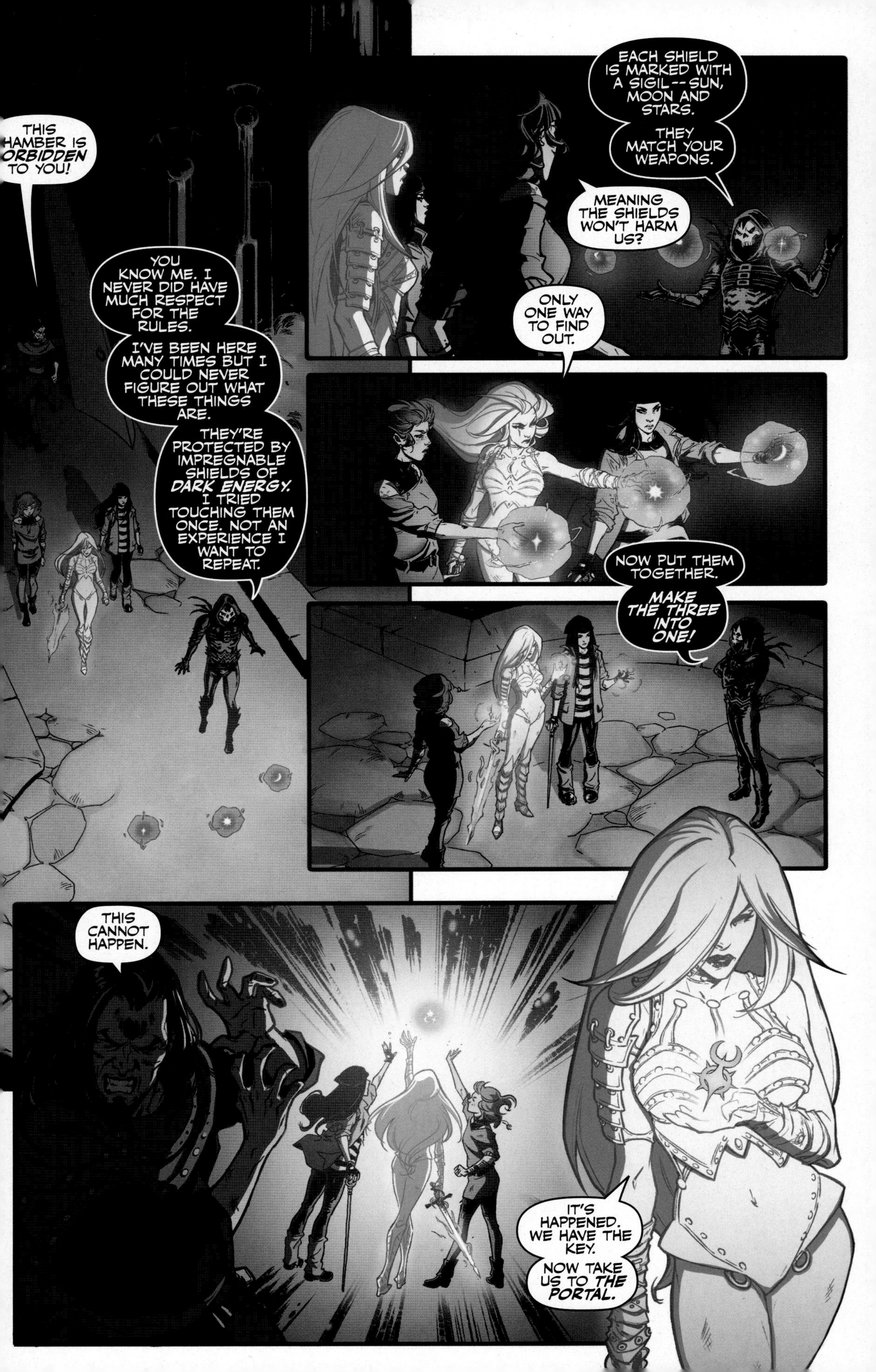
THIS HAMBER IS ORBIDDEN TO YOU!
YOU KNOW ME. I NEVER DID HAVE MUCH RESPECT FOR THE RULES.
I'VE BEEN HERE MANY TIMES BUT I COULD NEVER FIGURE OUT WHAT THESE THINGS ARE.
THEY'RE PROTECTED BY IMPREGNABLE SHIELDS OF DARK ENERGY. I TRIED TOUCHING THEM ONCE. NOT AN EXPERIENCE I WANT TO REPEAT.
EACH SHIELD IS MARKED WITH A SIGIL--SUN, MOON AND STARS.
THEY MATCH YOUR WEAPONS.
MEANING THE SHIELDS WON'T HARM US?
ONLY ONE WAY TO FIND OUT.
NOW PUT THEM TOGETHER.
MAKE THE THREE INTO ONE!
THIS CANNOT HAPPEN.
IT'S HAPPENED. WE HAVE THE KEY.
NOW TAKE US TO THE PORTAL.

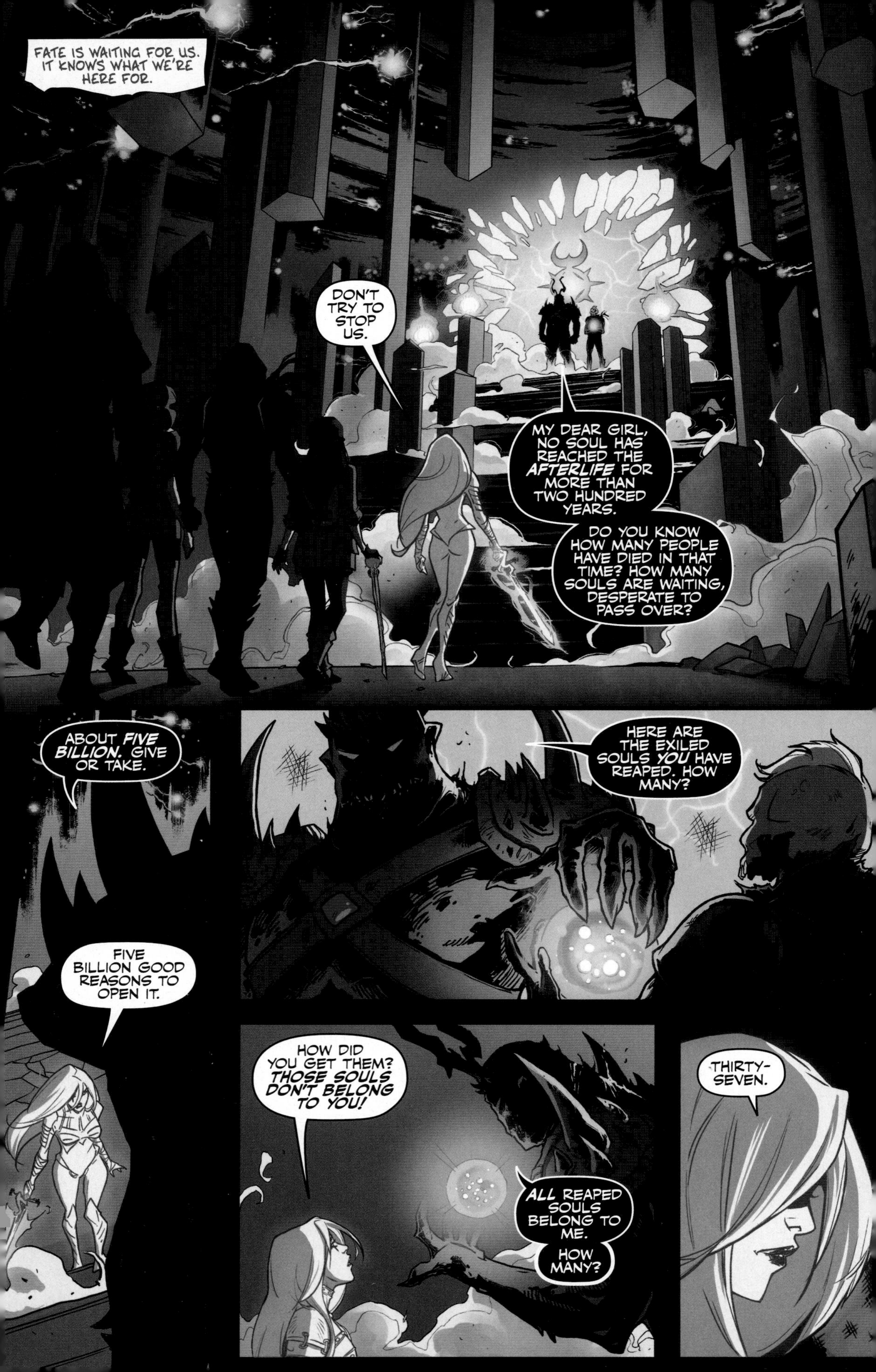
FATE IS WAITING FOR US. IT KNOWS WHAT WE'RE HERE FOR.
DON'T TRY TO STOP US.
MY DEAR GIRL, NO SOUL HAS REACHED THE AFTERLIFE FOR MORE THAN TWO HUNDRED YEARS.
DO YOU KNOW HOW MANY PEOPLE HAVE DIED IN THAT TIME? HOW MANY SOULS ARE WAITING, DESPERATE TO PASS OVER?
ABOUT FIVE BILLION. GIVE OR TAKE.
FIVE BILLION GOOD REASONS TO OPEN IT.
HERE ARE THE EXILED SOULS YOU HAVE REAPED. HOW MANY?
HOW DID YOU GET THEM? THOSE SOULS DON'T BELONG TO YOU!
ALL REAPED SOULS BELONG TO ME.
HOW MANY?
THIRTY-SEVEN.

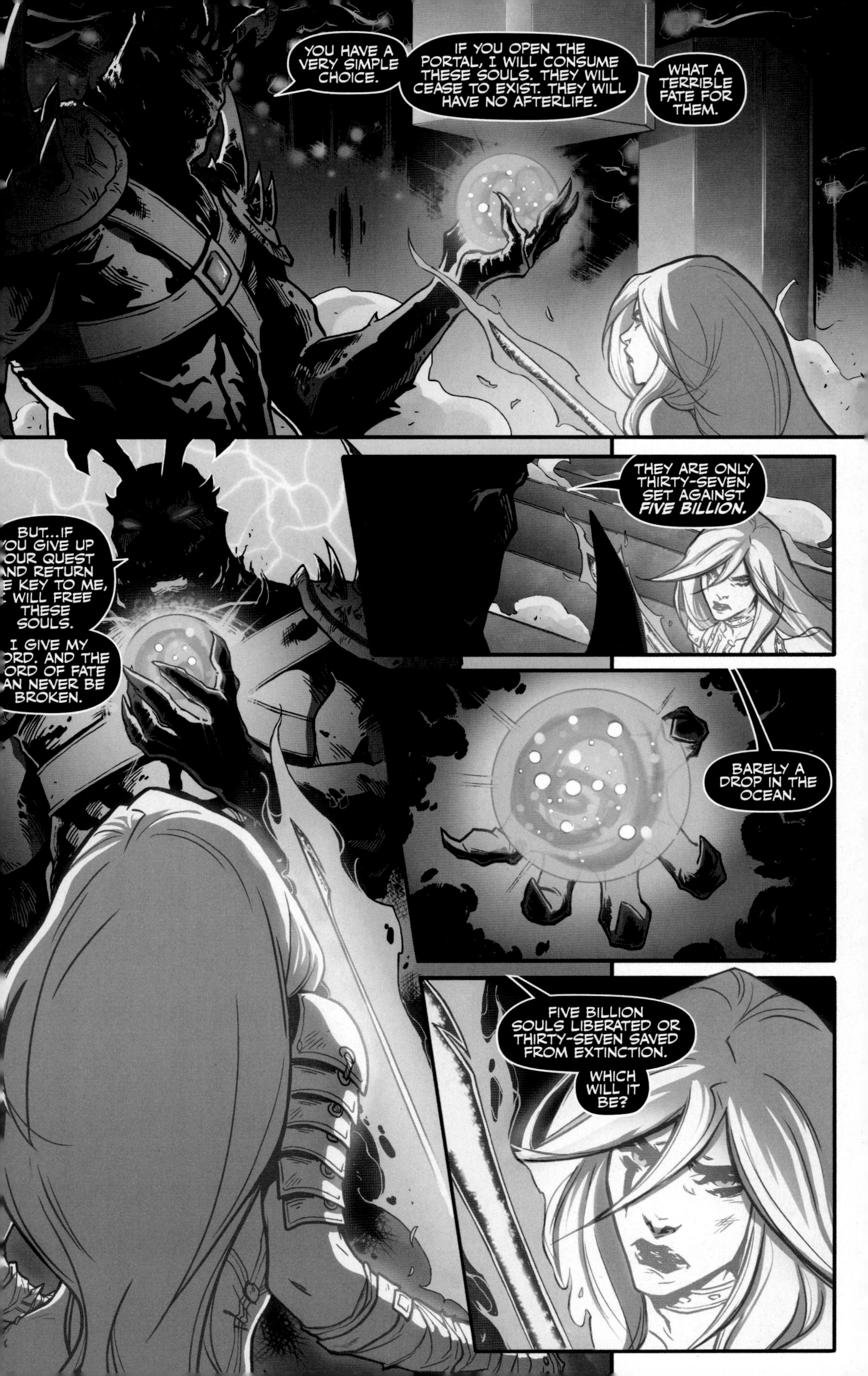
YOU HAVE A VERY SIMPLE CHOICE.
IF YOU OPEN THE PORTAL, I WILL CONSUME THESE SOULS. THEY WILL CEASE TO EXIST. THEY WILL HAVE NO AFTERLIFE.
WHAT A TERRIBLE FATE FOR THEM.
THEY ARE ONLY THIRTY-SEVEN, SET AGAINST *FIVE BILLION.*
BARELY A DROP IN THE OCEAN.
FIVE BILLION SOULS LIBERATED OR THIRTY-SEVEN SAVED FROM EXTINCTION.
WHICH WILL IT BE?

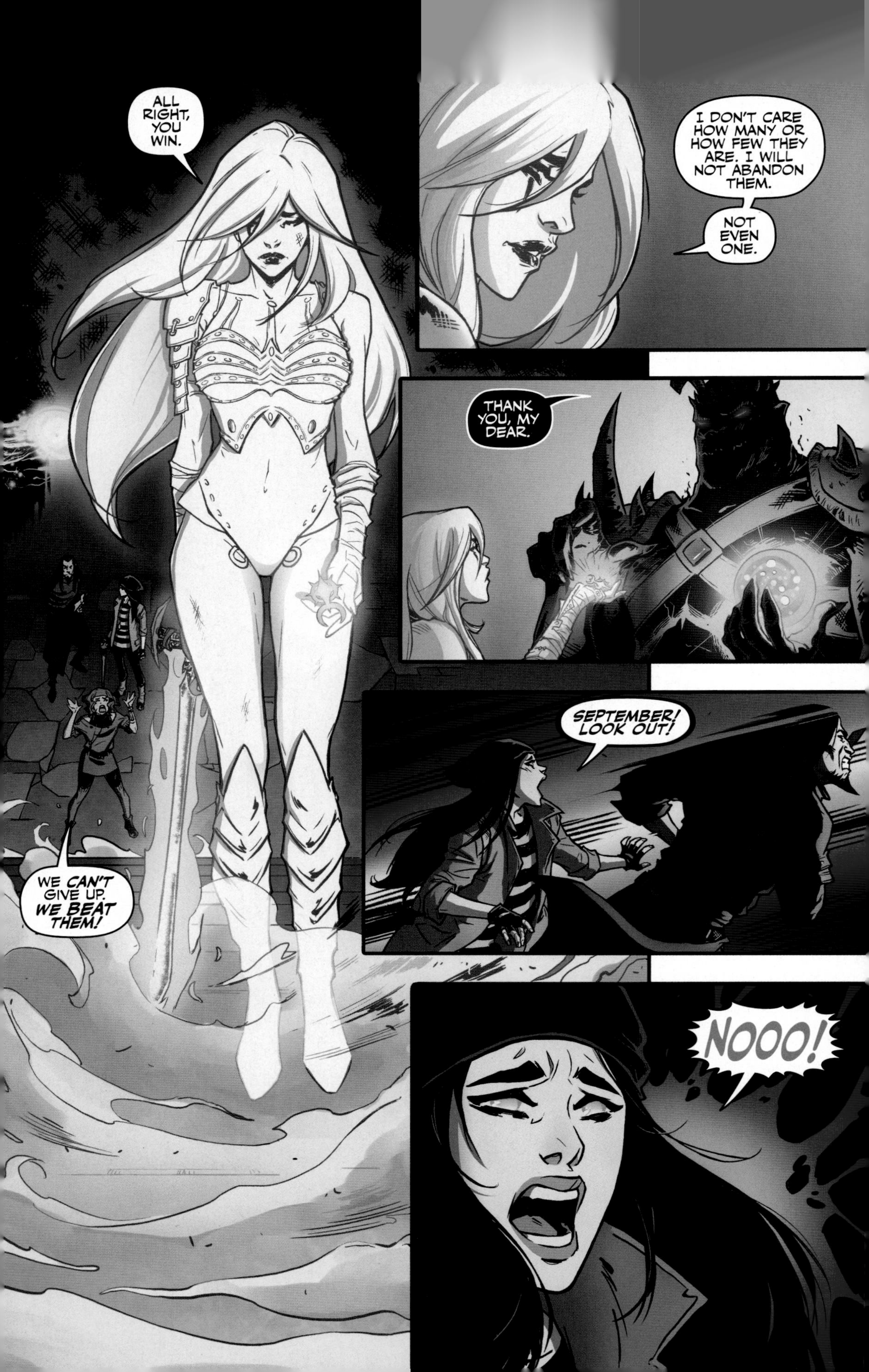

ALL RIGHT, YOU WIN.
WE CAN'T GIVE UP. WE BEAT THEM!
I DON'T CARE HOW MANY OR HOW FEW THEY ARE. I WILL NOT ABANDON THEM.
NOT EVEN ONE.
THANK YOU, MY DEAR.
SEPTEMBER! LOOK OUT!
NOOO!

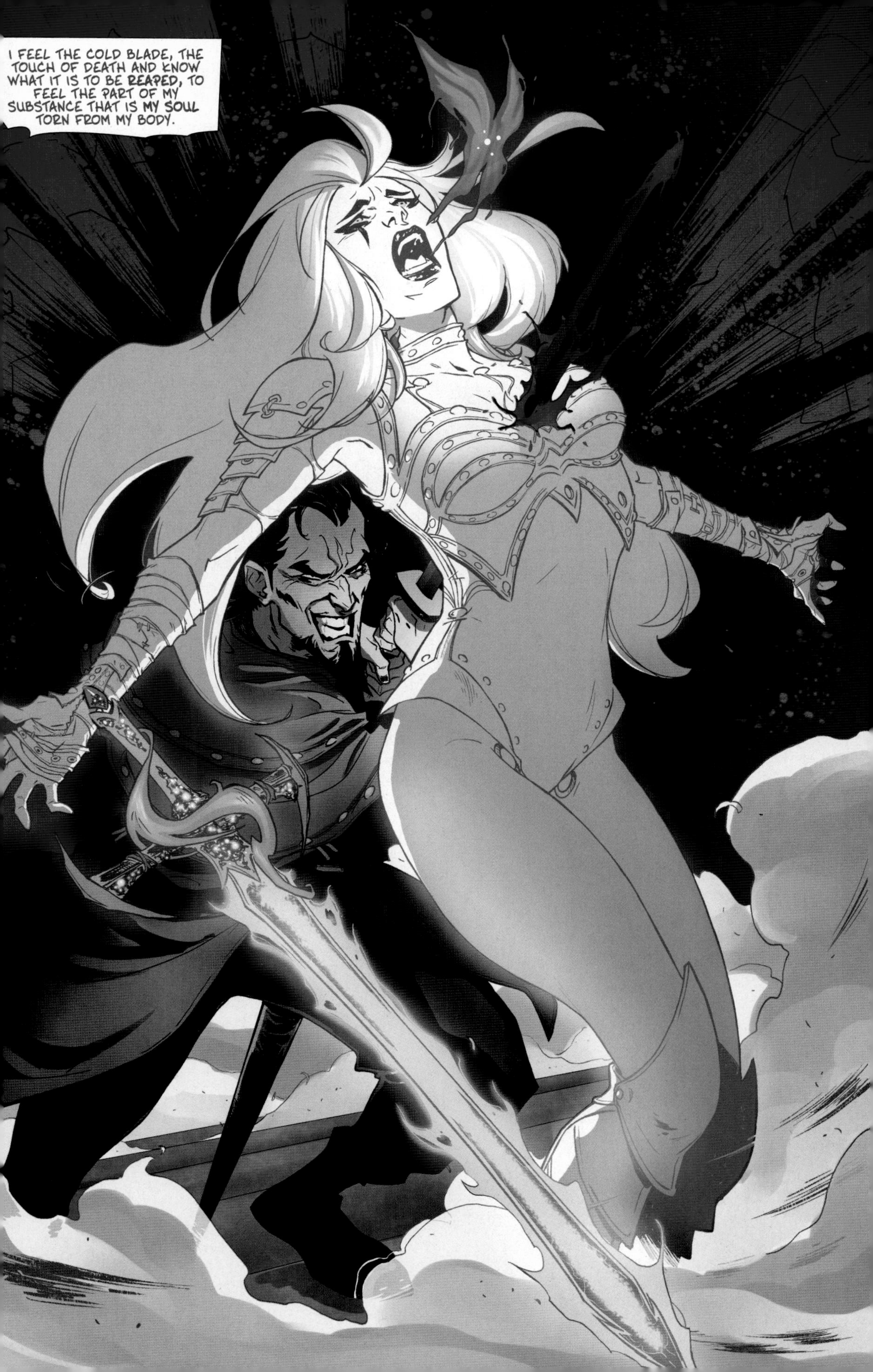
I FEEL THE COLD BLADE, THE TOUCH OF DEATH AND KNOW WHAT IT IS TO BE REAPED, TO FEEL THE PART OF MY SUBSTANCE THAT IS MY SOUL TORN FROM MY BODY.

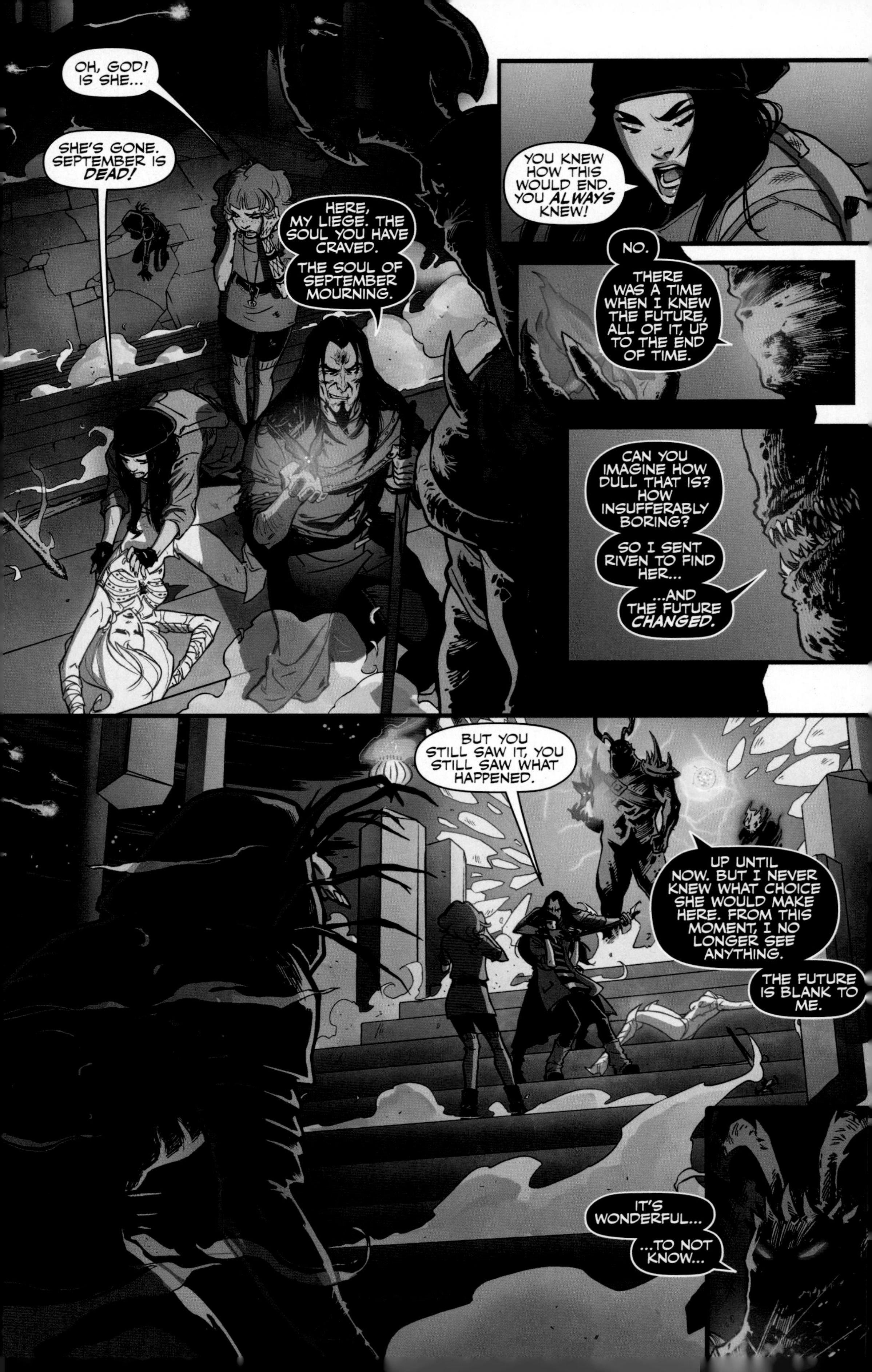
OH, GOD! IS SHE...
SHE'S GONE. SEPTEMBER IS *DEAD!*
HERE, MY LIEGE. THE SOUL YOU HAVE CRAVED.
THE SOUL OF SEPTEMBER MOURNING.
YOU KNEW HOW THIS WOULD END. YOU *ALWAYS* KNEW!
NO.
THERE WAS A TIME WHEN I KNEW THE FUTURE, ALL OF IT, UP TO THE END OF TIME.
CAN YOU IMAGINE HOW DULL THAT IS? HOW INSUFFERABLY BORING?
SO I SENT RIVEN TO FIND HER...
...AND THE FUTURE *CHANGED.*
BUT YOU STILL SAW IT, YOU STILL SAW WHAT HAPPENED.
UP UNTIL NOW. BUT I NEVER KNEW WHAT CHOICE SHE WOULD MAKE HERE. FROM THIS MOMENT, I NO LONGER SEE ANYTHING.
THE FUTURE IS BLANK TO ME.
IT'S WONDERFUL...
...TO NOT KNOW...

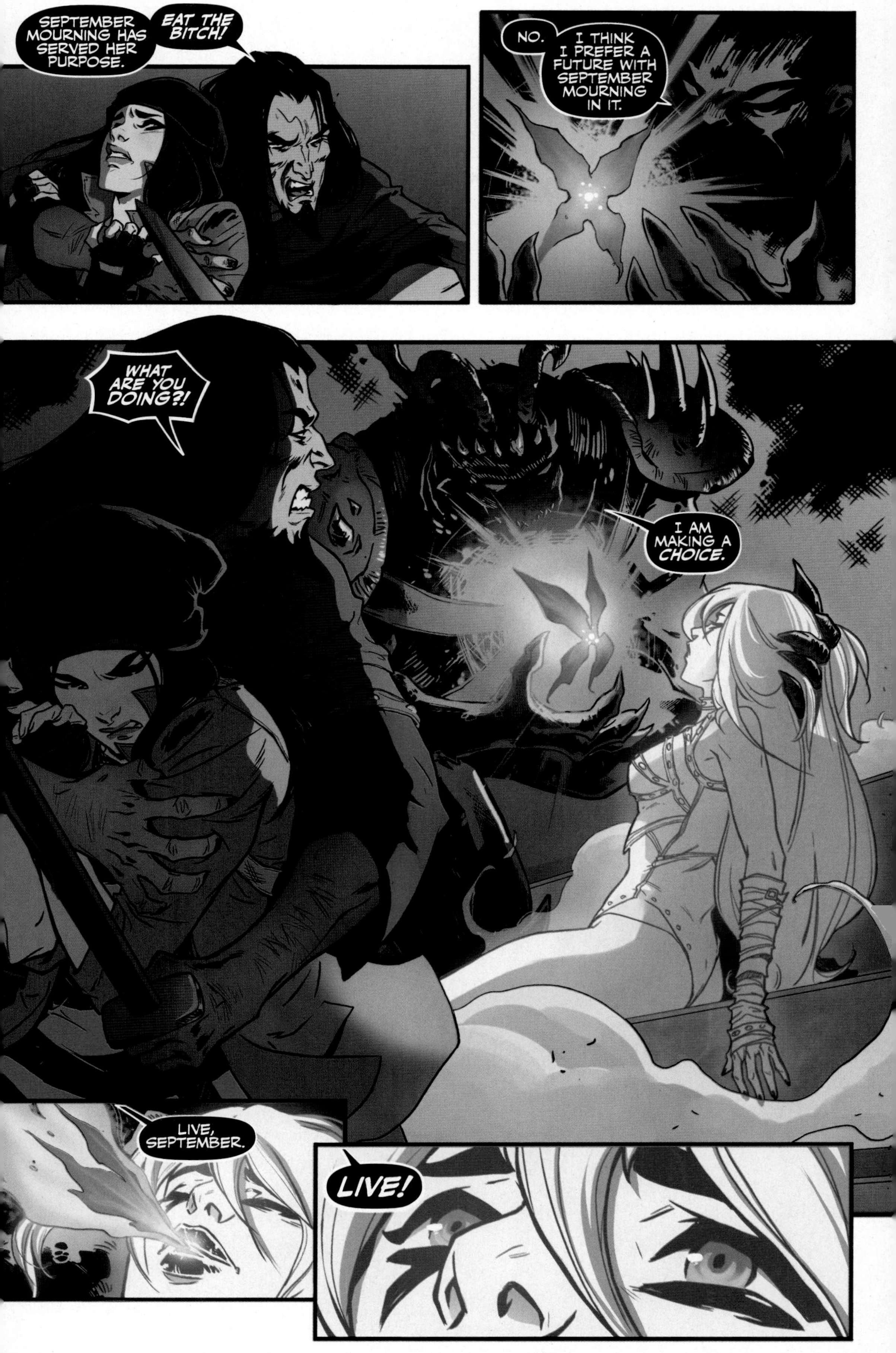
SEPTEMBER MOURNING HAS SERVED HER PURPOSE.
EAT THE BITCH!
NO.
I THINK I PREFER A FUTURE WITH SEPTEMBER MOURNING IN IT.
WHAT ARE YOU DOING?!
I AM MAKING A CHOICE.
LIVE, SEPTEMBER.
LIVE!

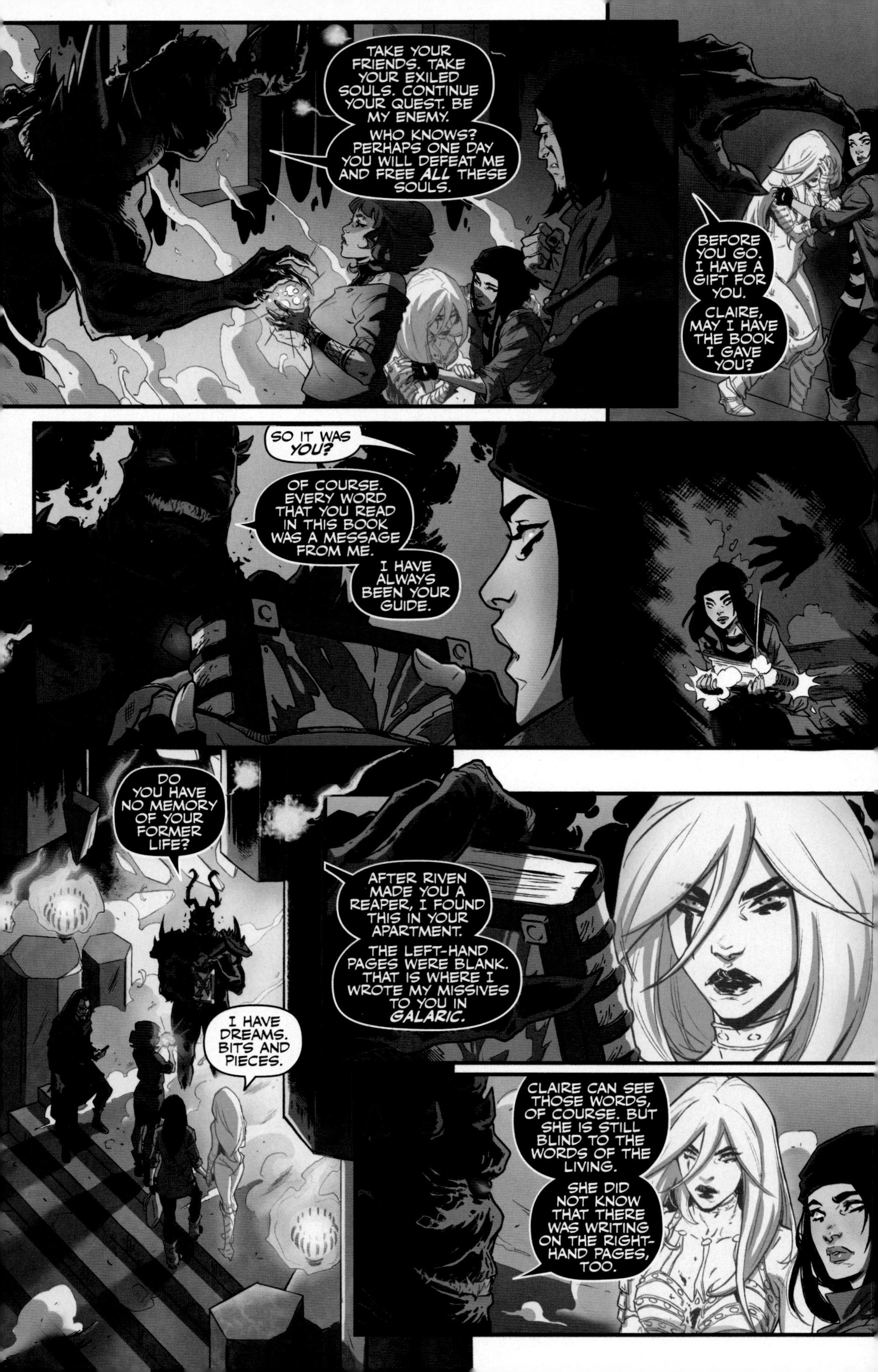
TAKE YOUR FRIENDS. TAKE YOUR EXILED SOULS. CONTINUE YOUR QUEST. BE MY ENEMY.
WHO KNOWS? PERHAPS ONE DAY YOU WILL DEFEAT ME AND FREE ALL THESE SOULS.
BEFORE YOU GO. I HAVE A GIFT FOR YOU.
CLAIRE, MAY I HAVE THE BOOK I GAVE YOU?
SO IT WAS YOU?
OF COURSE. EVERY WORD THAT YOU READ IN THIS BOOK WAS A MESSAGE FROM ME.
I HAVE ALWAYS BEEN YOUR GUIDE.
DO YOU HAVE NO MEMORY OF YOUR FORMER LIFE?
I HAVE DREAMS. BITS AND PIECES.
AFTER RIVEN MADE YOU A REAPER, I FOUND THIS IN YOUR APARTMENT.
THE LEFT-HAND PAGES WERE BLANK. THAT IS WHERE I WROTE MY MISSIVES TO YOU IN GALARIC.
CLAIRE CAN SEE THOSE WORDS, OF COURSE. BUT SHE IS STILL BLIND TO THE WORDS OF THE LIVING.
SHE DID NOT KNOW THAT THERE WAS WRITING ON THE RIGHT-HAND PAGES, TOO.

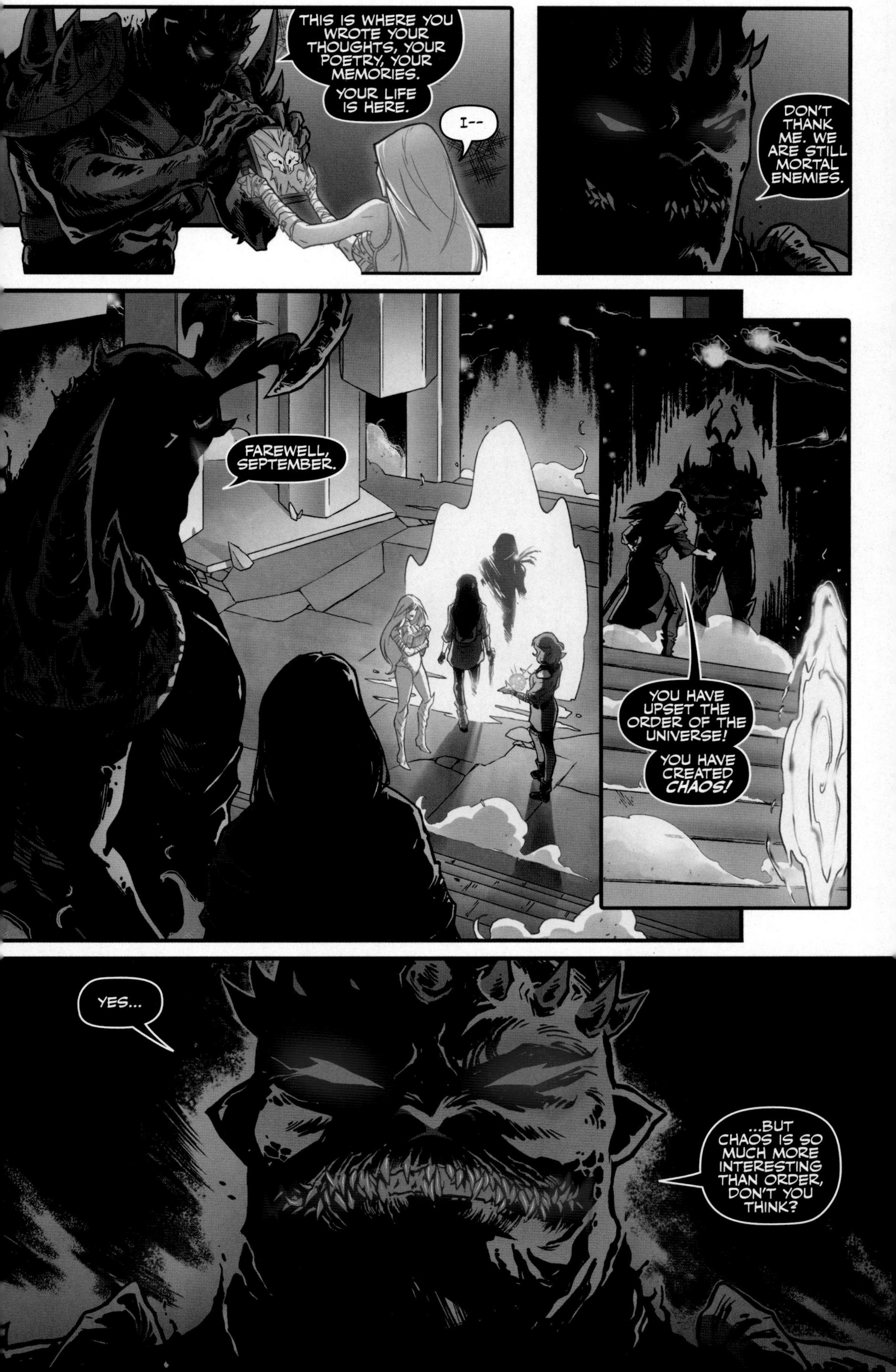
THIS IS WHERE YOU WROTE YOUR THOUGHTS, YOUR POETRY, YOUR MEMORIES.
YOUR LIFE IS HERE.
I--
DON'T THANK ME. WE ARE STILL MORTAL ENEMIES.
FAREWELL, SEPTEMBER.
YOU HAVE UPSET THE ORDER OF THE UNIVERSE!
YOU HAVE CREATED CHAOS!
YES...
...BUT CHAOS IS SO MUCH MORE INTERESTING THAN ORDER, DON'T YOU THINK?

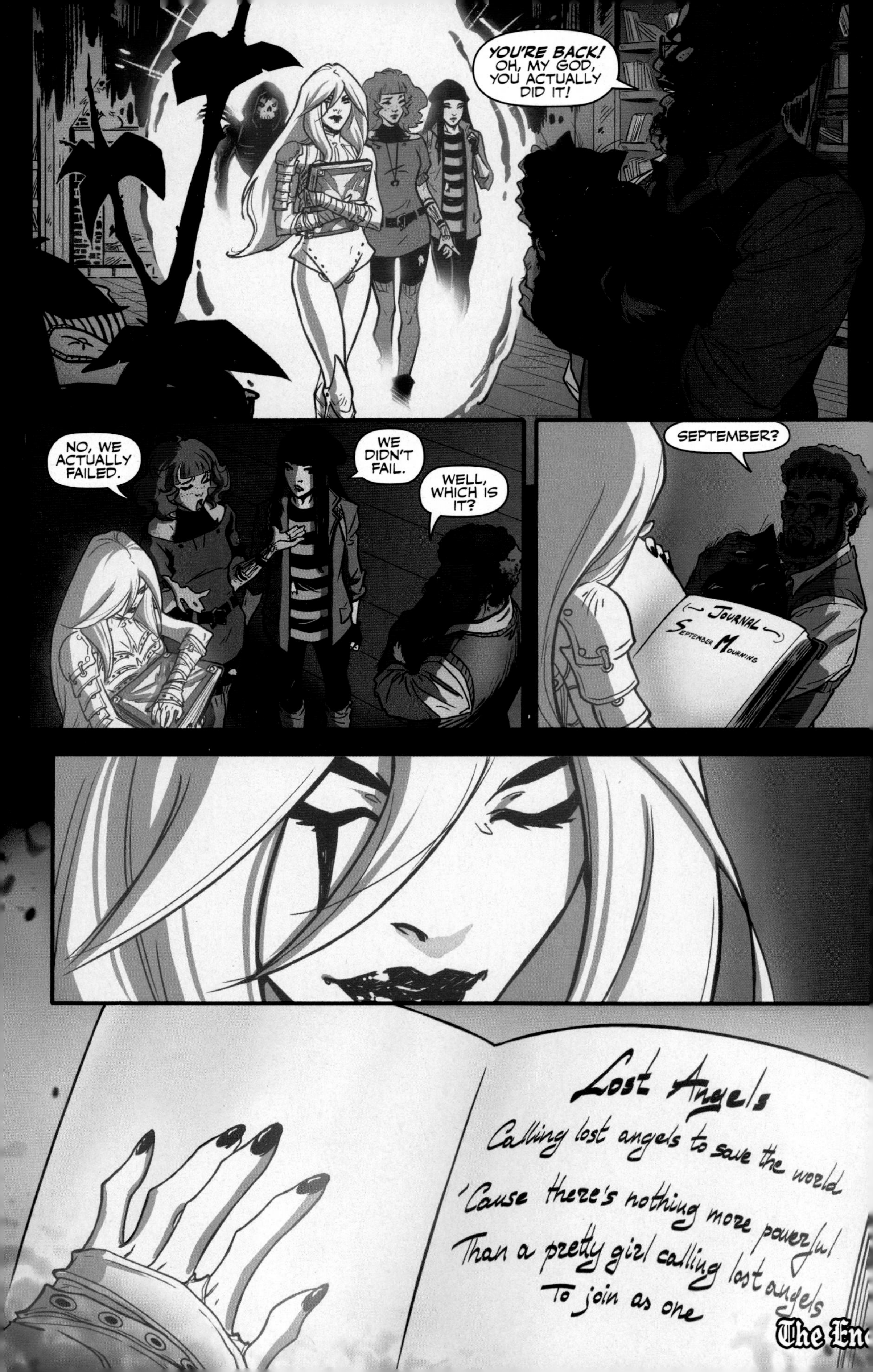
YOU'RE BACK! OH, MY GOD, YOU ACTUALLY DID IT!
NO, WE ACTUALLY FAILED.
WE DIDN'T FAIL.
WELL, WHICH IS IT?
SEPTEMBER?
JOURNAL
SEPTEMBER MOURNING
Lost Angels
Calling lost angels to save the world
'Cause there's nothing more powerful
Than a pretty girl calling lost angels
To join as one
The End

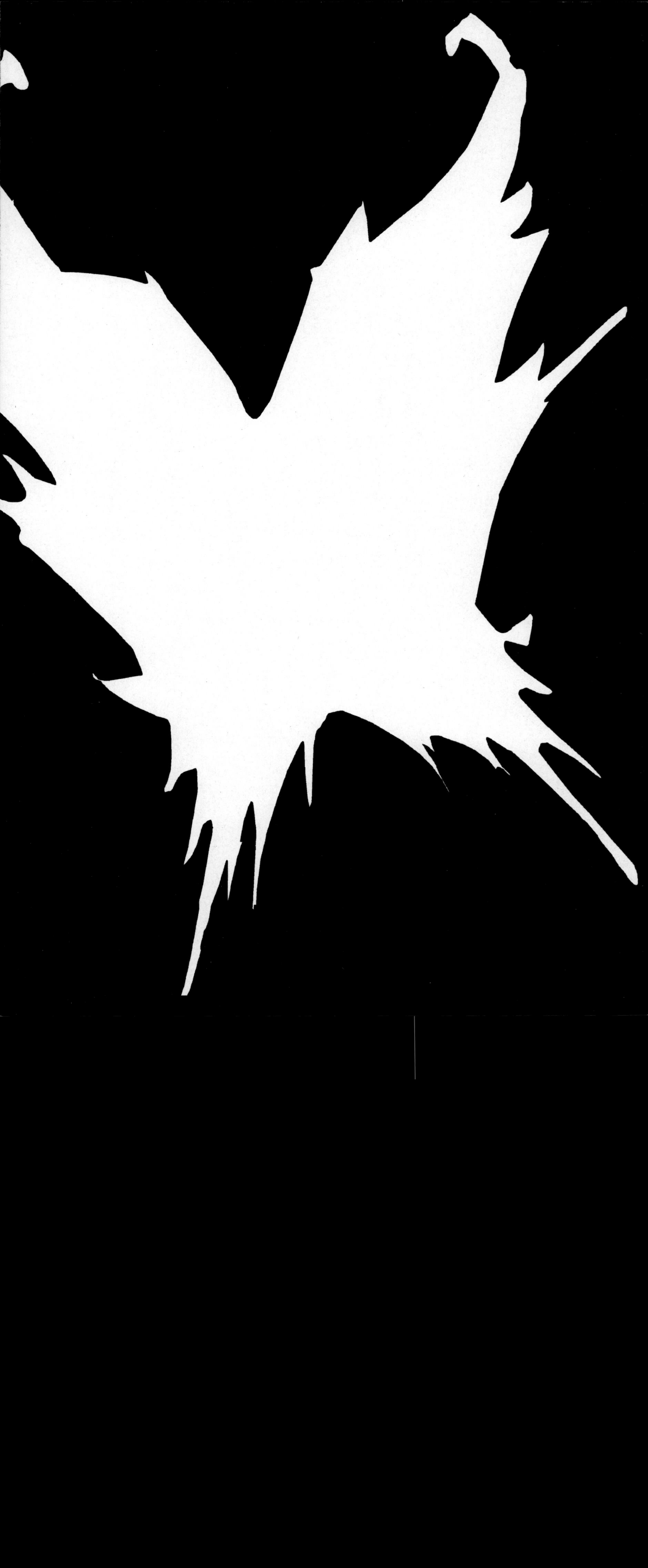

image COMICS
ILLUSTRATED QUALITY PAPER FULL BLEED COMIC PAGES
BOOK SEPTEMBER MOURNING ISSUE# 1 PG# COVER
xerox
stats
code
printed by BLUELINEPRO.COM

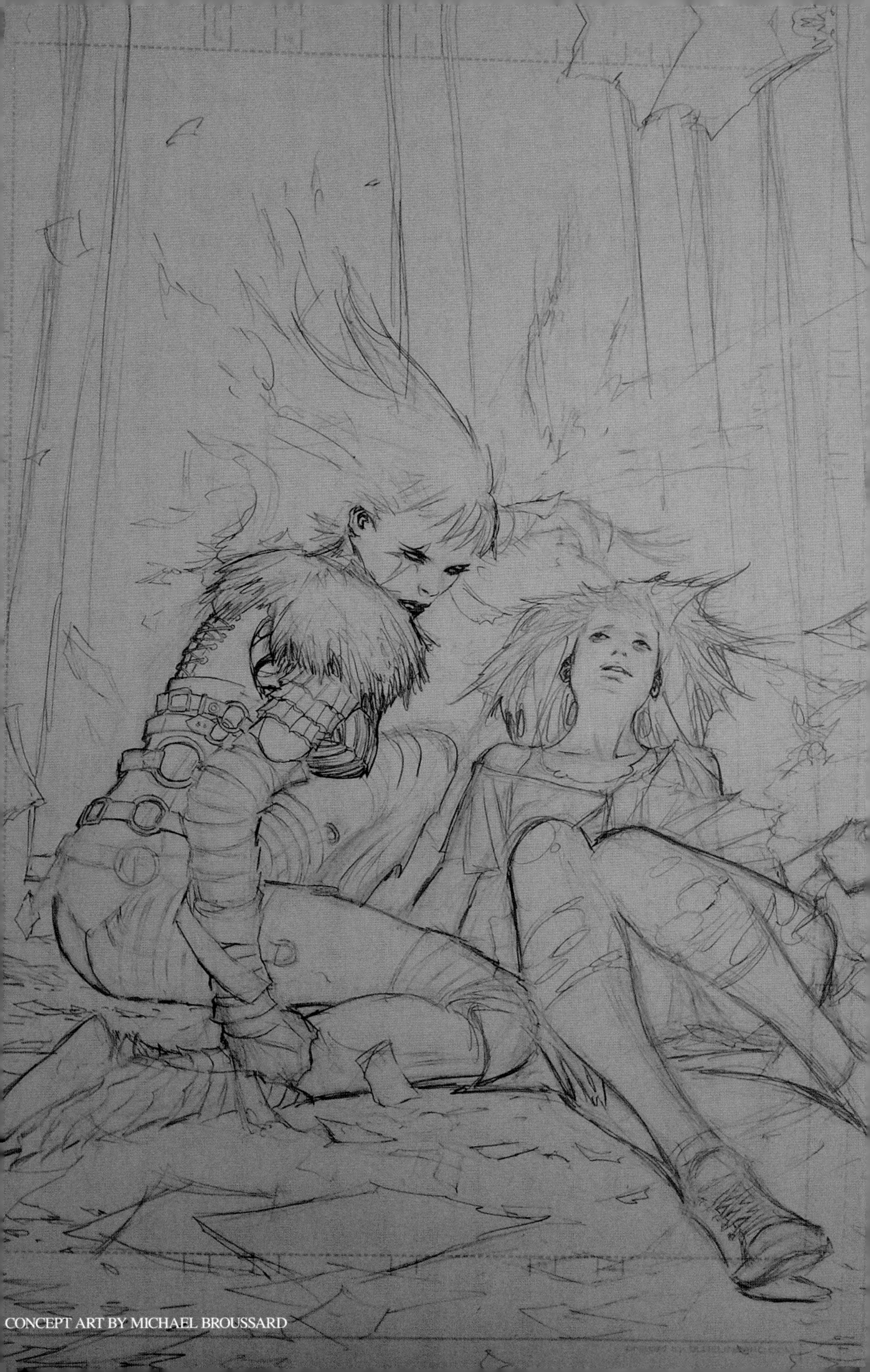

CONCEPT ART BY MICHAEL BROUSSARD

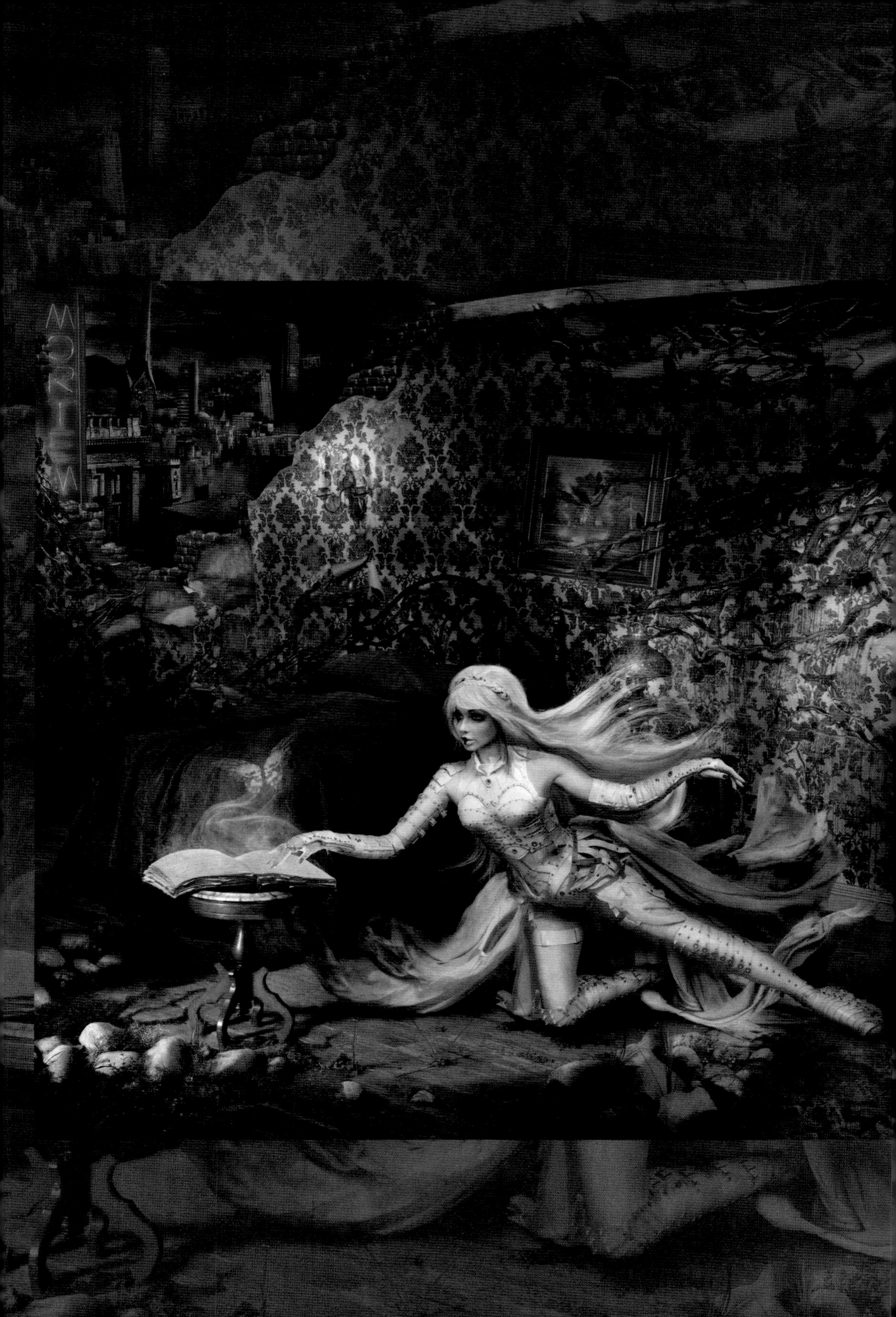

CONCEPT ART BY RANSOM & MITCHELL

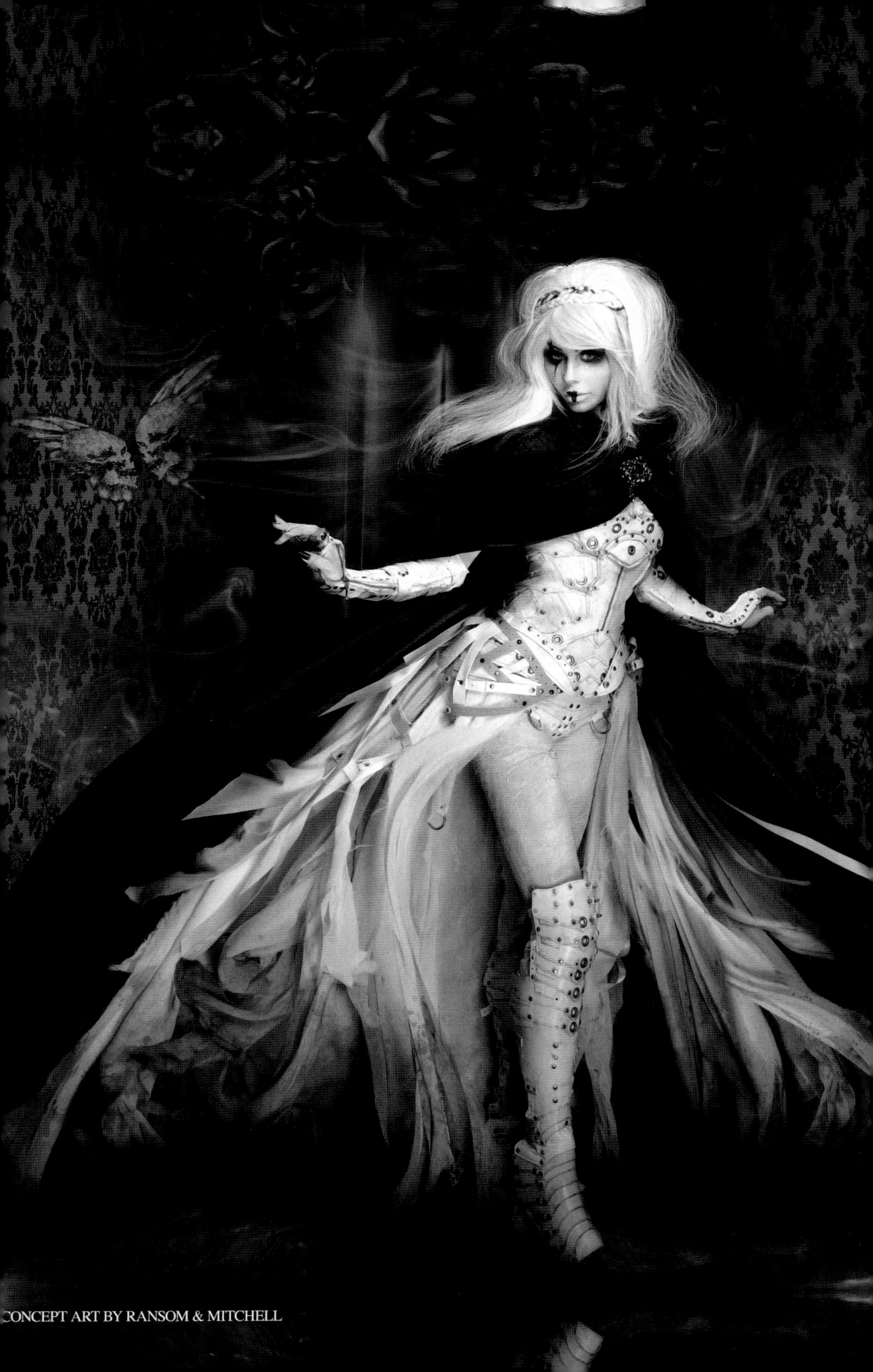

CONCEPT ART BY RANSOM & MITCHELL

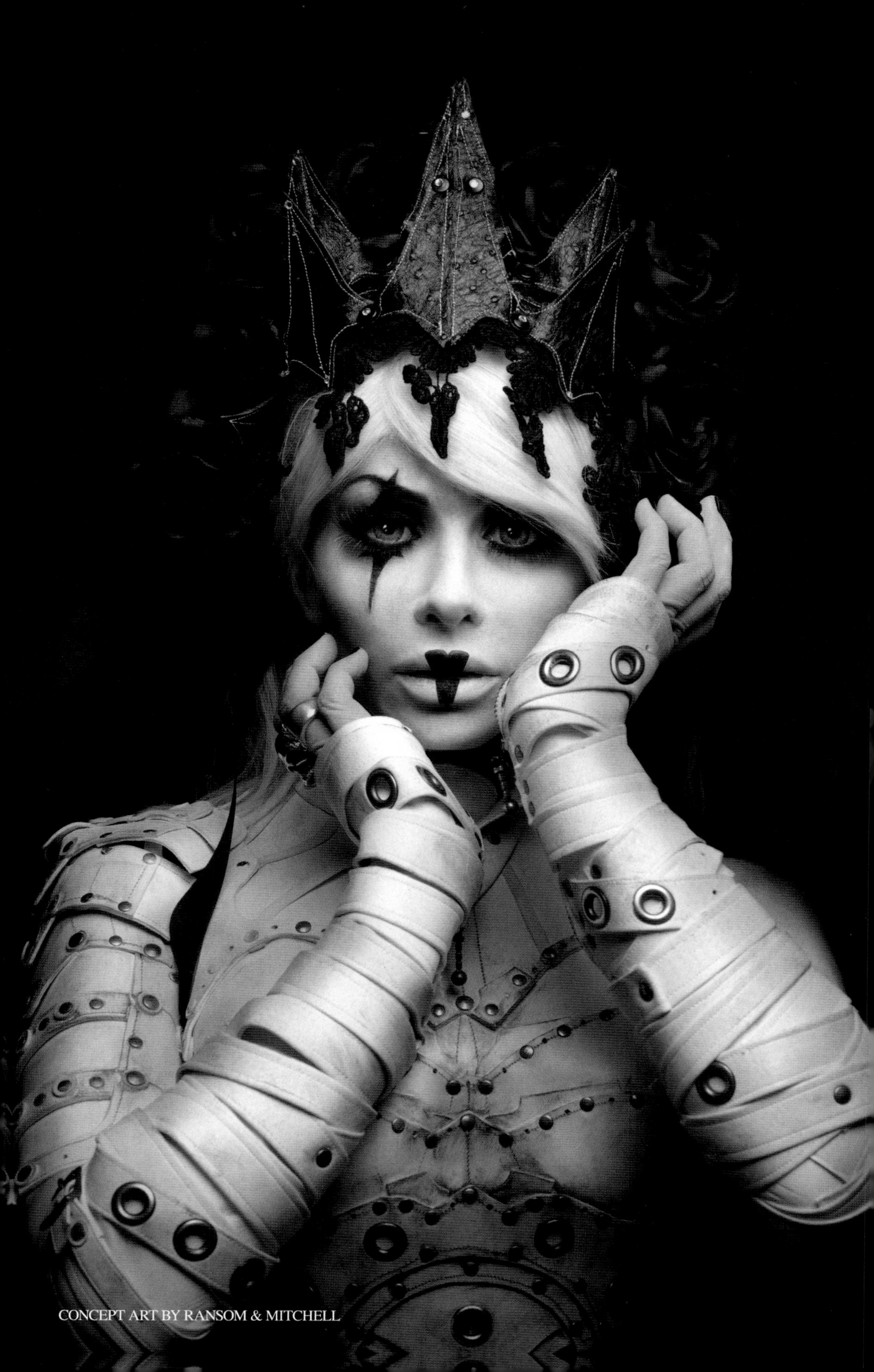

CONCEPT ART BY RANSOM & MITCHELL

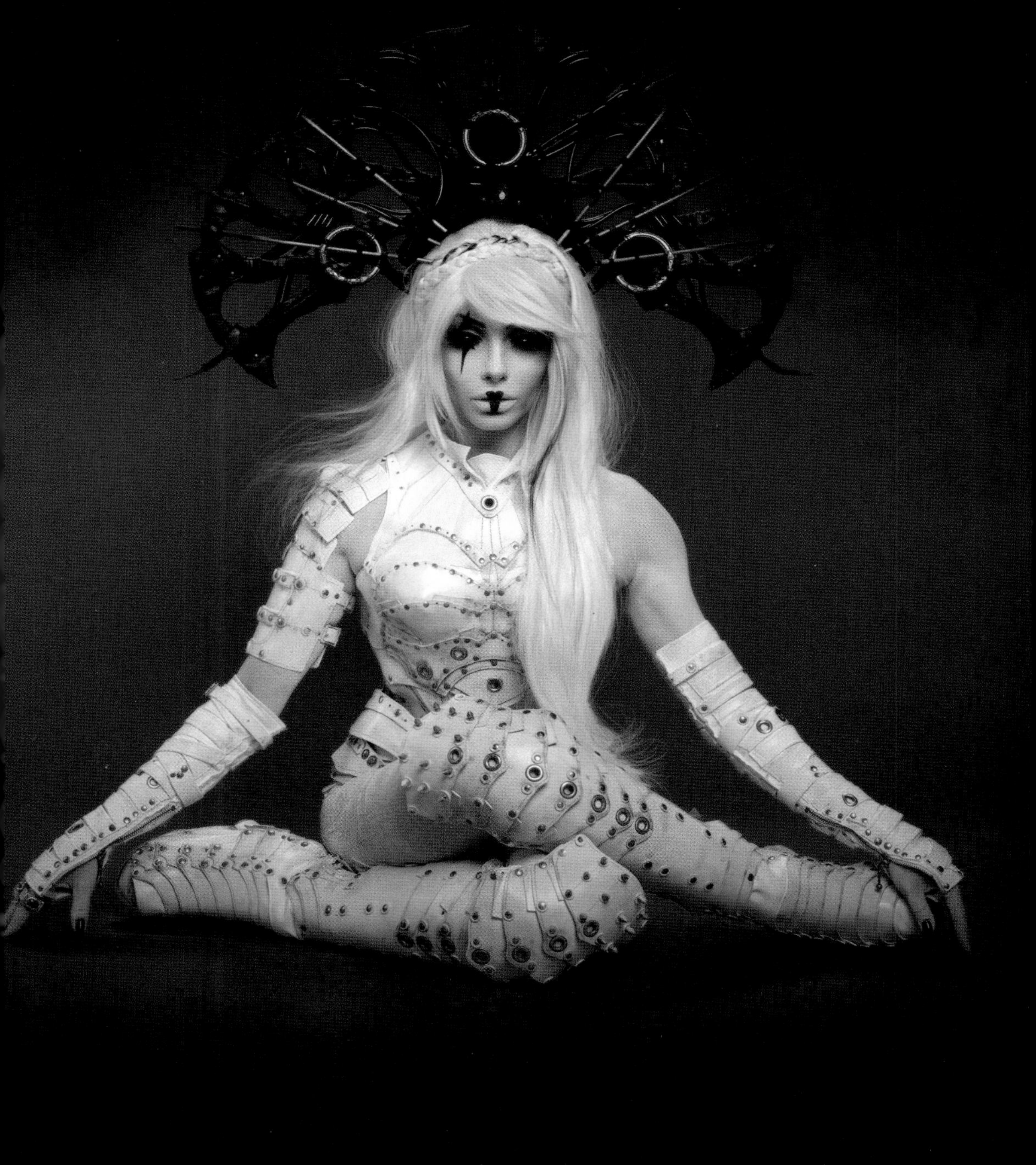

CONCEPT ART BY RANSOM & MITCHELL

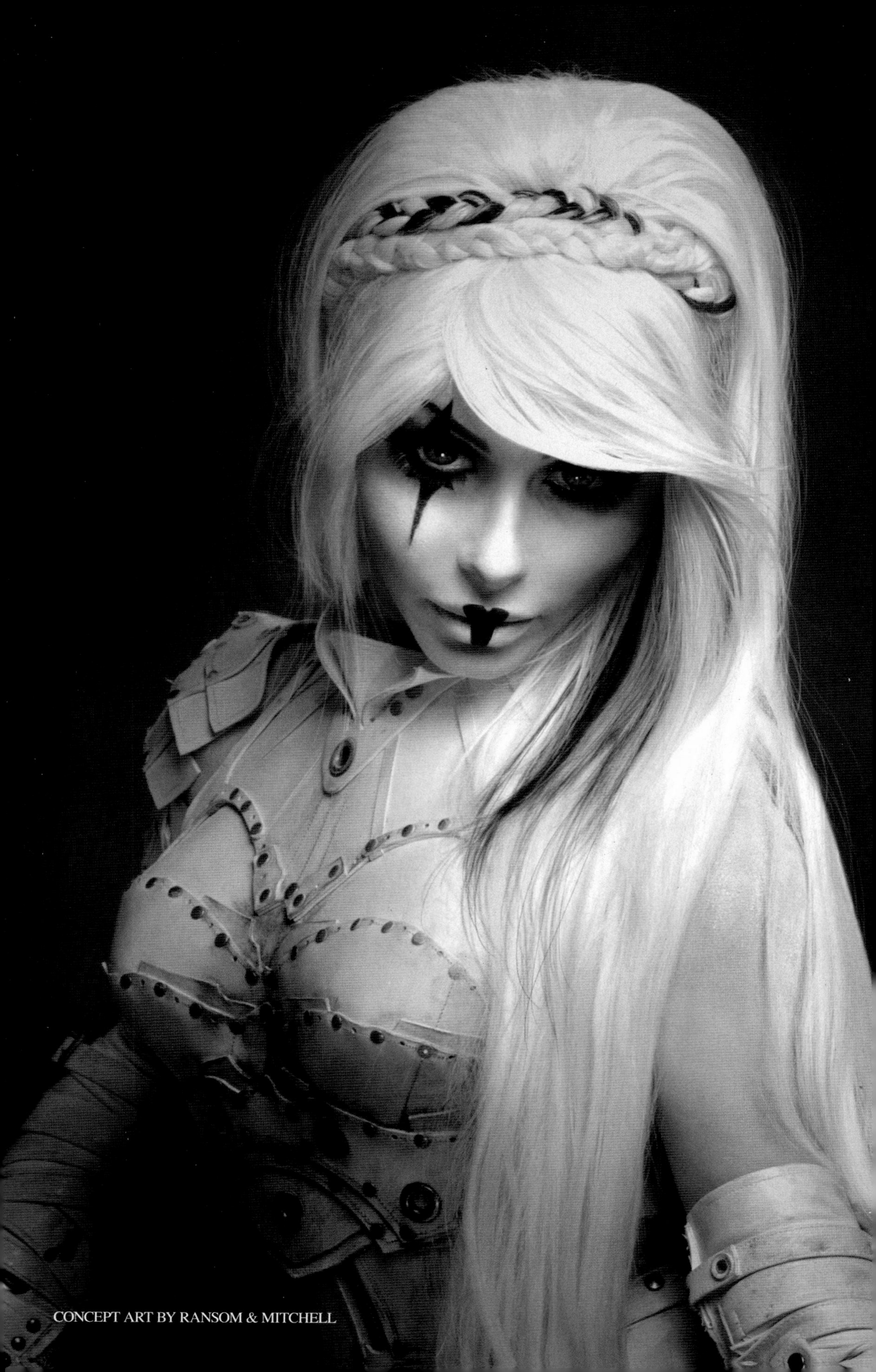

CONCEPT ART BY RANSOM & MITCHELL

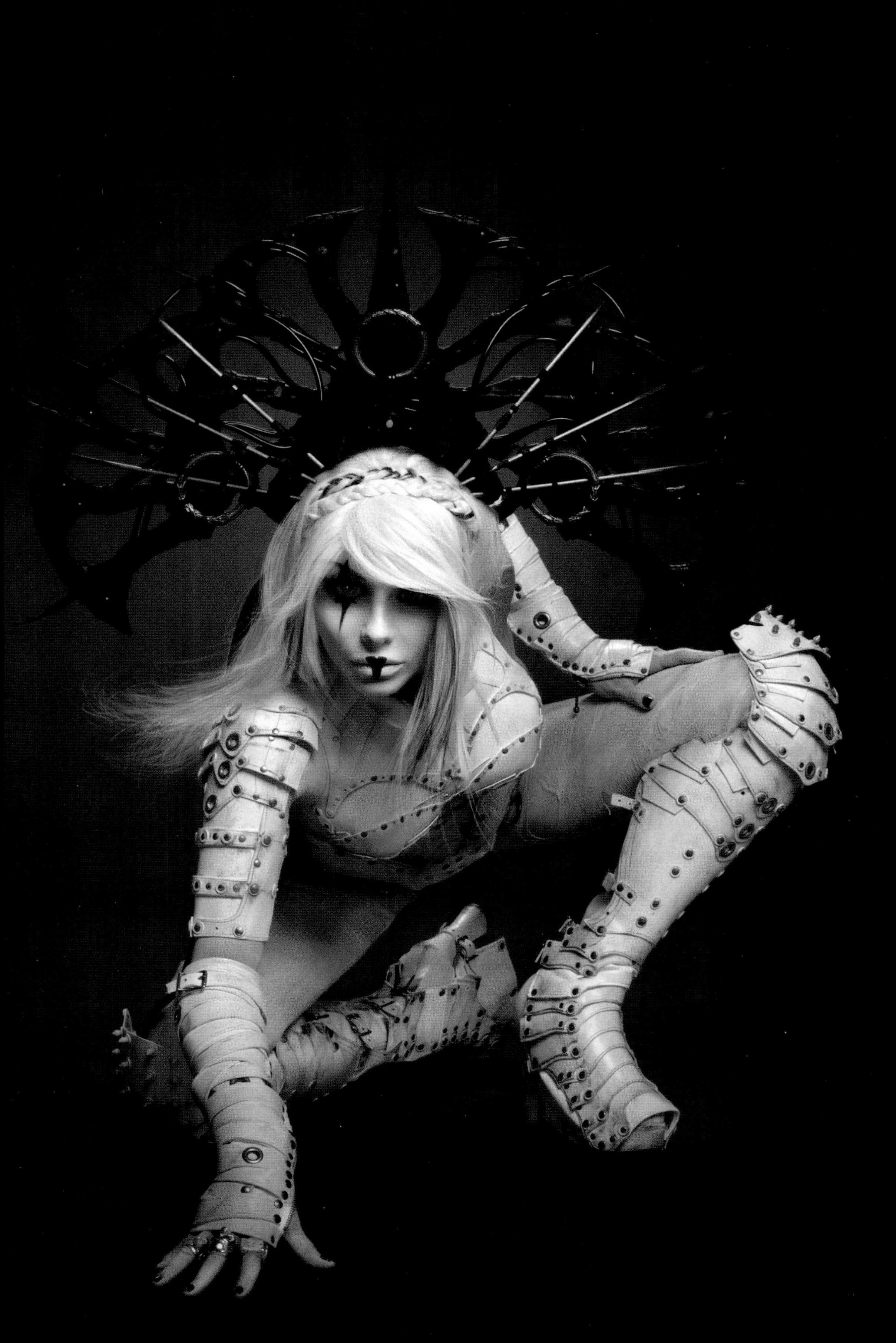

CONCEPT ART BY RANSOM & MITCHELL

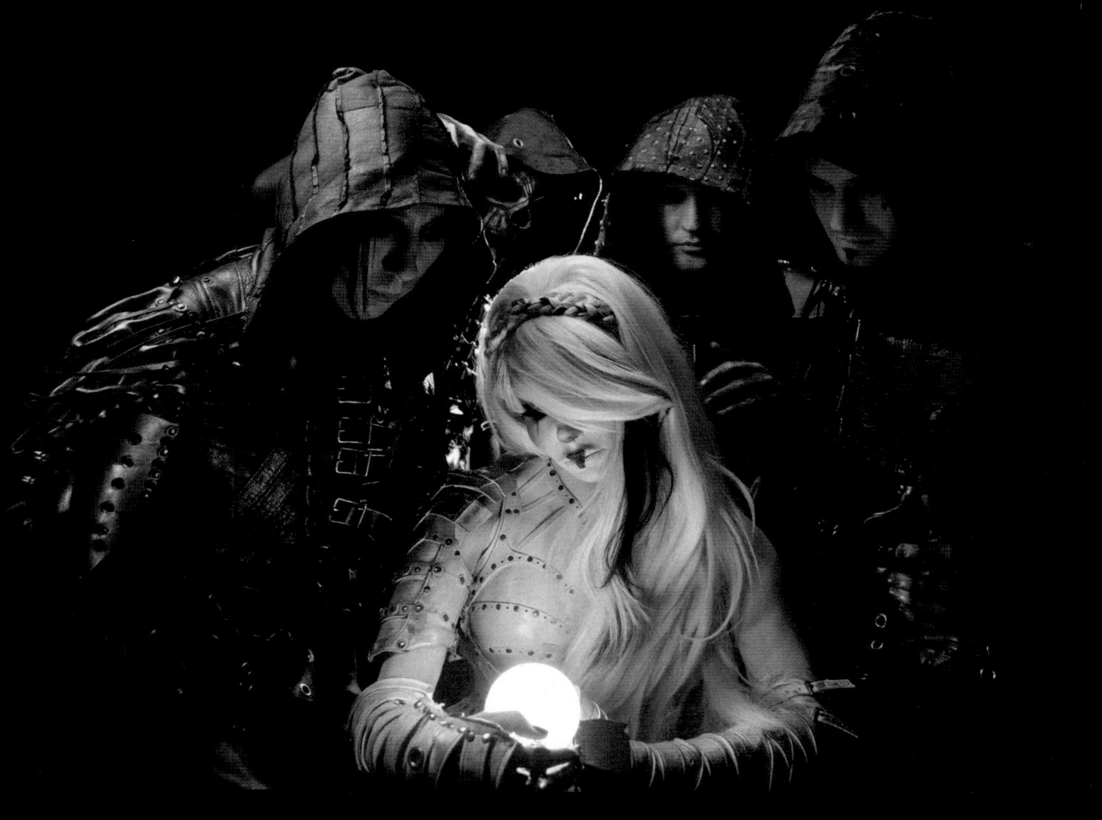

CONCEPT ART BY DEAN KARR

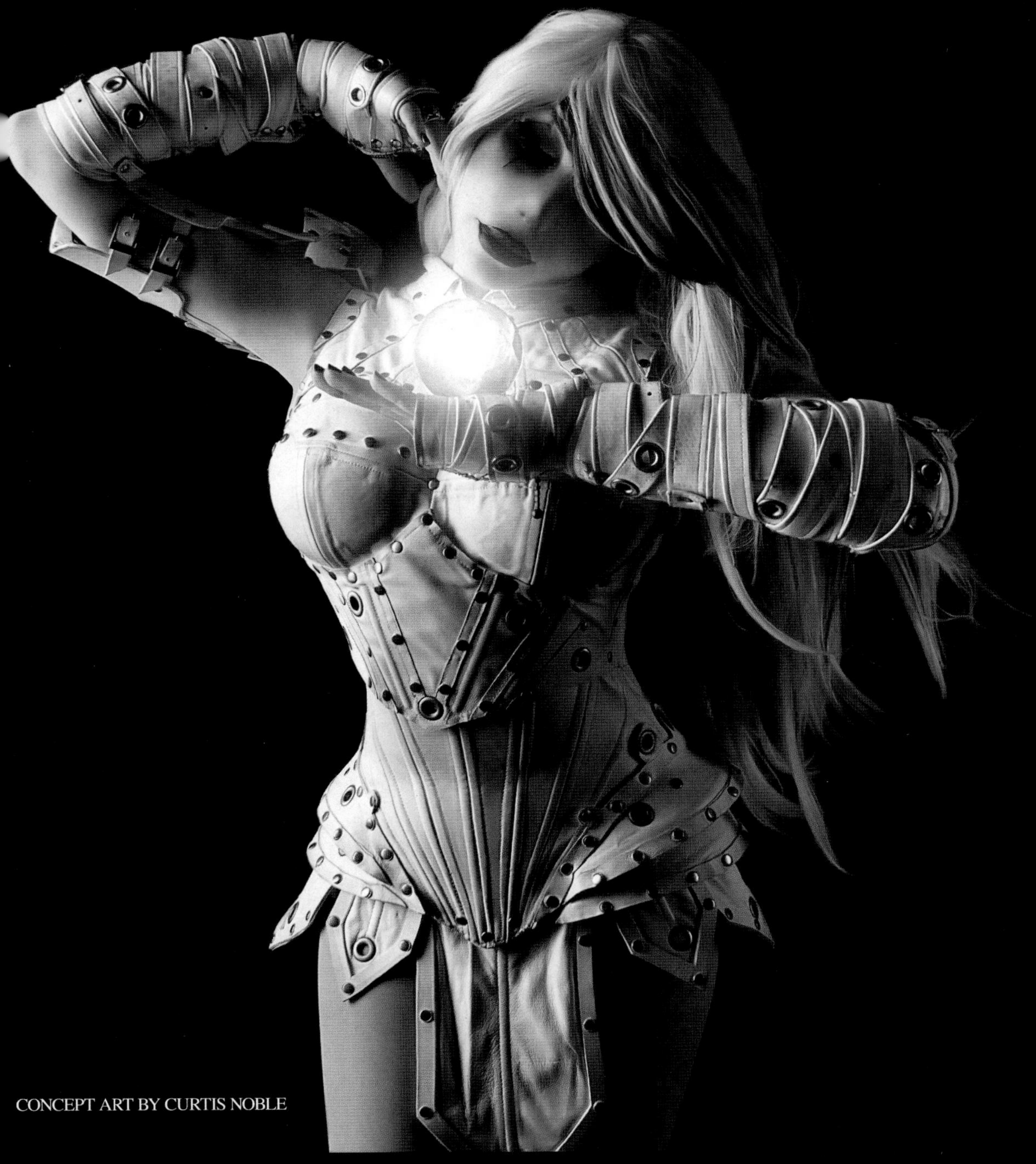

CONCEPT ART BY CURTIS NOBLE

CONCEPT ART BY CURTIS NOBLE

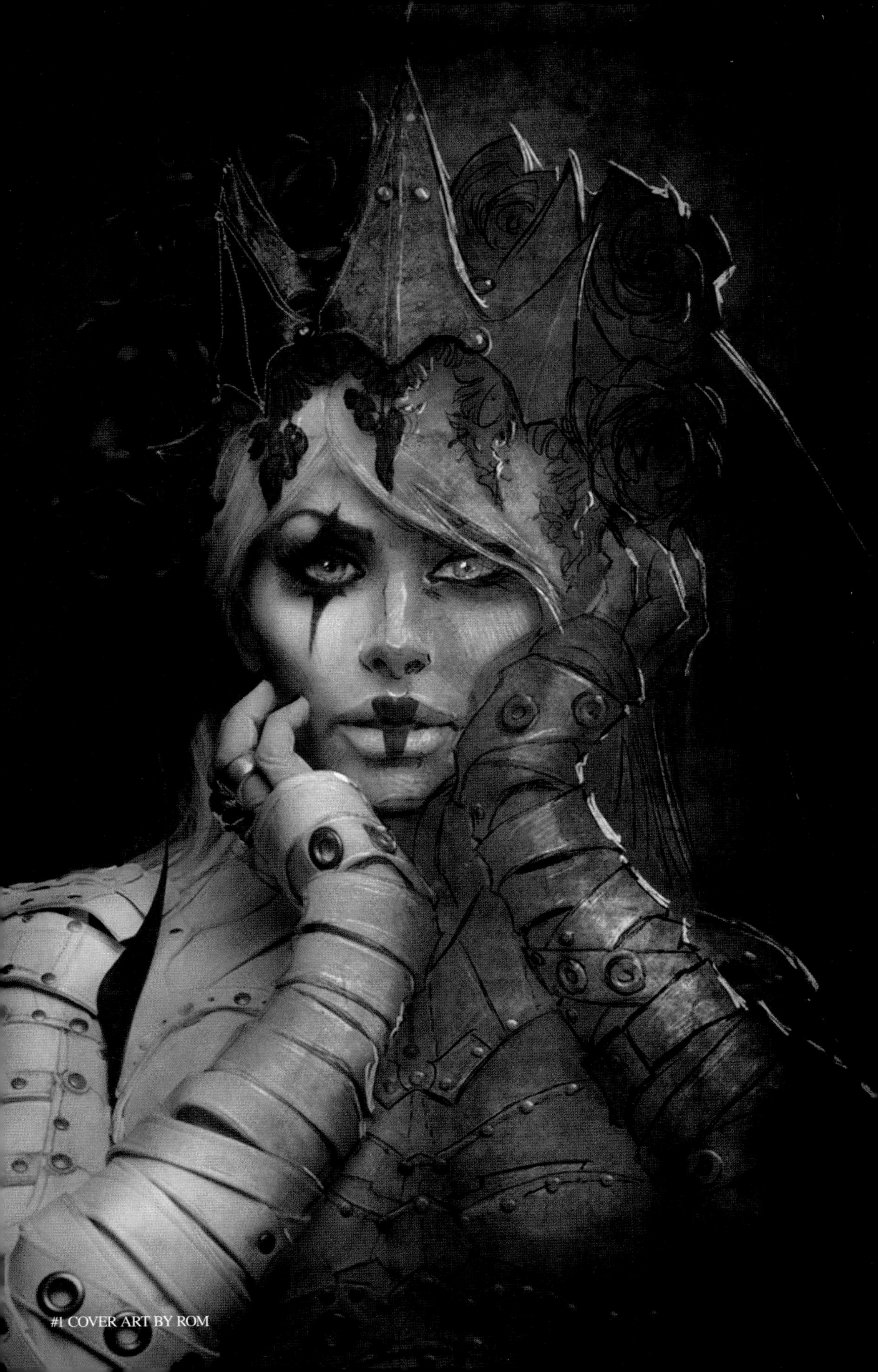

#1 COVER ART BY ROM

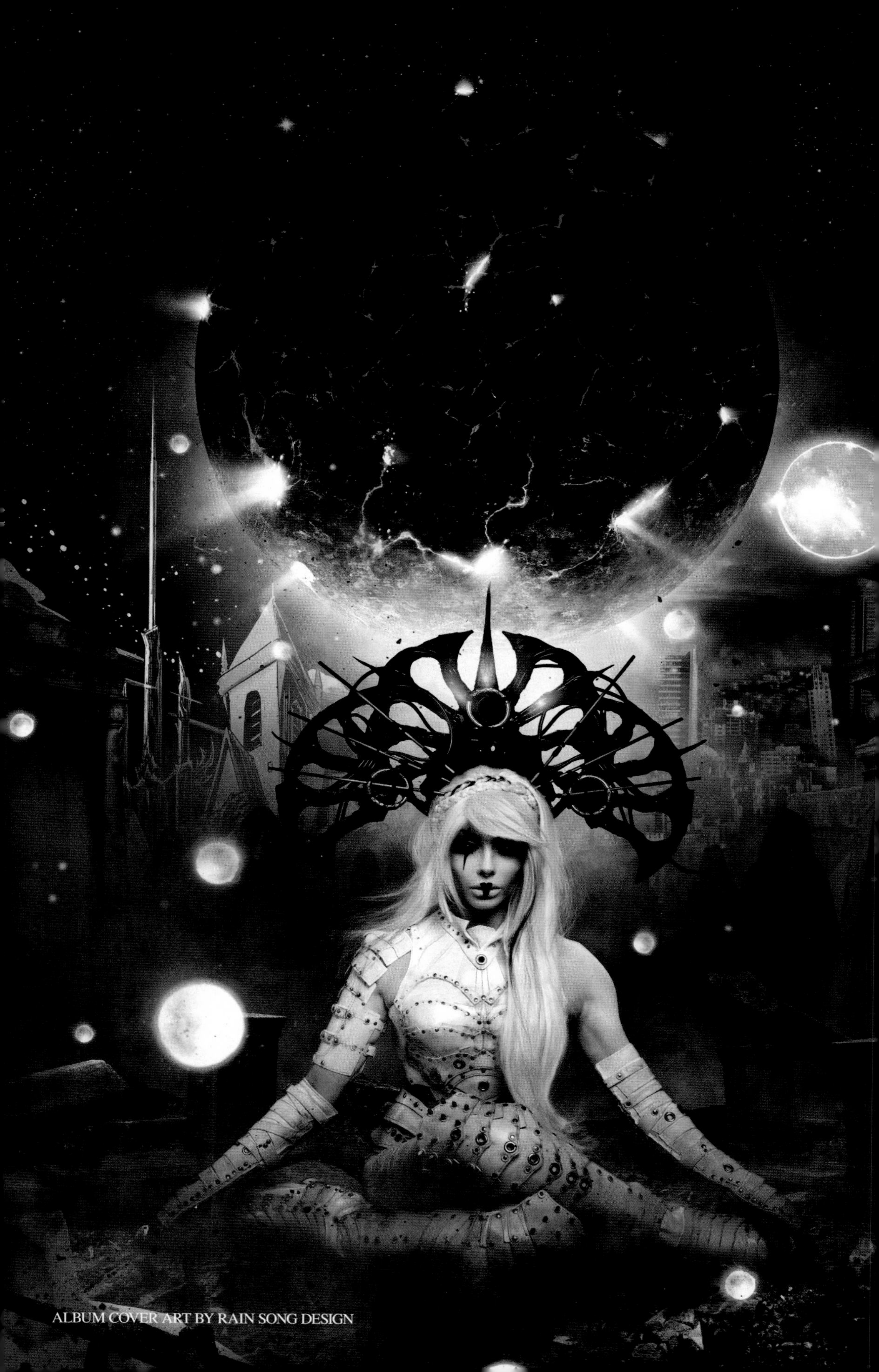

ALBUM COVER ART BY RAIN SONG DESIGN

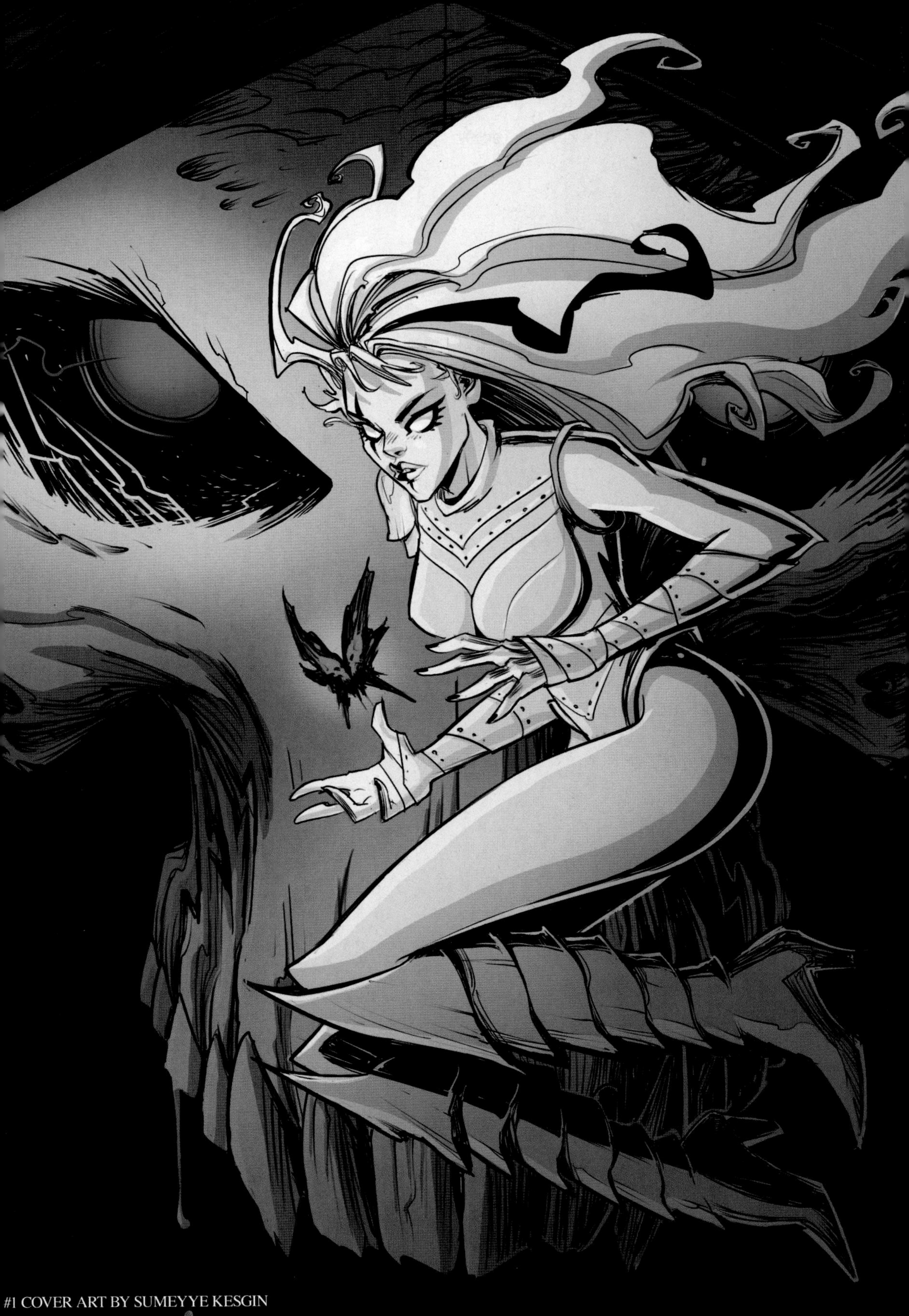

#1 COVER ART BY SUMEYYE KESGIN

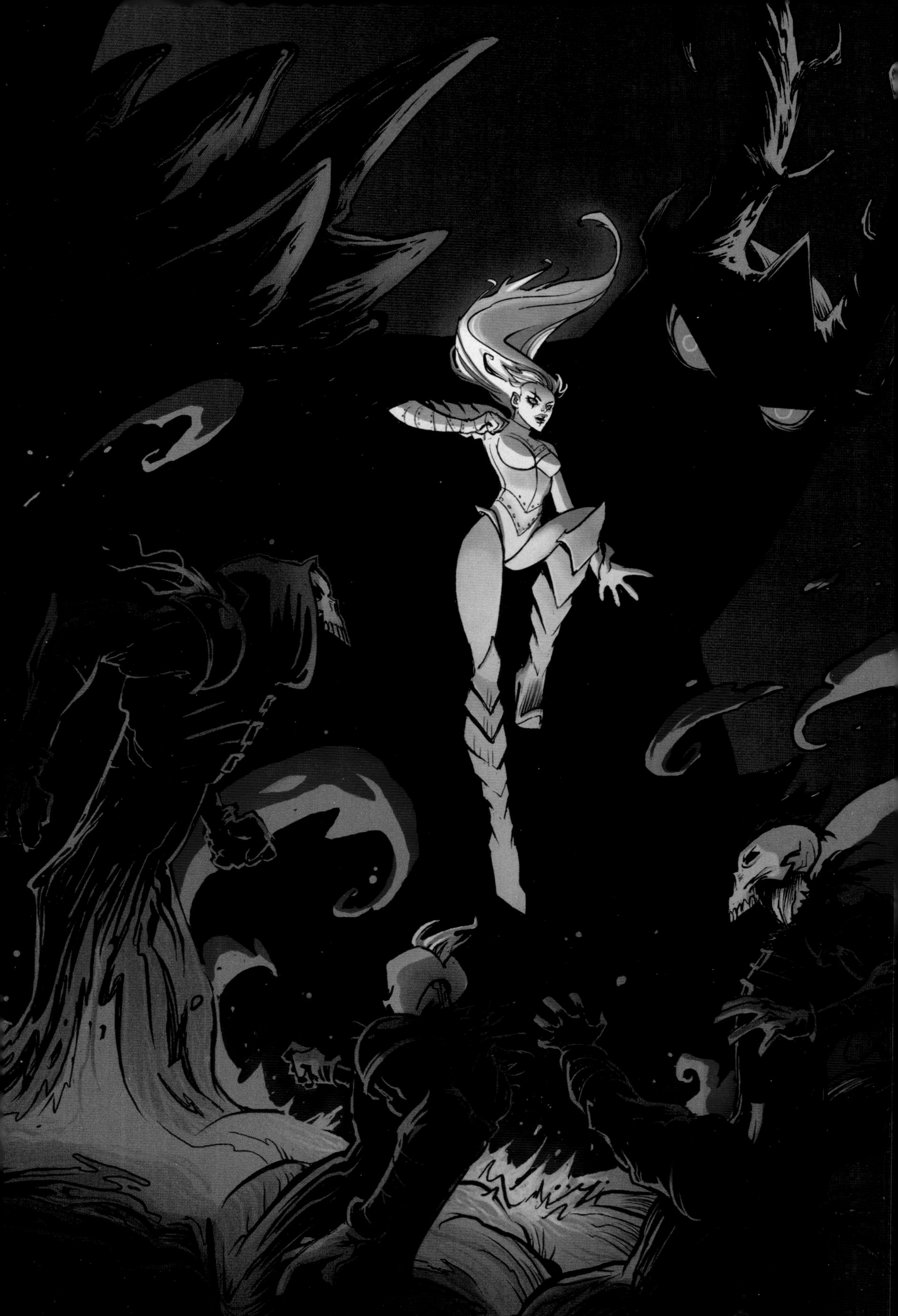

#2 COVER ART BY SUMEYYE KESGIN

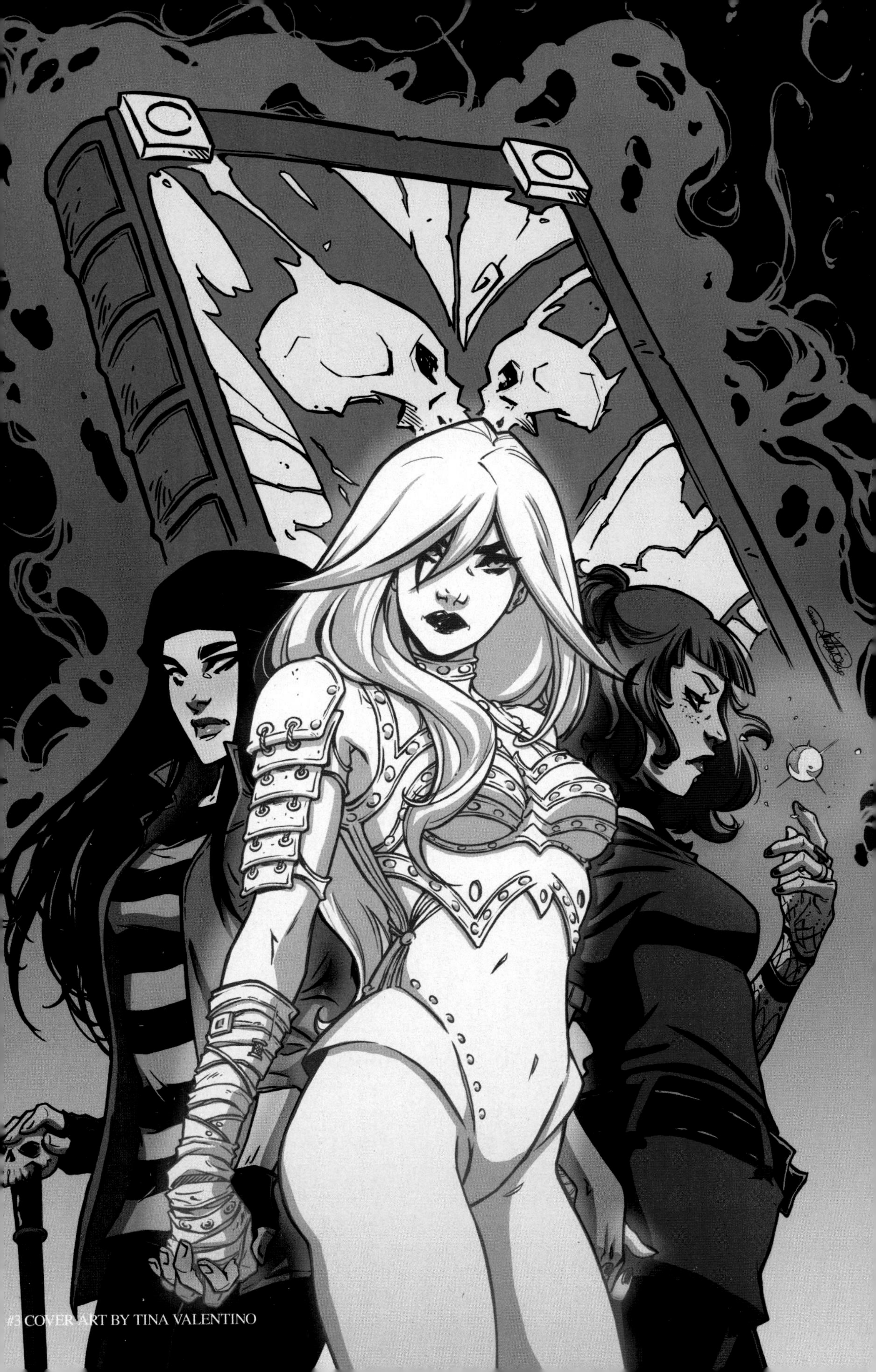

#3 COVER ART BY TINA VALENTINO

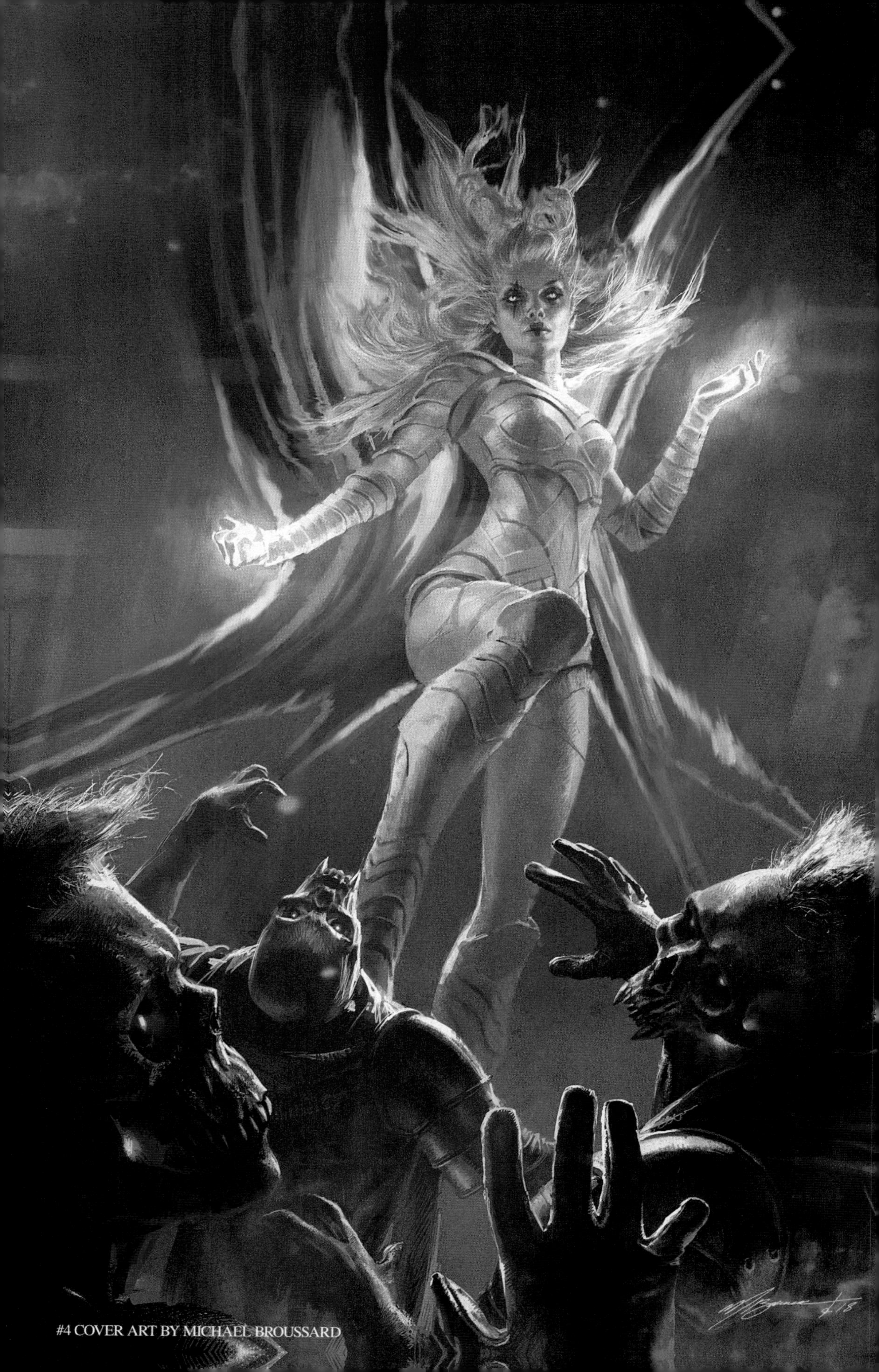

#4 COVER ART BY MICHAEL BROUSSARD

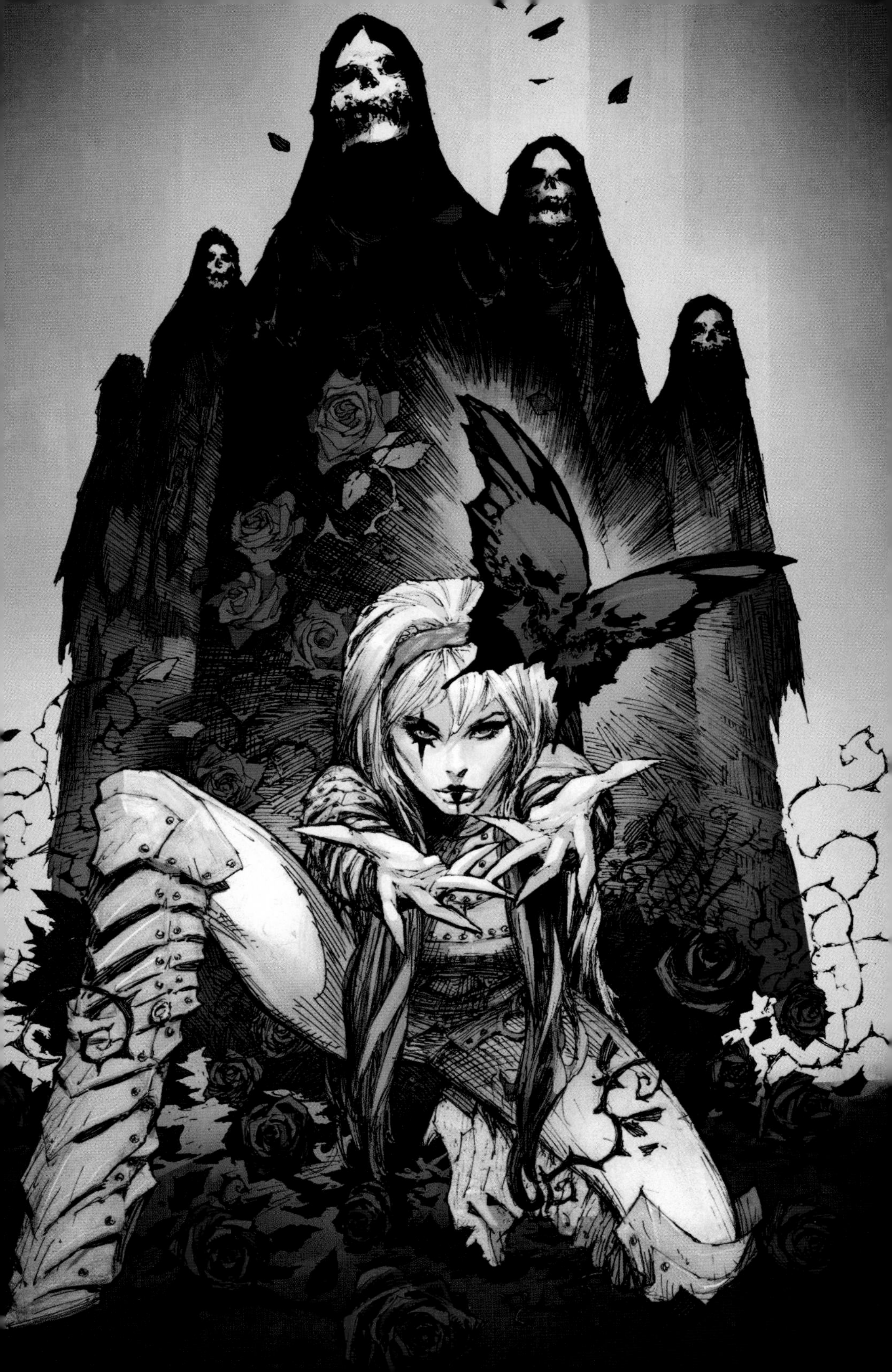

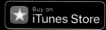  

<u>SEPTEMBER MOURNING IS</u>
† SEPTEMBER † RIVEN † WRAITH † SHADOU † STITCH †

ORIGINAL STORY AND CONCEPT
EMILY LAZAR & MARC SILVESTRI

FULL LENGTH ALBUM "VOLUME II" AVAILABLE ON SUMERIAN RECORDS

PRODUCED & ENGINEERED BY SAHAJ TICOTIN AT SUNGOD ROCK STUDIOS
ADDITIONAL PRODUCTION ON "CHILDREN OF FATE" BY HOWARD BENSON AT WEST VALLEY STUDIOS
ADDITIONAL RECORDING AT NRG RECORDING, ROOM 237, HOBBY SHOP & AVIAN AUDIO WORKS
VIOLIN ON "SKIN & BONES" & "'TIL YOU SEE HEAVEN" : JINXX OF BLACK VEIL BRIDES
MIXED AND MASTERED BY ALLAN HESSLER

SINGLES "EMPIRE" & "GLASS ANIMALS" AVAILABLE ON SUMERIAN RECORDS

"EMPIRE"
PRODUCED BY CHRIS LORD-ALGE, NICK SCOTT & JOSH NAPERT
PROGRAMMING BY NICK SCOTT
ADDITIONAL VOCAL RECORDING AT SUNGOD ROCK STUDIOS BY SAHAJ TICOTIN
GUITAR AND DRUM RECORDING AT SKYLIT SOUND BY JOSH BUMA
MIXED AND MASTERED BY CHRIS LORD-ALGE

"GLASS ANIMALS"
PRODUCED BY NICK SCOTT
PROGRAMMING BY NICK SCOTT
ADDITIONAL VOCAL RECORDING AT SUNGOD ROCK STUDIOS BY SAHAJ TICOTIN
GUITAR AND DRUM RECORDING AT SKYLIT SOUND BY JOSH BUMA
MIXED AND MASTERED BY CHRIS LORD-ALGE

A&R : ASH AVILDSEN & NICK WALTERS AT SUMERIAN RECORDS
MANAGEMENT : THE ORACLE MANAGEMENT
LEGAL : GUY BLAKE AT DAVIS & SHAPIRO, LLP
BUSINESS MANAGER : SCOTT ADAIR AT LONDON & CO., LLP
BOOKING : ALEX GILBERT AT ARTERY GLOBAL (USA) - LIAM SPENCER AT ARTERY GLOBAL (EUR/UK)
PR : ADRENALINE - MARIA FERRERO
ALBUM COVER ARTWORK : RANSOM & MITCHELL (PHOTOGRAPHY) - SUMEYYE KESGIN - (ARTWORK) - COLIN MARKS (DESIGN)
ALBUM PHOTOGRAPHY : DEAN KARR
ALBUM LAYOUT & SINGLE COVER DESIGN : DANIEL MCBRIDE AT MCBRIDE DESIGN

SEPTEMBER MOURNING PROUDLY ENDORSES
LEGATOR GUITARS, SCHECTER GUITARS, POSITIVE GRID, SENNHEISER WIRELESS, SALUDA CYMBALS, DDRUM, MAC COSMETICS, ROCKSTAR
WIGS, ULTIMATE EARS

SEPTEMBER MOURNING THANKS
MARC SILVESTRI, DEZ FAFARA, ANAHSTASIA FAFARA, ANDY GOULD, SAHAJ TICOTIN, ASH AVILDSEN, SARAH MARTIN, NOELLE CAMPBELL
STEVE STRANGE, GUY BLAKE, ALEX GILBERT, SCOTT ADAIR, NICK WALTERS, AMANDA FIORE, MIKE JAKUBOW, DANIEL MCBRIDE, STEVEN
CONTRERAS, DANNY WIMMER, MICHAEL PAPALE, TOP COW COMICS, MATT HAWKINS, ELENA SALCEDO, DAVID HINE, MARIAH MCCOURT,
SUMEYYE KESGIN, TINA VALENTINO, TOM AKEL, RANSOM & MITCHELL, CHRIS LORD-ALGE, NICK SCOTT, JOSH NAPERT, JOSH BUMA, JOHN
MCLUCAS, ZAC MORRIS, KYLE MAYER, PATRICK ROMANELLI, KASSIE ROQUE, EIRIK ASWANG, CARRIE SLEUTSKAYA, DRAGON PIETY, WAND
PIETY, ALLAN HESSLER, RON FAIR, HOWARD BENSON, MIKE PLOTNIKOFF, LENNY SKOLNIK, JONNY LITTEN, RYAN HARLACHER, TOM GEORG
DANNY HILLMAN, TRISTAN WALLACE, VICENTE CORDERO, BEN CHARLES EDWARDS, PETER AVVEDUTI, JAMIE KOALA, AVA JAZLYN, SARAH
MANKOFF, SHAWN WISEMAN, CURTIS NOBLE, ERIK RON, JIM KAUFMAN, MITCHELL MARLOW, KANE CHURKO, TREV LUKATHER, RUSSELL
ALI, XANDY BERRY, DAMON RANGER, KEVIN CHURKO, JOHN TRAVIS, ROY MAYORGA, JOHN 5, JOSH FREESE, PHIL X, CHRIS CHANEY, DEA
KARR, CURTIS FOREMAN, DRIVER RICK, RYAN VASSER, DAVID UNGAR, LOREN MOLINARE, SCOTT UCHIDA, BRIAN DOUGHERTY, TIM MOOR
WINN KROZACK, RICH HANSEN, ANTHONY RAMIREZ, JINXX FERGUSON, NATHAN ULRICH, TRI RUDOLF, STEPHEN LEE, ELLEN DOUGLAS, ER
SCHNIEBER, JAMIE COGHILL, ALL FRIENDS & RESPECTIVE FAMILIES (JUZWICK, ROMANELLI, MAYER), ALL REAPERS OF SEPTEMBER PAST.

EXTRA SPECIAL THANKS TO ALL CHILDREN OF FATE ACROSS THE WORLD FOR YOUR CONTINUED SUPPORT AND BELIEF IN OUR JOURNEY..
THIS WOULDN'T BE POSSIBLE WITHOUT EACH AND EVERY ONE OF YOU. WE ARE ONE!

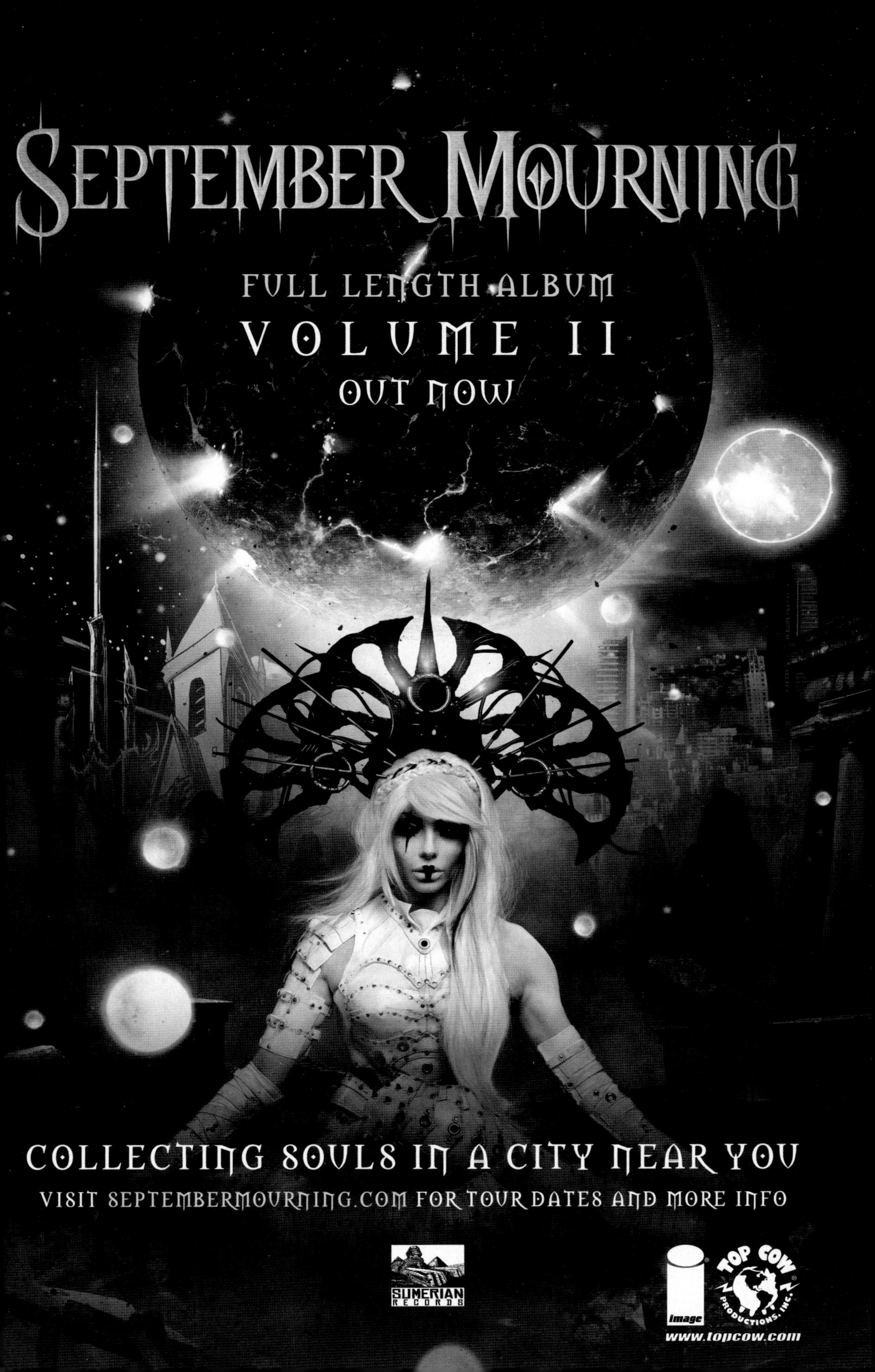

SEPTEMBER MOURNING

FULL LENGTH ALBUM
VOLUME II
OUT NOW

COLLECTING SOULS IN A CITY NEAR YOU
VISIT SEPTEMBERMOURNING.COM FOR TOUR DATES AND MORE INFO

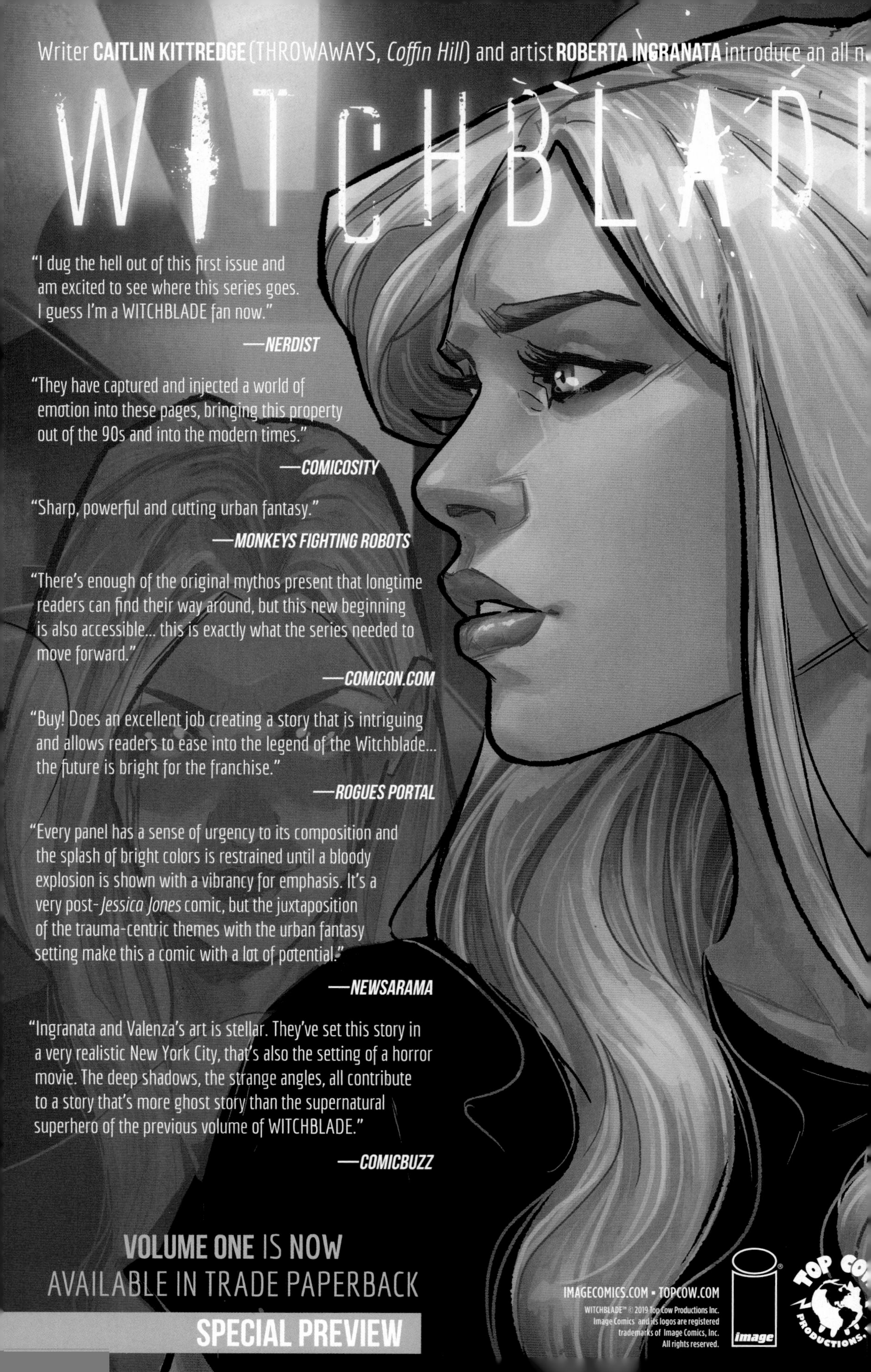
Writer CAITLIN KITTREDGE (THROWAWAYS, Coffin Hill) and artist ROBERTA INGRANATA introduce an all n
WITCHBLAD
"I dug the hell out of this first issue and am excited to see where this series goes. I guess I'm a WITCHBLADE fan now."
—NERDIST
"They have captured and injected a world of emotion into these pages, bringing this property out of the 90s and into the modern times."
—COMICOSITY
"Sharp, powerful and cutting urban fantasy."
—MONKEYS FIGHTING ROBOTS
"There's enough of the original mythos present that longtime readers can find their way around, but this new beginning is also accessible... this is exactly what the series needed to move forward."
—COMICON.COM
"Buy! Does an excellent job creating a story that is intriguing and allows readers to ease into the legend of the Witchblade... the future is bright for the franchise."
—ROGUES PORTAL
"Every panel has a sense of urgency to its composition and the splash of bright colors is restrained until a bloody explosion is shown with a vibrancy for emphasis. It's a very post-Jessica Jones comic, but the juxtaposition of the trauma-centric themes with the urban fantasy setting make this a comic with a lot of potential."
—NEWSARAMA
"Ingranata and Valenza's art is stellar. They've set this story in a very realistic New York City, that's also the setting of a horror movie. The deep shadows, the strange angles, all contribute to a story that's more ghost story than the supernatural superhero of the previous volume of WITCHBLADE."
—COMICBUZZ
VOLUME ONE IS NOW
AVAILABLE IN TRADE PAPERBACK
SPECIAL PREVIEW
IMAGECOMICS.COM • TOPCOW.COM
WITCHBLADE™ © 2019 Top Cow Productions Inc. Image Comics and its logos are registered trademarks of Image Comics, Inc. All rights reserved.

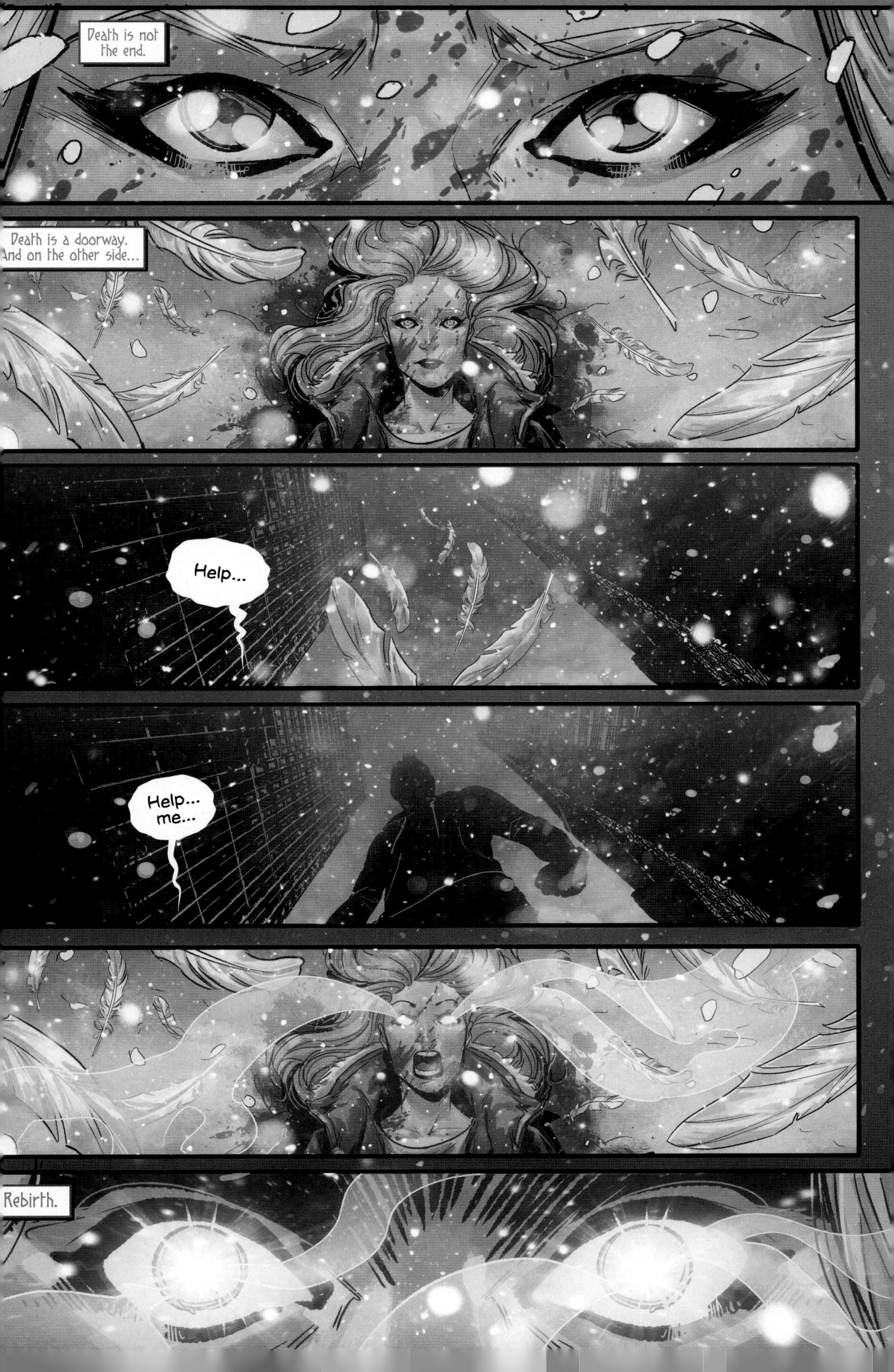
Death is not the end.
Death is a doorway. And on the other side...
Help...
Help... me...
Rebirth.

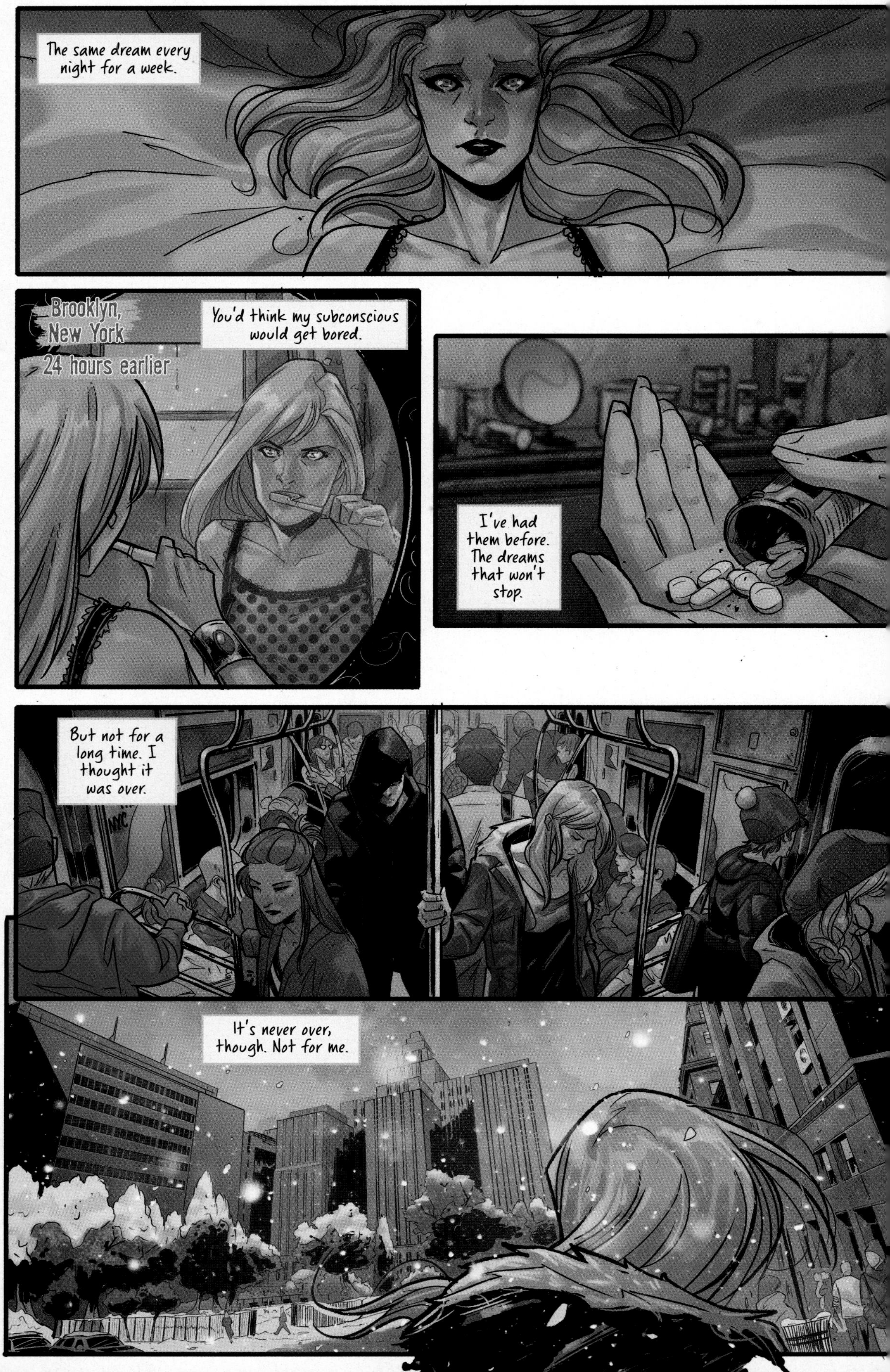
The same dream every night for a week.
Brooklyn, New York
24 hours earlier
You'd think my subconscious would get bored.
I've had them before. The dreams that won't stop.
But not for a long time. I thought it was over.
NYC
It's never over, though. Not for me.

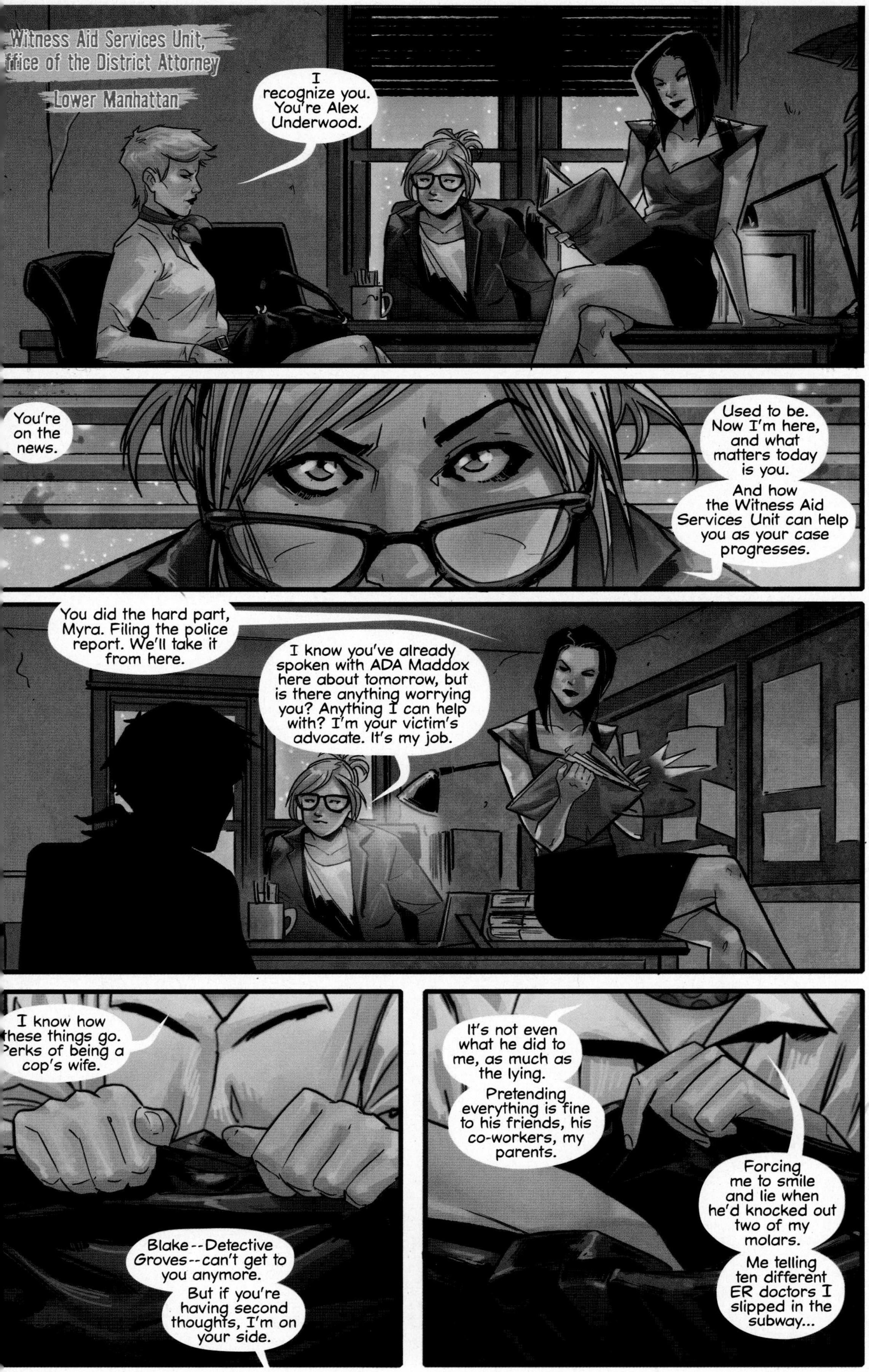

Witness Aid Services Unit, ffice of the District Attorney
Lower Manhattan
I recognize you. You're Alex Underwood.
You're on the news.
Used to be. Now I'm here, and what matters today is you.
And how the Witness Aid Services Unit can help you as your case progresses.
You did the hard part, Myra. Filing the police report. We'll take it from here.
I know you've already spoken with ADA Maddox here about tomorrow, but is there anything worrying you? Anything I can help with? I'm your victim's advocate. It's my job.
I know how these things go. Perks of being a cop's wife.
Blake--Detective Groves--can't get to you anymore.
But if you're having second thoughts, I'm on your side.
It's not even what he did to me, as much as the lying.
Pretending everything is fine to his friends, his co-workers, my parents.
Forcing me to smile and lie when he'd knocked out two of my molars.
Me telling ten different ER doctors I slipped in the subway...

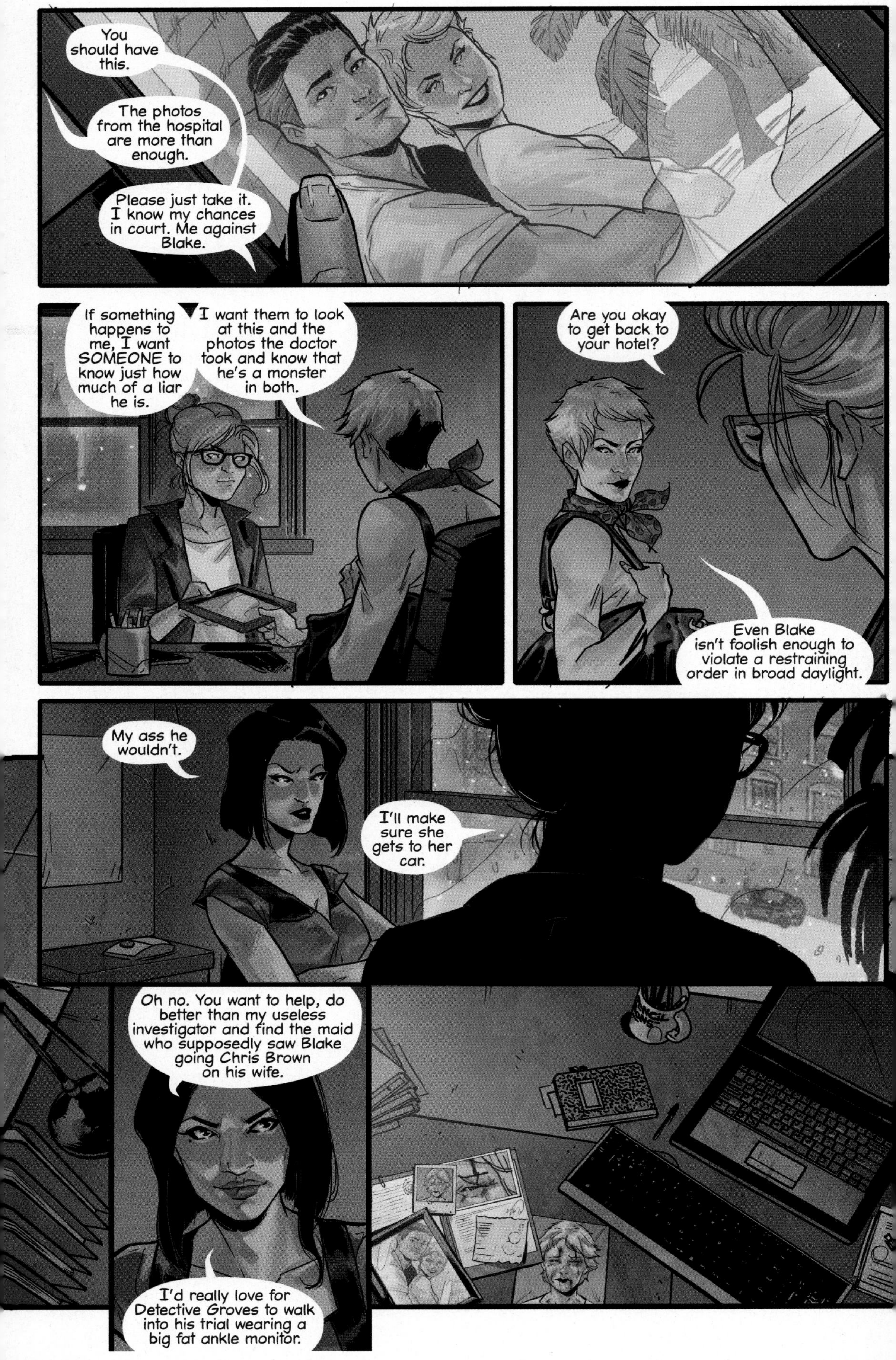
You should have this.
The photos from the hospital are more than enough.
Please just take it. I know my chances in court. Me against Blake.
If something happens to me, I want SOMEONE to know just how much of a liar he is.
I want them to look at this and the photos the doctor took and know that he's a monster in both.
Are you okay to get back to your hotel?
Even Blake isn't foolish enough to violate a restraining order in broad daylight.
My ass he wouldn't.
I'll make sure she gets to her car.
Oh no. You want to help, do better than my useless investigator and find the maid who supposedly saw Blake going Chris Brown on his wife.
I'd really love for Detective Groves to walk into his trial wearing a big fat ankle monitor.

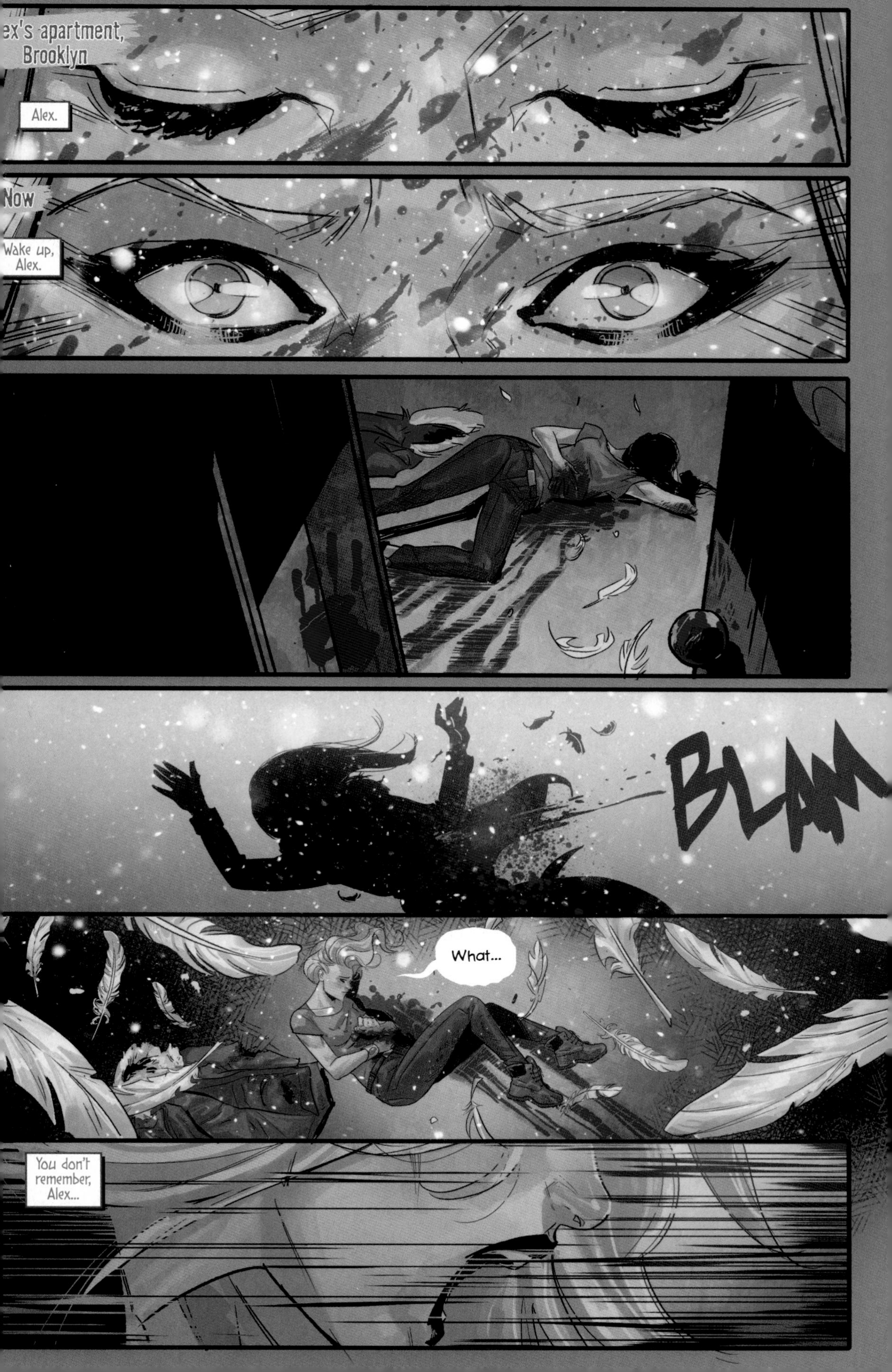
ex's apartment, Brooklyn
Alex.
Now
Wake up, Alex.
BLAM
What...
You don't remember, Alex...

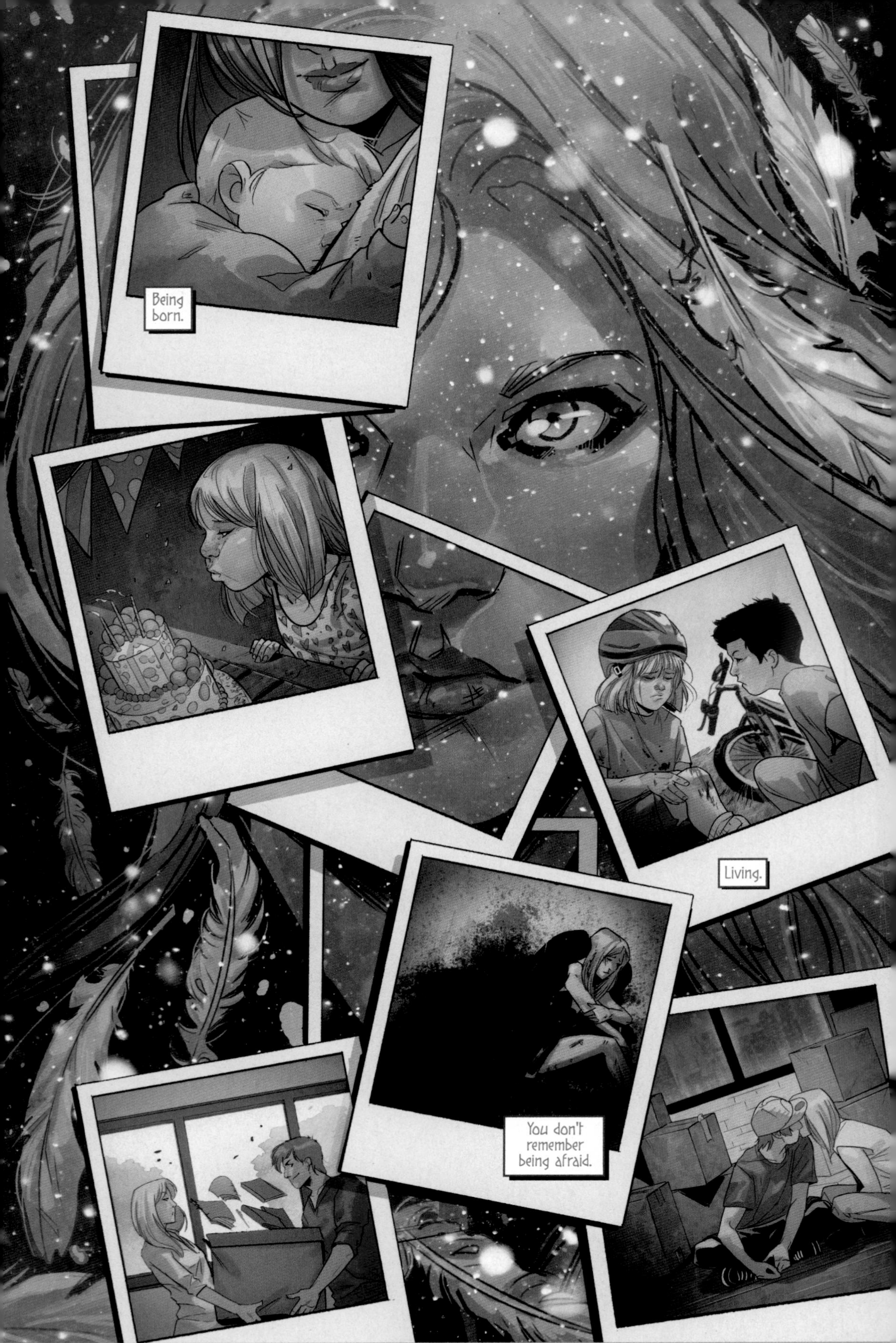
Being born.
Living.
You don't remember being afraid.

CONTINUED IN WITCHBLADE VOLUME 1, AVAILABLE NOW